# The World Bank Group, Multilateral Aid, and the 1970s

# The World Bank Group, Multilateral Aid, and the 1970s

John P. Lewis

Ishan Kapur

**Lexington Books**
D.C. Heath and Company
Lexington, Massachusetts
Toronto          London

**Library of Congress Cataloging in Publication Data**

Main entry under title:

The World Bank group, multilateral aid, and the 1970s.

Originated as talks at a seminar held at the Woodrow Wilson School of Public and International Affairs, Princeton University, in 1971.

Bibliography: p.

1. International Bank for Reconstruction and Development. I. Lewis, John Prior, ed.   II. Kapur, Ishan, 1948-    ed. III. Title.

HG3881.W593          332.1'53          73-10365

ISBN 0-669-90555-0

Published simultaneously in Canada.

Printed in the United States of America.

International Standard Book Number: 0-669-90555-0

Library of Congress Catalog Card Number: 73-10365

# Contents

**List of Figures**                                                    ix

**List of Tables**                                                     xi

**Preface**                                                           xiii

**Abbreviations**                                                     xvii

Chapter 1    The World Bank Group, Multilateral
             Aid, and the 1970s, *John P. Lewis
             and Ishan Kapur*                                           1

             Notes                                                     10


Chapter 2    The Challenges of the 1970s and the
             Present Institutional Structure,
             *Michael L. Hoffman*                                      13

             Comment: The Leopard's Spots,
             *Robert E. Asher*                                         21
             Comment: An Integrated Radicalism,
             *Carl I. Ohman*                                           27
             Notes                                                     34


Chapter 3    Determination of Priorities and the
             Allocation of Resources,
             *J. Burke Knapp*                                          37

             Comment: High Profile, Better Target,
             *William S. Gaud*                                         53
             Comment: The Raising of Resources,
             *Richard W. Richardson*                                   57
             Notes                                                     63

Chapter 4        Terms and Flexibility of Bank Lending,
                    *P.D. Henderson*                                    65

                 Comment: Grants, Loans, and
                    Local-Cost Financing
                    *John P. Lewis*                                     77
                 Comment: The Transfer of Resources,
                    *Mahbub Ul Haq*                                     83
                 Notes                                                 87


Chapter 5        Efforts to Influence Recipient
                    Performance: Case Study of India,
                    *I.P.M. Cargill*                                    89

                 Comment: Leaning Against Open Doors?,
                    *L.K. Jha*                                          97
                 Comment: A Bilateral Viewpoint,
                    *Maurice J. Williams*                              103
                 Notes                                                109


Chapter 6        The External Debt Problem,
                    *John H. Adler*                                    111

                 Comment: Debt Adjustment: The
                    Tyranny of Bankers, Brokers,
                    and Bondholders,
                    *Charles R. Frank, Jr.*                            123
                 Notes                                                130


Chapter 7        Relations with Other Multilateral
                    Agencies, *Richard H. Demuth*                      133

                 Comment: The World Bank and the
                    United Nations, *Stig Andersen*                    139
                 Comment: International Economic
                    Diplomacy, *Leon Gordenker*                        143
                 Notes                                                146


                 **Bibliography**                                      149

**Index** 159

**About the Contributors** 163

# List of Figures

2-1        Bank and IDA Lending by Purpose      23

3-1        Bank and IDA Lending by Area

                                                   44

6-1        World Bank: Outstanding Debt      112

# List of Tables

1-1        The Record for Ten Years, 1963-72                    3

3-1        Foreign and International Bond
           Issues by Market and Country
           of Borrower, 1967-71                                 40

3-2        India: IBRD Loans, IDA Credits,
           and IFC Investments by Sectors:
           1960-71                                              46

3-3        Cumulative Total of Bank and IDA
           Lending                                              48

4-1        Bank and IDA Commitments                             67

6-1        External Public Debt Outstanding of
           Selected Developing Countries,
           by Country and Type of Creditor,
           December 31, 1970                                    124

# Preface

This book originated at a seminar held at the Woodrow Wilson School of Public and International Affairs, Princeton University, on some of the prospects and problems of the World Bank Group in this decade. A series of senior Bank officials addressed themselves to certain policy issues and then were subjected to comment and questioning by other participants, mostly from outside the Bank. They included recipient country representatives, bilateral-aid officials, academics, and spokesmen for other multilateral agencies.

The book, like the original seminar, is not in any sense an official project of the International Bank for Reconstruction and Development or its affiliates. However, we are grateful to President Robert S. McNamara of the World Bank for informally approving of the undertaking at its inception. His interest undoutedly facilitated our recruitment of key Bank officials; their identity and the seriousness with which they accepted their assignments in turn aided the enlistment of the other participants.

Views expressed are those of individual contributors, not necessarily of institutions with which they are affiliated. Aside from the first chapter, the contents of the book began as seminar talks, typically from notes. While a great deal of working over of the taped record of those sessions by authors and editors alike has, we think, yielded a thoroughly readable text, it is only fair to the authors to note that the material was originally prepared for the ear rather than the eye; that, despite considerable updating, the principal ideas and emphases date from early 1971; and that responsibility for all the notes and tables lies with the editors.

A word is also in order about the scope and structure of the argument. The topical coverage of the seminar was designed to be highly selective, and aside from certain points added in our own first chapter, we have left the book the same way. Thus, some subjects of importance to the Bank, such as project appraisal and country planning analysis, are wholly or largely neglected. In addition, where seminar participants strayed beyond their assigned themes (often very provocatively), while eliminating overlaps, we have not tried to slice up and reshuffle contributions to conform to the original outline. It seemed better to let each writer say his piece whole.

What remains is an informed and multifaceted discussion of selected topics in multilateral development assistance for the 1970s that has no parallel in the available literature. The World Bank contributors do not turn out to be monolithic in their opinions, nor are other contributors diffident in voicing criticisms of the Bank's structure, operations, philosophies, and constraints. Nevertheless, the principal value of the volume is as a statement of how the World Bank saw itself and some of its principal problems, early in this decade and in a nonofficial format, as it was moving towards a more central role in the development assistance enterprise.

In the first chapter, the editors discuss the World Bank's projected role in the overall context of multilateral development assistance. They point to the need for new forms of concessional transfer and the pivotal role that the Bank will have to play in the coming decades.

In Chapter 2, Michael Hoffman presents the formal structure of the Bank as it has evolved from the original Articles of Agreement, Robert Asher analyzes whether the Bank is really the development agency it purports to be, while Carl Ohman argues for a radical approach to the Bank's sectoral lending with more emphasis on areas of high social benefit.

In the third chapter, Burke Knapp discusses the problems of allocating funds, sectorally as well as geographically. William Gaud poses the interesting question of the Bank's public profile getting higher and the consequent adverse effects on the Bank's operations in various countries. Richard Richardson's comment has the bulk of this volume's discussion of the Bank's own borrowing, an operational aspect that will become critically important in the coming decade.

In Chapter 4, David Henderson deals with the terms on which the Bank and IDA lend money and compares this to the terms of bilateral assistance. Mahbub Ul Haq and John Lewis comment on issues of project versus program lending and on local-cost financing.

Some recent literature has vehemently criticized the World Bank for the exercise of "leverage" in its efforts to influence the economic performance of recipient countries. We decided to take a specific case study, and as a result, Chapter 5 has three papers on the Bank's operations in India, its largest single client. Peter Cargill presents the main argument; L.K. Jha offers an Indian response. Maurice Williams presents insights into performance conditioning from a bilateral viewpoint.

The entire issue of debt relief and the external debt problems of developing countries is discussed in considerable detail by John Adler and Charles Frank, Jr. in Chapter 6.

Finally, in Chapter 7, Richard Demuth, Stig Andersen, and Leon Gordenker deal with the delicate and sensitive question of the formal and informal relationships of the World Bank with other multilateral agencies. There is a divergence of opinion on whether greater power and influence should be given to the UN Development Program or to the World Bank Group.

Finally, abstracting from the current mayhem on the foreign-exchange markets, it should be pointed out here that almost all data used in this book are denominated in United States dollars prior to May 1972, at a par value of US$1.00 per Special Drawing Right (SDR), unless otherwise specified.

Our thanks go to Mrs. Judith Duff and Mrs. Shirley Epton for transcribing the original seminar tapes, to Miss Linda Lavers and Mrs. Manya Vas for typing the manuscript, and to Mrs. Dorothy Rieger for seeing to it that the logistics of putting together a volume of this kind went smoothly.

The Editors

*Princeton, New Jersey*
*and*
*Washington, D.C.*
*July 1973*

# Abbreviations

| | |
|---|---|
| AsDB | Asian Development Bank |
| AfDB | African Development Bank |
| AID | Agency for International Development |
| CIAP | Inter-American Committee of the Alliance for Progress |
| DAC | Development Assistance Committee |
| DD II | Second Development Decade |
| ECOSOC | Economic and Social Council |
| FAO | Food and Agricultural Organization |
| GATT | General Agreement on Tariffs and Trade |
| GNP | Gross National Product |
| IBRD | International Bank for Reconstruction and Development |
| IDA | International Development Association |
| IDB | Inter-American Development Bank |
| IFC | International Finance Corporation |
| ILO | International Labor Organization |
| IMF | International Monetary Fund |
| LDCs | Less Developed Countries |
| ODA | Official Development Assistance |
| OECD | Organization for Economic Cooperation and Development |
| SDRs | Special Drawing Rights |
| UNCTAD | United Nations Conference on Trade and Development |
| UNDP | United Nations Development Program |
| UNESCO | United Nations Educational, Scientific, and Cultural Organization |
| WHO | World Health Organization |

# 1 The World Bank, Multilateral Aid, and the 1970s

John P. Lewis and Ishan Kapur

The International Bank for Reconstruction and Development has become the largest, and perhaps the most dynamic, external agency in the overseas development field. Observers' mounting interest, however, in the Bank is based on more than just its size or importance. There is also fascination with the ambivalent role in which the Bank has been cast and is casting itself.

On the one hand, the Bank has entered the 1970s with a reputation for considerable competence, earned during its first quarter-century of operations since 1946. It has an institutional style and *esprit* rivaled by few other international or, for that matter, bilateral agencies. Recently, with its scale of operations expanding at a tremendous rate, it has become the world's largest supplier of development assistance. It has strong, imaginative leadership. In its organization of country consortia and consultative groups, and in its negotiations with governments and with other multilateral agencies, the Bank has become increasingly active as an analyst, promoter, and coordinator of development policies. Its span of attention is rapidly spreading to a broader range of development issues and sectors, into areas such as agriculture, population control, education, and nutrition. The institution's research capacities are being impressively strengthened.

For many developing countries, since recipient governments share in its overall control and management, the Bank continues to appear more professional, to be relatively less suspect of political motives, and to seem less foreign than many bilateral aid programs. At the same time, donor governments, some of which have growing preferences for shifting their resource transfers from bilateral to multilateral channels, value the formal control that weighted voting gives them over the World Bank Group. They approve of the Bank Group's avoidance of the operational rigidities, such as national personnel quotas, that tend to characterize multilateral agencies governed on a one-flag, one-vote basis.

So much for the favorable side of the image. On the other hand, it can be argued that the Bank Group is acquiring its pre-eminence by default. One can say that the Bank is moving into a vacuum created, on the one hand, by the relative decline of bilateral assistance and, on the other, by the unreadiness of other multilateral instruments. It has been asked whether the institution is genuinely well cast for the assignment. Most of what it presently has to offer consists of the Bank's own loans—rather than much softer-term International

1

Development Association (IDA) credits—at interest rates high enough to repay the Bank's own borrowings in the international financial markets. Development assistance on these hard terms is not what the Bank's poorer clients need, especially those already burdened by large external debts initially caused by borrowings on inappropriately hard terms. Expansion of the Bank's own loan portfolio may be no better than a "second-best" solution to the resource gap problems projected for the 1970s.

There are also doubts as to whether the World Bank, in acceding to the role of the dominant development institution, is ready to be more than just a financial intermediary. Can it adequately respond to shifts in the development priorities of countries and bring to bear creative insights into the institutional and technical texture of the development process? The significance of the fact that the Bank itself has never conducted technical-assistance operations can be overdrawn: it has for a long time built requirements for technology transfers into its project agreements, and even into its program loans. For several years the Bank has been cultivating joint ventures with specialized UN agencies, such as FAO, WHO, and UNESCO, with technical expertise in particular sectors; and for at least a decade the Bank has been guiding its own programs with well-articulated views of national development programs that have also identified needed changes in the domestic policies of recipient countries. Nevertheless, some major doubts about the World Bank's ability to be an all-encompassing development agency remain. In particular, those who criticize IBRD for its overriding concern with the banking aspect of its lending and borrowing wonder whether its operations do not continue to inject an unwholesome capital-intensive bias into the technology being transferred to developing countries. They ask also whether the Bank's preoccupation with the rates of return on investment and the promotion of balance of payments improvements will dull its responsiveness to the poor countries' attempts to cope with problems of mass poverty and underemployment.

Finally, questions are being raised about the governance of the Bank. On the one hand, as its relative prominence as a supplier of development assistance increases, how successful will the Bank Group be in preserving its present degree of autonomy from operational control by donor governments and their parliaments? For example, will the growing disposition of elements in the United States Congress to subject World Bank operations to detailed inspection by the General Accounting Office prevail? Such efforts pose threats to the present governance of the Bank from one side of its constituency. Conversely, among the developing countries there is open questioning of how long an institution under the predominant control of donor governments representing a small minority of the world's population, though a majority of its income, will remain acceptable to the Third World even as a principal dispenser of development assistance, let alone as the major architect of world development policy.

These doubts are no longer confined to "New Left" critiques of the Bank,

**Table 1-1**
**The Record for Ten Years, 1963-72 (Millions of United States Dollars)**

| Fiscal Year | 1963 | 1964 | 1965 | 1966 | 1967 | 1968 | 1969 | 1970 | 1971 | 1972 |
|---|---|---|---|---|---|---|---|---|---|---|
| **World Bank** | | | | | | | | | | |
| Loans: Number | 28 | 37 | 38 | 37 | 46 | 44 | 84 | 70 | 78 | 72 |
| Loans: Amount[a] | 449 | 810 | 1,023 | 839 | 877 | 847 | 1,399 | 1,680 | 1,896 | 1,966 |
| Countries | 19 | 28 | 26 | 27 | 33 | 31 | 44 | 39 | 41 | 40 |
| Disbursements | 620 | 559 | 606 | 668 | 790 | 772 | 762 | 722 | 955 | 1,182 |
| Repayments to Bank | 113 | 117 | 137 | 166 | 188 | 237 | 298 | 329 | 319 | n.a. |
| Gross Income | 204 | 219 | 267 | 292 | 331 | 356 | 410 | 504 | 578 | 646 |
| Net Income | 83 | 97 | 137 | 144 | 170 | 169 | 171 | 213 | 212 | 183 |
| Total Reserves | 813 | 846 | 895 | 954 | 1,023 | 1,160 | 1,254 | 1,329 | 1,444 | 1,597 |
| Borrowings: Gross | 121 | 100 | 598 | 288 | 729 | 735 | 1,224 | 735 | 1,368 | 1,744 |
| Borrowings: Net | −5 | −32 | 250 | 64 | 503 | 215 | 698 | 299 | 819 | 1,136 |
| Subscribed Capital | 20,730 | 21,186 | 21,669 | 22,426 | 22,850 | 22,942 | 23,036 | 23,159 | 23,871 | 26,607 |
| Member Countries | 85 | 102 | 102 | 103 | 106 | 107 | 110 | 113 | 116 | 117 |
| **IDA** | | | | | | | | | | |
| Credits: Number[b] | 17 | 18 | 20 | 12 | 20 | 18 | 38 | 56 | 53 | 68 |
| Credits: Amount | 260 | 283 | 309 | 284 | 354 | 107 | 385 | 606 | 584 | 1,000 |
| Countries | 9 | 8 | 11 | 8 | 13 | 14 | 28 | 33 | 34 | 38 |
| Disbursements | 56 | 124 | 222 | 267 | 342 | 319 | 256 | 143 | 235 | 261 |
| Usable Resources, cumulative | 767 | 1,451 | 1,593 | 1,682 | 1,767 | 1,807 | 2,176 | 3,182 | 3,343 | 4,016 |
| Member Countries | 76 | 93 | 94 | 96 | 97 | 98 | 102 | 105 | 107 | 1,108 |
| Professional Staff | 429 | 463 | 532 | 662 | 724 | 752 | 961 | 1,170 | 1,348 | 1,568 |

[a]Excludes loans to IFC of $100 million in FY1967, $100 million in FY1970 and $60 million in FY1972.
[b]Joint Bank/IDA operations are counted only once, as Bank operations.
Source: IBRD *Annual Report 1971-72*, World Bank, Washington, D.C., p. 3.

such as those given prominence at the Bank's annual meeting in Copenhagen in September 1970.[1] As will be evident from the views expressed in this volume, many of the Bank's senior officials and some of its friendlier outside observers are grappling with the same questions; indeed, they have been sensitive to them for a long time.

It is not the intellectual or political fashion in the West at the moment, particularly in the United States, to emphasize the importance of the development-assistance situation in the 1970s. As recently as the summer of 1970 representatives of the United States Government participated very positively in the decisions, first of the UN Economic and Social Council, then of the General Assembly, to designate the 1970s the Second Development Decade. In DD II, the General Assembly asserted, real gross national product in the developing countries should average a growth rate of 6 percent annually; to this end, there should, during the decade, be annual net transfers of external resources equivalent to 1 percent of the GNPs of donor countries; and at least 70 percent of these transfers should flow through official channels and be on concessional terms.[2]

Already, in many sophisticated circles in the United States and elsewhere, these goals are regarded as unrealistic and passé. Conventional wisdom is backsliding from the DD II objectives on two grounds. The first is the claim that the foreign-aid aspect of the goals is beyond reach, mainly in the case of the United States. While most other developed nations have been expressing a willingness to play a larger part in the cooperative development effort, the United States has reduced its official development assistance (ODA) from $3.6 billion in 1963, .6 percent of Gross National Product (GNP), to $3.0 billion in 1970, or .3 percent of GNP, $3.3 billion in 1972, or *less* than .3 percent of GNP, and the immediate future looks extremely bleak.[3]

The other argument for downplaying development assistance is reassuring to those Americans of good will who have already given up on the aid front. The claim is that, due to new developments and new awarenesses of the past few years, we can now see that the 6 percent GNP growth target for the poor countries was not an adequate objective in any case. There are two principal strands to this rationalization. In the first place, in the developing countries themselves the interconnections between economic and political development have proved to be more complex and puzzling than official planning had frequently surmised. Many countries have concluded recently that their economic development efforts have been focusing too single-mindedly on average GNP-per capita growth with insufficient attention to equity and distribution issues. In the second place, in the developed countries the wave of concern with environmental problems has superseded the cause of overseas development for many people—and prompted the corollary that if growth implies pollution, then encouragement of its pursuit should be either stopped or diminished.

As arguments against the continuing importance of economic development and of net transfers of resources to assist that process, all of this conventional wisdom is exceedingly shallow. As for the feasibility of aid, the case overweights the importance of the United States in a period when other donors have been slowly developing a countertrend of their own. In the United States itself, the argument probably extrapolates too much from a particular conjunction of economic and political circumstances. Among other phenomena, there has been in Congress a strong reaction against direct US involvement in either the economic or political affairs of less developed countries; in part a spillover from the Vietnam war. Worst of all, the view that more ambitious levels of net-resource transfers are beyond practical political reach ignores the considerable possibilities (itemized in part below) that now exist for moving resources via unorthodox channels whose principal burden does not fall on budgetary appropriations by donor parliaments.

The rationalizations of aid erosion that cast doubt on the importance of productive expansion in the developing countries are equally shallow. It is true that many poor countries are belatedly recognizing a dangerous neglect of the income-distribution and employment dimensions of their development process. But the emphasis on equity objectives is being largely added to, not substituted for, their growth targets. To be sure, there is in some situations a trade-off between growth and equity, so that when choices are being made about how specific investable resources are to be employed, more attention to distributive and equity objectives may dictate slower growth rates than would otherwise be the case. In an important sense, however, countries with very low per capita incomes will need aggregate growth dividends even more, not less, if they are to find the resources for making significant inroads on poverty problems. Some countries are beginning to project just such antipoverty strategies, which, by mobilizing underemployed, low-productivity manpower into new development tasks, will raise the aggregate GNP growth rate, at the same time tilting the distribution of the increment to the very poor. Foreign-aid donors may safely assume that the new equity and employment emphasis in the developing countries will in no sense diminish the need for net transfers of external resources. On the contrary, whether because of adjustments caused when allocative decisions are no longer single-mindedly aimed at GNP growth and the attainment of balance in international payments or because of the incremental activity launched for antipoverty purposes, aid requirements are likely to increase.

The ecological case against growth and development assistance is also weak. The fact that the convergence of the world's income inequalities among nations must be worked out within a frame of planetary natural resource constraints surely is no argument for the poor countries staying or being kept as poor as they are. It may say more about the longer-term prospects for real incomes in the rich countries. As the documentation for the United Nations' Stockholm

Conference on Environmental Issues in June 1972 indicated, the developing countries are not about to be deterred from growth by environmental admonitions. Nor should they be. In their own interests it will be economical for them, as they develop, to avoid some of the local environmental wastage and abuse into which the advanced economies have blundered. But most growth-related pollution is highly localized and highly relative to income; developing countries would be as foolish to build advanced-economy standards against it into their cost structures as they would be to adopt advanced-economy wage rates.

The developing countries, accordingly, will continue to have a need and appetite for as vigorous economic growth as they can manage consistent with their internal equity objectives. We know of no reason to think that the appropriate development assistance goals for the 1970s do not remain at least as high as those that were chalked out in the Second Development Decade exercise.

The World Bank itself has reached the same conclusion: There is no question of the importance of a bold development-assistance effort in this decade. The issue the present volume addresses is how well the Bank Group is equipped to play a central role in that effort. Subsequent chapters treat a number of its facets. Here at the beginning we would add comments of our own only on two questions, both already noted. The first is whether the World Bank's claim to a central role in the supply of external resources to the developing countries in the seventies rests on the premise that the latter must settle for "second-best" solutions in the form of high-interest loans whose terms are dependent on those available to an institutional borrower operating in private financial markets. The second question concerns the Bank's capacities and limitations as a leader and mobilizer of worldwide development policy in this decade. Both of these are comparatively sweeping, basic issues. They need close and frontal consideration, we think, in a book that accords the World Bank such a central role.

It is quite true, as Mr. Knapp among other subsequent contributors notes, that the Bank's capacities in the years ahead for making conventional IBRD loans are very much larger than its probable, let alone assured, capacities for extending soft (IDA) credits. Under present ground rules for its own loans, the Bank is constrained to charge interest rates nearly as high as it must pay in the private financial markets of the industrialized countries. It is also true that, given their poverty, limited foreign-exchange earnings prospects, and existing debt burdens, many developing countries cannot afford to pay such costs for external credit.

As Mr. Adler's paper makes plain, the Bank itself just now is a leading analyst of such matters. Setting minimal projections of the developing countries' needed net transfers of external resources against what it believes to be reasonable estimates of likely IDA replenishments as well as future levels of bilateral aid, the Bank is finding a compelling case for a multiple expansion of conventional Bank loans before this decade is over. Given its interest in the scaling up of international transfers in the near future, the Bank is presently doing a fairly convincing job of persuading itself that all but the poorest developing countries will be able to digest the substantial expansion of debt-servicing burdens that such funding will imply.

We suspect this last argument is correct and, barring better answers, we agree that the Bank should stand ready to boldly enlarge its conventional loan portfolio on its normal terms. At the same time, as we see it, this course would constitute a poor answer to the capital needs of the 1970s. It would painfully exacerbate and prolong the process of appropriate resource transfers from the rich countries to the poor. More efficient and unidirectional vehicles for accomplishing these transfers are urgently needed. Moreover, we are convinced, in one form or another such vehicles with much heavier grant elements than conventional World Bank loans are not beyond reach.

However, the single issue that concerns us at the moment is the dominance of the development-assistance role the Bank is likely to play in this decade. The point, as far as this issue is concerned, is that successful substitutions of other vehicles that are superior to conventional World Bank loans as devices for net resource transfers will not mean a parallel diminution of the institutional role of the Bank in the composite development-assistance process. Instead, most of the potential alternative means for increasing the net resource flow to the developing countries under softer terms would in fact heavily involve the World Bank Group.

The first and conceptually simplest idea, although perhaps politically the most difficult, is the possibility for larger-than-projected contributions to IDA by donor governments. This would by definition augment the aid-dispensing role of that agency.

Second, and perhaps most important, is the possibility of supplementing development assistance through the use of the Special Drawing Rights (SDRs), created by the International Monetary Fund in January 1970.[4] Though designed to deal with international monetary and liquidity problems, SDRs can be used to increase the transfer of resources to developing countries, and it can be hoped that they sooner or later will be.[5]

In their first introductory round SDRs have been the only reserve currency ever passed out free to those desirous of liquidity. Their distribution has been modeled on the pattern of IMF quotas and therefore skewed toward the have nations and away from have-nots. Now that the SDRs have won their spurs as a reserve asset, have proven that in the eyes of many holders they are indeed as good as gold (and have become quite conspicuously better than dollars), there appears to be no good reason why subsequent rounds of SDR distributions should not go predominately to the developing countries, the advanced economies who want increased liquidity being forced to earn it by exchanging some exports for the desired reserve assets. Nor, in the aggregate, should this requirement be perceived as onerous by the developed economies, most of whom now seem determined to run trade surpluses, which they can do collectively only if the developing economies run a collective deficit. This would be an acceptable state of affairs for the latter if they can find orderly, nononerous adequate financing, such as continuing distributions of SDRs, metered, it should be noted, to the world's liquidity, not its development, needs.

For our purposes the point regarding these SDR possibilities is that while the World Bank Group would not automatically or necessarily be involved in their implementation, in fact, the likelihood is that it would be. Actually, there would be a strong case for sparing the whole procedure from the conventions of development assistance and for distributing the SDRs to the poor countries, directly through the IMF, simply as block grants allocated by a fixed formula. Such a procedure would maximize the flexibility and timeliness of the transfers and avoid the discriminatory tendencies between recipients that characterize all discretionary aid donors. Very probably these gains would more than offset the misuses of SDR distributions that, with an automatic distribution, might occur in a few cases. But such a procedure may be too freewheeling to garner the support of the rich countries, as has been proven at the discussions of the Committee of 20 this year during the international monetary reform negotiations. The developed nations, if they can be persuaded to support the "link" scheme, are likely to insist that increased channeling of SDRs to poor countries be administered by an experienced development-assistance agency against responsible program and project proposals. If so, the agency elected to this role almost surely will be IDA.

Third, it is becoming increasingly evident that a significant part of the net resource transfers between rich and poor countries in the seventies will have to be accomplished by one form or another of debt relief.[6] That is to say, the algebraic sum that is net aid will be increased in part by rescheduling or otherwise reducing the reflow of interest and amortization payments from the poor countries to the rich.

In a large number of developing countries, the basic problem is not so much a chronic overindebtedness but a short-term liquidity problem arising out of large amortization liabilities incurred on relatively short-term debt. World Bank and OECD studies have indicated the severity of this problem and pointed to the large amounts, gross, that countries have had to borrow in order to obtain a relatively small net transfer of resources. In theory, it is still possible for countries to avoid external debt problems from getting out of hand if there are good possibilities for rolling over amortization of short-term debts through borrowing. Amelioration or avoidance of external debt problems will depend on the provision of adequate quantities of free foreign exchange or on the flexibility with which donor countries are prepared to match their assistance to the import requirements of the developing countries.

Here, on the one hand, the World Bank's need to maintain its credit standing in the international financial markets greatly inhibits its ability to include its own conventional loans in debt-adjustment exercises. On the other hand, however, the Bank is already the world's leading institutional analyst of the debt-burden problem. It has taken the lead in organizing limited debt-adjustment exercise on behalf of certain clients. If debt adjustment does prove to be an assistance vehicle of which donors make greater collective use in the seventies, almost surely this will happen only with the help of continuing World Bank leadership.

Fourth, there are various alternatives of the "Horowitz Proposal" leading to a subsidy on interest payments charged on IBRD loans that have originally been raised at commercial rates in private markets.[7] Resources raised elsewhere than in the private financial markets (for example, via donor government contributions or from SDRs) would be used to subsidize the interest rates charged from borrowing countries and also to provide risk guarantees for some of the latter's own borrowings in private markets.

There are, indeed, some hypothetical possibilities for transferring resources to the poor countries which probably would *not* involve the World Bank. One of the more exotic, and potentially more important, of these is the effective internationalization of all rights to, and royalties from, economic exploitation of the world's oceans and seabeds. The challenge now is to do this before further national encroachment on the seas and seabeds occurs. However, the prospects for early action seem dim. Between them, those maritime developing countries who are trying to extend their territorial waters to the two-hundred-mile mark and those advanced countries who are allergic to all restraints on their exploitation of the oceans seem to have effectively stalemated the cause of global management of the ocean's resources.

As already noted, there may be a strong case for not involving the Bank in future SDR distributions. For our present purposes, the conclusions are quite obvious. It is indeed to be hoped that most developing countries will not, for their concessional transfers in this decade, need to rely as heavily on conventional World Bank loans as the Bank itself now surmises in some of its more pessimistic analyses. But as better alternatives do come to hand, the financing agency that recipient countries are most likely to find themselves dealing with is going to be the World Bank Group.

We shall deal only briefly with the Bank's prospects as a leader in making and coordinating worldwide development policy. On the general issue, our point is simply that the Bank has an impressive head start. Obviously, it cannot go it alone as a designer, promoter, or mediator of sensible international development policies. But in terms of the comparative capacities of the various agencies on the multilateral development scene—their analytic, programming, and negotiational capacities as well as the resources they command—it is hard to imagine any promising evolution of international development strategies in the near future in which the Bank will not play a key role.

The international scene is in grievous disarray. A world of global linkages, balances, and inequities is still overwhelmingly dominated by the nation-state. Most multilateral organizations are still little more than nation-state collectives organized on the principle of one-flag, one-vote. On the one hand, these multilateral agencies are the hostages of their minor members and are distrusted by the major powers. At the same time, the polarization of the postwar world by the superpowers is ending. Old blocs are breaking up and new ones coalescing— with many implications that are as yet uncertain. Meanwhile, the activities of multinational corporations seem to elude the control of national governments and international agencies alike. It is not, to say the least, an easy scene in which to work out coherent strategies for the advancement of the poor countries.

As a central actor in the piece, the World Bank, it seems to us, may need to effect at least two structural adjustments. First, it may need to modify its present weighted voting pattern. It probably should do so only gradually and at a pace that does not lose it the confidence of the donor countries. In particular, it is to be hoped that such a change in voting patterns will not be in a manner that merely mimics the rest of the UN system's habit of counting flags rather than heads. Instead, as the Bank accords a growing voice to the poor countries, it may begin to lead the rest of the multilateral community toward patterns of representation weighted by national populations.

Second, if it is to play the major role that its resources suggest, we would assume the Bank will need to affiliate more members from among the Socialist bloc. At present it has Yugoslavia and Rumania, and declares itself ready to receive others whose applications conform to its existing rules. But to promote the Socialist bloc's affiliation, the Bank probably will need to modify some of its rules. In particular, it may wish to loosen the bracketing of IBRD membership with IMF membership that exists under the Bretton Woods formula.[8]

In addition, the Bank must take great care in its operation, as it seems increasingly disposed to do, to be neither arrogant in its relations with its clients nor uncooperative with other multilateral bodies. But with all of this said, this fact remains: Of all multilateral agencies on the development policy scene, the World Bank Group presently is far and away the one with the strongest institutional identity, the greatest depth of technical and analytical capacity, the greatest ability to talk firmly both to host governments and donor governments, and the most promising combination of globalism and pragmatism in its operating philosophy. If it does not stay in the middle of this decade's development strategy game we will be in even worse trouble than otherwise.

### Notes

1. See, for example, Teresa Hayter, *Aid as Imperialism*, Penguin Books, 1971.

2. United Nations, International Development Strategy: *Action Program of the General Assembly for the Second United Nations Development Decade*, New York: United Nations, 1970 (St/ECA/1939).

3. *Development Assistance Review*, Efforts and Policies of the Members of the Development Assistance Committee, Paris: OECD, 1971, pp. 38-39, 165; and United States Agency for International Development, Washington, D.C.: 1973.

4. See International Monetary Fund, *Annual Report, 1970*, pp. 28-31 and 144.

5. For samples of the extensive discussion of this subject, see Thomas Balogh, "Old Fallacies and New Remedies: the SDRs in Perspective," *Bulletin of the Oxford University Institute of Economics and Statistics*, vol. 32, no. 2, May 1970; and The Third UNCTAD, Santiago, Chile, May 1972, Papers and Proceedings.

6. International Bank for Reconstruction and Development, *Annual Report, 1972*, Washington, D.C., pp. 50-56; See also papers by John H. Adler and Charles R. Frank, Jr. in Chapter 6 of this volume.

7. International Bank for Reconstruction and Development, *The Horowitz Proposal, A Staff Report*, Washington, D.C.: February 1965. This idea is also discussed further by Richard W. Richardson in Chapter 3 of this volume.

8. International Bank for Reconstruction and Development, *Articles of Agreement*, as amended December 17, 1965; see article II, section 1 and article VI, section 3.

# 2

## The Challenges of the 1970s and the Present Institutional Structure

Michael L. Hoffman*

In order to try and set the stage for a critical consideration of the Bank's role in the 1970s, we have to understand how the institution works and how it got where it is today. What I am going to present is an insider's view, for which I make no apologies. I like to think it possible both to understand how the thing works in a way that only an insider can and at the same time be able to stand at some distance and look at the creature in its environment.

It is necessary to remind ourselves how the world environment has changed since the Bank was conceived and organized. I would like to mention a few of the more striking and significant differences between the world of the 1970s and the world that was anticipated by the founders of the Bank at Bretton Woods.

In 1944 the war was ending; there were "allies"—who also constituted the original United Nations—and defeated enemy powers. Though the imperial powers had won, a lot of people believed that the era of empires was over. However, no one had any experience of a world with nation-states but no empires. Consequently, the founders had no real notion of what those sovereign states now known as "less developed countries" would be like. With a few exceptions, about which almost nothing was known, only Latin America offered any examples. Even in Latin America, moreover, nobody thought of Uruguay or Argentina as "underdeveloped."

In 1945, a year after Bretton Woods, when the UN was organized, there were only 55 nation-state members; now there are 131 countries in it, plus non-members. The important fact is that practically all of the new countries are of a species that could not have been identified or described by the founders, and much less, could their habits have been understood.

The main interest of the founders of the Bretton Woods "system" was in the International Monetary Fund.[1] The Fund continued to be the center of intellectual interest for almost twenty-five years, and the Bank has only recently become a focus for intellectuals. So far as the founders thought at all about the Bank, it was the reconstruction aspect that concerned them most. This was well before the Marshall Plan had even been imagined. However, the concept of development was included in the title of the new agency, and this was virtually its first appearance on the international scene.

*Currently, Director, Department of International Relations, International Bank for Reconstruction and Development, Washington, D.C.

13

When the Bank was created, experience with international organizations was very limited. Of the present family, only the International Rhine Commission, International Telecommunications Union (ITU), Universal Postal Union (UPU), and the International Labor Office (ILO) existed. The ILO was largely a convention-drafting outfit and not an operational agency. The notion of technical assistance by international agencies, or for that matter by one sovereign government to another, hardly existed. In fact, even the term did not exist and cannot be found in the Articles of Agreement as one of the functions of the Bank.

The founders, as well as the first four presidents, had been impressed, and some of them seriously burned, by the experience of the 1920s and the 1930s with international loans. A large amount of bonds had been sold for general purpose financing, mostly by Latin American and European municipalities. The proceeds were not well applied, and nobody made any attempt to evaluate what we call the performance or even the creditworthiness of the economies before selling bonds. The result was large scale defaults in the 1930s. The founders of the Bretton Woods system were determined not to repeat this experience, and this gave rise to the "project approach" to lending that is so deeply imbedded in the Articles of Agreement.[2] The intention was to insure that funds were well used, and the founders sought to do this by tying funds to projects. These issues will be more fully examined later; for now, I just want to explain how the project approach got built into the Bank's operations. This is also why the Articles of Agreement appear to restrict the Bank's freedom of action in two areas: first, the financing of local expenditures and, second, what is now known as program lending.[3]

Perhaps most important of all these points is the fact that an institution like the Bank had never existed before and had absolutely no standing as a borrower in capital markets. For the first ten years or so of its existence this meant, in effect, the US capital market. I am sure that the wildest estimates of the most enthusiastic founder would never have envisaged that over $8 billion could be raised in the next quarter of a century by an institution borrowing on competitive market terms and investing primarily in projects in poor and largely unknown parts of the world. The establishment of World Bank Bonds as Triple A securities took time. This was mainly the work of Eugene R. Black, but the founders had the genius to lay the foundations for this kind of new high-grade securities.

In fact, the founders did not think the Bank would be a lending institution to any great extent, if at all. Testimony by the US Secretary of the Treasury at the time clearly indicates that he thought the Bank would mainly guarantee the obligations of borrowing countries floated in international capital markets. Ironically, the guarantee powers have not been used at all. It quickly became evident that if the Bank was to establish its credit, then it was much better for it to issue its own obligations. This, naturally, was also better for the borrower. We may still use the guarantee powers, but probably in situations not envisaged by the founders, as for example in the case of big regional projects involving a large debt burden or of countries on the verge of being able to market their own obligations. Neither, however, is a very important possibility.

One of the commonest criticisms of the World Bank is that it is an Anglo-Saxon institution. This is true, but is a characteristic that has to be judged in the context of the Bank's environment. In the world of 1944 it could hardly have been otherwise; Europe badly needed reconstructing, and Japan and Germany were defeated powers. Russia was present at Bretton Woods but provided no intellectual input, and finally did not join. Had the United States and the United Kingdom not largely agreed on the methods and objectives, and largely worked out the scheme between them, there would have been no World Bank or Fund. Naturally, the institutions bear a strong imprint of Anglo-Saxon legal and organizational concepts and ideals. It took just over eighteen months to negotiate the Fund and Bank Articles of Agreement from the first Fund draft to ratification. It is inconceivable that his could have been done except through domination by two governments thinking fundamentally very much along the same lines.[4]

One could go on citing things that the founders could not have known or foreseen about the world of the 1950s and 1960s, much less the 1970s. So far I may have given the impression that I have been laying the groundwork for a case that the Articles of Agreement are obsolete and inappropriate for the 1970s. On the contrary, my main thesis is that the Articles of Agreement have proved to be an extraordinarily far-sighted and flexible document, enabling the Bank to operate on a scale and in ways certainly not envisaged by the founders but without contravening their fundamental principles and purposes for the institution. They are a very good foundation on which to build the Bank's program for the 1970s. The Fund's Articles have been changed more than ours but have also stood up very well in comparison with other international agreements negotiated at the time.

Let me go on to identify some of the Bank's strong points (which seem to me still to be strong points for the years ahead) that are rooted in the Articles of Agreement or in other conventions that have grown up around the Articles. I want to emphasize characteristics peculiar to the Bank that distinguish it from other international organizations.

First, there is the powerful leverage of "joint and several guarantees" written into conditions governing the 90 percent uncalled capital subscription.[5] Each member is obligated up to the limit of its unpaid capital subscription. And each member's obligation is independent of the others; that is, default by one member does not excuse any other member from its obligations to pay if called upon. The total effect is that members share proportionately the risks involved in the Bank's loans, and each member's full credit is behind Bank obligations to the extent of the uncalled portion of its own capital subscription. At first only the guarantee of the US Government was important in the international capital markets; today, guarantees of the Federal Republic of Germany, Japan, France, and others have almost equal market standing. By the stroke of a pen, the founders created an entirely new Triple-A asset, but it took the market several years to realize this fact. Recently, an even newer kind of asset has been created: short-term obligations sold to central banks and treated as secondary reserves. Nearly $800 million has now been mobilized through two-year bonds.

There are certain obvious criticisms of the system of weighted voting in the Bank, which contrasts with all other international organizations with the exception of the IMF. In particular, the political arms of the United Nations sometimes get very irritated at the fact that we do not conform to the UN system of one-country, one-vote. But two points need to be made. First, decisions by the Board typically, and especially in the case of loans, are unanimous. Thus, the weights attaching to different directors' votes have no ostensible function. The second point is that whereas weighted voting has not, therefore, had a major effect on Bank policies and project determinations, its existence has been indispensable to the scale of the Bank's operations. Without it the institution would not have been entrusted with the resources it now has at its disposal.

The third distinctive set of characteristics concerns the powers of the President of the World Bank. These particularly warrant discussion because some of the most significant ones are not written into the Articles of Agreement but are only implied. There is long established acceptance of the basic principle that Executive Directors cannot initiate proposals for loans or credits in the interests of their constituents. The President proposes and the Board of Directors accepts, amends, or rejects.[6] The Board is not a political bargaining body; there has been no case of the rejection of a loan proposal, though withdrawals of proposals have occasionally occurred when it became clear that the Board was divided. It is worth emphasizing the contrast between this method of operation and that of other international agencies. One result is that the Bank reflects the ambitions, objectives, personality, and prejudices of its presidents more than most other institutions—the change in attitude, for example, between Eugene Black and George Woods, the latter being far more willing to take bigger risks. In McNamara's case, there has been the introduction of the programming approach and the move away from using GNP indices as the sole criterion of development performance. The attitudes towards, and the policies of, the International Finance Corporation (IFC) have also altered under McNamara and tended to make that organization more important and larger in its operations.

The Board of Directors itself is a very small body with nearly all the powers of the Governors delegated to it. There are a few exceptions. The original Board of twelve has now grown to twenty-one, and each elected Executive Director now represents roughly the same number of votes.

The Articles of Agreement give full and unquestioned authority to the

President to organize his staff. The hiring of personnel is not bound by a nationality-quota system, as in other international agencies. An effective effort is made at broad internationalization, but there are no constitutional restraints on hiring the best professionals available.

The Articles of Agreement established other lasting characteristics of the Bank's operation. For example, even before the United Nations existed, the Articles stated that the Bank "shall co-operate with any general international organization and with public international organizations having specialized responsibilities in related fields."[7] That is as near as they could come in those days to the notion of a specialized agency. In Article 5, Section 8b, the Bank is enjoined to give consideration to the views and recommendations of competent international organizations. All this has become much more important for the Bank politically, in recent years.

However, the last contribution of the founders that I would emphasize here was their articulation of the mission of the Bank. I have said earlier that everyone in 1944 was more reconstruction-minded than development-minded. Nevertheless, the founders imposed an obligation upon the Bank to develop "productive resources of members thereby assisting in raising productivity, standard of living and conditions of labor in their territories."[8] To so charge an international institution endowed with substantial resources was an entirely novel idea. It took us a long time to realize the implications of this obligation, and new ones are emerging every year. Among other things, this led to the development of completely new techniques of finance. The IBRD had to look at a country as a whole as client and borrower, in a way similar to a country banker who knows all about his client's family, relatives, business, prejudices, and so on. The "whole country" approach grew out of this system and from these roots and is now widely accepted throughout the UN structure.

The question of flexibility in the Bank's operations has often arisen. The Bank can do practically anything it wants to do in pursuit of its objectives (except default on its bonds). The Executive Directors are not only the institution's governing board but its supreme court for interpreting the Articles of Agreement and their implications for operational work.[9] A whole new world of development finance has grown up under the Articles of Agreement. Many of the concepts and mechanisms first evolved under these auspices now have been accepted by other institutions. The important issues to discuss are not whether the Bank *can* do this or that but whether it *should* and *how*.

There are also certain characteristics that the Bank has evolved that were not preconditioned by the Articles of Agreement. One is a rather distinctive tripartite operational approach. Our practice is to bring to bear on any project or policy problem the expertise of technical staff, trained economists, and negotiators with intensive knowledge of their countries. The result is a continuous state of intellectual tension on every issue. With increasing frequency a fourth vector is the contact between the Bank and other agencies within the UN system.

Also, the Bank has evolved a comparatively centralized operation. It has been and predominantly remains a headquarters-centered agency that relies on frequent missions abroad by its staff for its knowledge of facts and situations in member countries. Compared to other agencies, it has been characterized by a high degree of continuity in professional staff association with particular countries. This, however, has diminished in recent years with the rapid expansion that the Bank has undergone and the creation of new departments.

Despite its considerable centralization, the Bank now has fifteen resident offices apart from its Paris and Tokyo offices, and they show a great variation in function. There is a fairly strong view prevalent in the Bank at the moment, subscribed to among others by Hollis Chenery, formerly Economic Advisor to the President of the World Bank and now Vice-President, Development Policy, that more decentralization is both inevitable and desirable.

So far I have been talking about the Bank only. However, the Bank is the centerpiece of three institutions. It is worth keeping in mind that without the Bank and its record there would be no International Development Association (IDA) or International Finance Corporation (IFC). Some of the points I have mentioned here, such as the question of credit standing, are not logically related to the IDA but nevertheless are politically important. In considering the role of the World Bank Group in the 1970s the role and the potential of IDA are crucial.[10] Admirable as it may be, the World Bank, depending essentially on borrowing in capital markets, could not possibly finance many development projects in the very poor countries that have emerged and joined the UN and the World Bank Group during the past fifteen or twenty years. We think that a twenty-year amortization period and a 7 1/4 percent rate of interest are pretty good terms for loans, but there are a good many countries that for years to come will not be able to afford even those terms. These countries have a high growth potential, but only over a very long-run period. (Countries can change their positions faster than we think; the change in the relative positions of Taiwan and Italy over the past twenty years is one example.)

Despite a story propagated by some of the more enthusiastic critics of the World Bank, IDA was not forced on to a reluctant Bank. The concept was developed in the Bank headquarters, and the reasons for such an institution grew directly out of the Bank's experience. By 1956 it was already apparent to professionals in the Bank that the development problems of many of the new countries could not be met to any significant extent by loans on the Bank's terms—and in those days our rate of interest was around 4 1/2 percent.

The animal I have tried to describe—the Bank—has a twin in IDA. The two bear an unmistakable family resemblance to each other, but there is a deep, if narrow, difference. It concerns the source of funds and the consequent terms of lending. IDA does not depend on capital markets for its resources, but instead on appropriations by individual governments. And its credits are soft: fifty-year amortization period, ten-year grace period, and no rate of interest. (IDA credits have a 3/4 of 1 percent service charge on them, but no interest is levied.) These, however, are the terms to the governments or the initial borrower, not necessarily to the ultimate beneficiary institution—and definitely not if it happens to be a revenue-earning entity. Otherwise, nearly all of what I have said about the Bank as an institution applies to IDA also.

The existence of IDA has meant considerably more government concern with the running of the Bank Group institutions. This is reflected in the gradual increase in the Board discussions of policy issues. The Bank's resources, in a very real sense, "belong" to the institution as such: it borrows its money, and the President, while he needs government acquiescence, is independent of periodic legislative procedures. IDA's money, however, is *government* money in a quite different sense, and governments have not been slow to make this clear.

So far IDA has been run simply as a fund on which the Bank can draw to meet situations where Bank terms are inappropriate.[11] The original idea was that it should in fact be a fund, and not a separate institution. It has the same standards as the Bank on projects, and the same standards on country economic and fiscal performance. Whether this is right or not is a question that will have to be discussed and faced. Some economists, such as W. Arthur Lewis, believe that this adoption of Bank standards is not the correct criteria for IDA's operations.

In conclusion, it is important to emphasize that the Bank Group operates through a continuing dialogue with member governments, not through legislation, passing resolutions, or political bargaining in the Board of Directors. A large program of sector studies, economic country missions, consultative meetings, and academic research forms the essential basis for this dialogue. Since there are numerous worthwhile projects for the Bank Group to support and finance, some sort of order of priority has to be established, given the limited resources available. The present institutional structure of the Bank Group, I think, facilitates the determination of these priorities. The question then is: Is this kind of institution useful for the problems of the 1970s?[12]

# Comment: The Leopard's Spots

The World Bank seems destined to play a leading—in all probability, the leading—role during the 1970s in nurturing and coordinating the international development effort. Virtually all the high-level commissions, committees, and task forces studying international development now recommend a shift from a predominantly bilateral approach to a considerably more multilateral, if not predominantly multilateral, approach. As one who was advocating greater reliance on multilateral machinery long before it was fashionable to do so, I am immensely gratified to find myself at last fully in fashion. As an employee of an independent, private research institution, however, I can be more ornery and provocative than others in this series who are senior employees of the Bank or the IFC.[13]

Take, for example, the vaunted flexibility of the Bank. The Bank has, in truth, demonstrated considerable capacity to adjust to changing times and meet changing requirements, particularly by comparison with some of the other UN agencies. In many respects, however, the much-maligned US aid program has been more innovative, more pioneering, more flexible than the Bank.

The United States pioneered in developing the technical-assistance concept; in introducing soft lending; in providing nonproject (or program) assistance; in demonstrating the potentialities of aid on a generous scale; in responding to crises; in consistently emphasizing agriculture, education, and health work; and in other ways. For most of its life the Bank, I would say, has been a follower rather than a leader in thinking about the nature of the development process and how to expedite and enrich that process. It has been financially oriented rather than development oriented.

One of the basic questions about the World Bank Group that I would like to raise is: Can the leopard change its spots? Can an agency that at first closely resembled a bank and until fairly recently has continued to make noises like a bank, be transformed into an institution that could more accurately be termed a development agency?

Unfortunately, we do not yet have universal agreement on what is meant by the term "development," except that it means considerably more than an increase in the gross national product. Neither can any widely accepted

*At time of writing, Senior Research Fellow, Foreign Policy Studies Program, Brookings Institution, Washington, D.C. Currently, an independent international economic consultant.

21

definition of the term "development agency" be cited to illuminate the transformation I have in mind when I contrast a bank with a development agency. However, the essence of the difference between a bank and a development agency, in my view, is the greater concern of the latter with development goals, strategy, and performance, with the social and civic, as well as the economic and financial, aspects of development, with meeting the most urgent needs as well as with providing foreign exchange for necessary projects, and with rationing its resources in such a fashion as to take all claims upon them properly into account.

Judgments concerning the leopard's ability to change its spots are further complicated because the Bank, in effect, denies that it has any spots to change. Ever since the late 1940s, when the Bank withdrew from the reconstruction business in favor of the Marshall Plan, its leaders have thought of it as a development agency. President McNamara's predecessors, no less than Mc-Namara himself, have regarded the Bank as a counselor to its less developed members on investment priorities, on project preparation and appraisal, and on economic and financial policies conducive to self-sustaining growth. Thus, what may have been transformed during these last two decades is not the Bank's conception of its function but its judgment concerning the most appropriate ways of fulfilling that function. In other words, those of us who allege that the Bank for too long behaved too much like a bank may simply be saying that, in our view, its conception of development, its ideology, for too long remained rigid and narrow.

If question number one is: "Can the leopard change its spots?" and question two is "Does it have any spots to change?," question three is "Even if it has spots, should it change them?" Do the members of the World Bank family, who may readily concede that the Bank knows what it is doing when it makes an economic and technical appraisal of an electric power project, have the same confidence in its judgment when it seeks to devise or appraise a development strategy?

During the first ten or twelve years of its existence, the Bank's capital contributions to the less developed world consisted of a relatively small annual flow of funds. The funds were devoted almost entirely to financing the foreign-exchange costs of specific projects, three-quarters of which were public utilities projects. While this concentration of effort may have been expedient, in the light of the Articles of Agreement and the need to make the new institution respectable in the banking community, it was promptly given a fancier rationale. As the Bank's Annual Report said in 1951:

It is only natural that, except for the early reconstruction loans, the Bank's lending operations have been concentrated in the field of basic utilities. An adequate supply of transportation facilities is a precondition for the most productive application of private savings in new enterprises. It is also the first step in the gradual industrialization and diversification of underdeveloped countries. These basic facilities require large initial capital outlays which, because of the low level of savings, often cannot be financed wholly by the countries themselves. Moreover, most of the machinery and equipment used in the construction of these facilities must be imported. Therefore, the resources of the Bank are called upon to provide the foreign exchange necessary for the building of these vitally important facilities.[14]

The leaders of the Bank had tremendous faith in private enterprise and private investment as the real engines of growth. Not only did they consider the absorptive capacity of the less developed countries for foreign capital extremely limited, but even the Bank's relatively small contribution to that flow could, in

(Millions of US dollars)

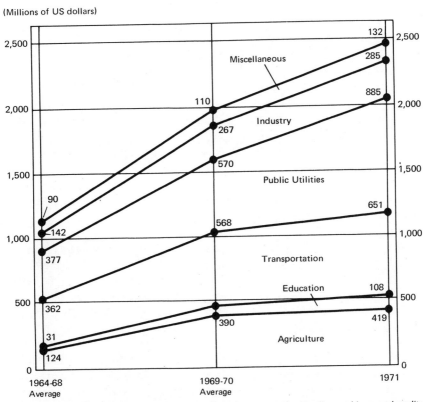

*Miscellaneous includes industrial imports credits and other non-project lending, and loans and credits for population, tourism, engineering and project preparation. Loans and credits to development finance companies are included under industry.

**Figure 2-1.** Bank and IDA Lending by Purpose. *Source:* IBRD *Annual Report 1970-71*, World Bank, Washington, D.C.

their view, be justified only if borrowing countries followed "sound" policies. In general, "sound" policies meant settling outstanding obligations on defaulted pre-World War II bonds, pursuing conservative monetary and fiscal policies, generating sufficient public savings to cover the local currency costs of capital infrastructure projects, and providing a hospitable climate for foreign and domestic private investment. It meant recognizing that oil refineries, steel mills, fertilizer plants, national development banks, and virtually everything but major public utilities ought to be privately owned.

The Bank's views on development included almost no concessions to the views being expressed vigorously in the United Nations and in the academic community. There it was asserted that the Bank took far too dim a view of the creditworthiness of poor countries, that those countries were capable of putting to productive use a considerably larger volume of external assistance than the Bank was making available, and that the Bank (and its sister institution, the Fund) were more interested in stability than in growth. Poor countries, it was argued in the United Nations, needed help in building their social as well as economic infrastructures—their water and sanitation facilities, schools, hospitals, etc.—and in meeting the local currency as well as the foreign-exchange costs of development programs. Grants and soft loans as well as hard loans were needed.

In the eyes of its management, however, the Bank was doing about all that could be reasonably expected of it. When planning and programming were still in their infancy, the Bank was encouraging investment programming on a national scale; and good country-development programs could make clear the volume and types of outside aid required. Its managers thought that about the most serious deficiency of the Bank as a development institution was its inability to assist the private sector more directly by lending to private enterprises in developing countries without obtaining a guarantee of repayment from the government of the country in which the enterprise would be located.

The need for an International Finance Corporation (IFC) was recognized early in the Bank's history, and the Bank was inventive enough, even before the IFC came into being, to meet part of the need by helping to establish, and by lending to, national development banks, which in turn could finance domestic private investment. Until about 1968, however, the Bank held tightly to the idea that such development banks had to be privately owned.

Although Michael Hoffman has said that the IDA, the soft-loan affiliate of the World Bank, was not forced on a reluctant Bank, my memory (refreshed by some research not too long ago) indicates that, on the whole, it was. The Bank vigorously opposed the soft-loan concept till about 1958. When the build-up for a soft-loan agency had become almost irresistible, the then President of the World Bank, Eugene Black, decided that if there was going to be such an agency, he might as well run it.

The result, I have not doubt, is a more competent, faster-growing agency than we would otherwise have. Yet I would say that the Bank was slow to see the role that soft lending could play in meeting recognized needs for foreign capital. The admirably simple-minded solution of the Marshall Plan era was to provide 80 percent of the assistance on a grant basis and end the period of dependence as soon as possible. But yesterday's beneficiaries of Marshall Plan grants are as determined as reformed alcoholics to save the less developed countries from the perils of such benevolence. So grants today are rare, and soft loans unavailable in large enough volume.

The creation of the IDA can be viewed as a major milestone in the as-yet-incomplete transformation of the World Bank Group into a development agency. The need to ration precious resources involved the Bank Group more deeply in evaluating development performance. This, in turn, has raised serious questions about what is being done by borrowers to reduce unemployment, to see that the fruits of productivity increases are equitably shared, and to encourage popular participation in the development effort. IDA has helped the Bank Group increase its lending for agriculture, education, and other previously neglected sectors.

Edward S. Mason nevertheless makes the following comment in one of the chapters of our analytical history of the World Bank Group.

One would have thought that the systematic attention given by the Bank Group over long periods of time to the development of its member countries might have led, through country comparisons, to a grouping of these countries into significant development cases or models of use in formulating development strategies. . . . There are labor surplus economies, export-oriented economies, characteristic differences between the structure of production of small and large economies at similar per capita income levels, and among economies of similar size at different per capita income levels. In fact, the only grouping of developing economies that emerges from Bank experience is the product of administrative organization rather than politico-economic analysis.

The geographic organization of the Bank Group into area departments differentiates the economies of Latin America from those in Africa south of the Sahara, the Middle East, etc., but this administrative division hides more than it reveals in understanding developmental processes. The functional or projects departments have built up over the years a uniquely competent staff of project appraisers in those fields in which the Bank has done the bulk of its lending. This comparative advantage of the Bank over other sources of development finance has reinforced the Bank's dedication to the project approach and has accounted for some of its resistance to a substantial broadening of its fields of lending and of interest. "Why mess around with nonproject lending, education and things like that, if you are really best at financing electric power projects and there are still electric power projects to be financed?"

Until quite recently, development to the World Bank Group (as well as to many others) meant primarily an increase in GNP; the Bank's concern with development performance was virtually limited to policies and practices thought to affect fairly directly the rate of growth of GNP: rates of investment, savings rates, export prospects, and so forth. Under McNamara, there has been a tremendous increase in the volume of Bank Group lending, and also in the breadth of the Bank's concern with noneconomic matters considered relevant to the development process, family planning, for example. There is talk in the President's speeches and in the Board of Directors about distributing income increases more equitably, reducing unemployment and malnutrition, and influencing other social and environmental aspects of development. Though lending for agriculture and education has increased significantly, some of the other new considerations have not yet been reflected to any great extent in the Bank's loan commitments. With the best of good will, moreover, there are obstacles to translating them effectively.

I fear that my remarks about the Bank have sounded more critical than I am. The Bank has not yet become a development agency, but it has been picking up momentum since the day it started lending. I am sorry that the World Bank antedates the IDA, thereby making the IDA a part of the World Bank Group instead of the Bank a member of the IDA Group. But the combination is beginning to sound less and less like a bank, and I have hopes that before we are too far into the 1970s it will become the full-fledged development agency the world so desperately needs.

# Comment: A Social Radicalism

Carl I. Ohman*

What is the role of the Wold Bank Group in the seventies? There are, of course, other questions just as meaningful. Will development aid as a whole adjust better to the needs of developing countries? Will the World Bank be a leader or a follower? Will the Group adjust to the lowest common denominator that everyone can willingly support? Or will it reach out to the highest common denominator, the maximum that, albeit with hesitation, most would accept? Will the IBRD Group, dealing with countries as different as Upper Volta and New Zealand, Nepal and Brazil, continue as virtually one organization? Will the present, rather mixed-up leopard continue with some changes in its spots, or will it have to split up into two leopards with somewhat different spots?

The development aid efforts for the next few years will, in all probability, take place within the general framework of the strategy for the Second United Nations Development Decade, unanimously adopted by UN General Assembly in October 1970. The strategy focuses on social and human development as at least as vital as economic development. It stresses that economic development becomes meaningful only if its proceeds are equitably distributed.

How does the Bank Group fit into that pattern? How does it behave as a member of the UN family? I would like to hint at some desirable changes, some of which are substantive, in the Bank Group's relationship with the UN family and with its member countries. Increased cooperation with other international bodies would seem necessary. Concentrated efforts are being made to improve the coordinating role of the UNDP, in close connection with national planning organizations. The Bank Group, presently enjoying a special reputation for efficiency, should continuously adjust its activities to fit in with the general coordinating work undertaken.

Although the definition of "developing country" varies, depending on the context, one can say that the developing countries as a group have only a bit more than one-third of the voting power in the IDA and in the Bank. If, for some reason, weighted voting power is considered a must, it would seem

*At the time of writing, Alternate Executive Director for Denmark, Finland, Iceland, Norway, and Sweden, International Bank for Reconstruction and Development, Washington, D.C., from 1970 to early 1973. Currently, at the Ministry of Foreign Affairs, Office for International Development Co-operation, Sweden.

equitable to have the votes equally distributed between "lending" and "recipient" countries in the two organizations. If this is difficult to achieve in the Bank, a 50-50 distribution should at least be possible in the IDA to facilitate the sense of partnership which is one of the basic ideas of the UN development strategy for the 1970s. It is true that votes are seldom taken, but discussions on controversial issues always take place with the voting figures in mind.

Does the membership of the World Bank really correspond to its name? The answer clearly is "No." It is an organization of predominantly Western industrialized countries and of most of the developing countries, whereas most of the so-called Socialist bloc countries are conspicuous by their absence. The organizations would be wise to adopt an open-door policy, trying to find imaginative ways of facilitating entry for countries now on the outside. A more representative membership for an organization that claims to be worldwide would not only make it more generally acceptable in many quarters but, just as important, would bring in important additional resources, including personnel with fresh ideas, to help the Bank Group broaden its approach to development.

One obstacle against a wider membership seems to be that, in order to become a member of IDA, a country must first be a member of the Bank. In order to become a member of the Bank, a country must be a member of the International Monetary Fund. It is difficult to see why this cumbersom chain of conditions should be necessary. Most Socialist bloc countries might find difficulties in complying with some of the rules of the Fund. Why this should deprive them of possibilities to participate in the Bank's multilateral aid efforts is difficult to see.

Incidentally, that same chain of conditions poses seemingly unnecessary burdens on some of the poorer of the developing countries, candidates for IDA resources, who also might consider it difficult to comply with some of the Fund's harsher regulations.

The Bank Group must ensure that its country programs can be continuously adjusted to the priority needs of each recipient country. It is an indication of strength to be able openly to admit mistakes and thus allow others to learn from them. In many fields, of course, the Bank Group has just as much to learn from recipient countries. Probably it should endeavor to be more country and problem oriented and relatively less project oriented. Efforts to achieve certain quantitative goals, highly laudable as such, might create certain problems. If a coordinator of project work has to choose between two projects in different countries, both requiring equal staff time, there might be tendency to favor the big, capital-consuming, safe, and relatively easy project, possibly in a country with which people concerned are already familiar.

Again, efficiency is valuable, but not at the expense of an adequate input into more general country and program analysis. In this connection, there is much to be said for substantially strengthening the role of Area Departments relative to the Project Departments, the Area Departments being in the best position to coordinate projects and to look at overall needs, in close cooperation with the recipient countries.

As an example, I shall take the IDA-Bank attitude towards nationalizations. According to the rules, no new commitments can be made to a country that has nationalized foreign property without making serious efforts to achieve agreement on compensation. There are many decisions by national governments that might adversely affect foreign interests. (And there are many activities by foreign parties that might seriously affect national interests!) The act of nationalization seems to have been singled out as the most harmful element. Whatever one might think of the desirability of granting equitable compensation, it seems dubious as a principle to use multilateral resources, and especially IDA money, as leverage to obtain bilateral settlements. The Bank Group should make efforts to show understanding for the needs of developing countries, with varying tools at their disposal, to achieve necessary restructuring of their societies.

The Bank Group has at times shown reluctance to lend to countries with certain types of economic difficulties. Those same countries have tended to attract very limited amounts of capital from other sources. A vicious circle is created. Maybe the concept of "lender of last resort" could be used to break some such circles. A generous and understanding attitude by the Group would thus possibly lead the way for others to follow.

The Bank has been accused of interfering excessively, and also accused of not using its influence sufficiently, in recipient countries.[15] Whether one calls it influence of interference, the Group cannot avoid having an important impact on development in many countries. This stems not only from the size of its resources, the technical quality of its assistance, but also from its leadership in important aid-coordination groups and the role of its economic documentation in development aid planning. Activity is influence, but nonactivity, where activity would be called for and possible, is in a way also influence. As a general rule, of course, the Bank should try to adjust its activities to the expressed wishes of the recipient countries. In many cases, the expressed wishes might not correspond to unanimously or even generally held opinions. Then, suggestions and encouragement by the Bank Group might give the upper hand to those latter views, possibly more in line with the real needs of the country in question. But this is very tricky ground, since governments change and so do their priorities. Although the Bank must be flexible, certain undertakings are by their very nature of a long-term character, and it would therefore seem advisable, where this is the case, to have certain relatively fixed policies, preferably coordinated with other donors and in line with UDNP efforts. Logically, those policies to prevent possible reversal should aim at achieving the best possible social and economic benefits for the largest number of needy people.

It has often been said that this or that project or approach was impossible because of its possibly negative impact on the Bank's ability to borrow on the international capital markets. What are the facts? In the 1971-72 budget year, the Bank planned to commit roughly twice as much as IDA in money terms. If the grant element is taken as a measure, however (and this would seem to be what really matters), the commitments of *IDA would be as important as those of the Bank*. And IDA's resources originally come from taxpayers in the industrialized countries. Secondly, I seem to recall that, say, 40 percent of the capital in use by the Bank comes from other sources (paid-in capital, reserves, Central Banks) and not from the open capital markets. When the Bank issues bonds on the capital markets, it pays the going rate. The investors buy the bonds, because they consider them profitable. They are also considered safe, presumably because the Bank's multibillion capital serves as a guarantee subscribed by member governments.

It would therefore seem possible and desirable to concentrate even more on the inevitable social effects of projects, to take slightly bigger risks with difficult, but potentially more fundamental, projects, and to insist less on certain rates of return and levels for public utility tariffs, if those are contrary to the general policies of the recipient country. Rates of return should only be used as guidelines, together with unquantifiable benefits, to determine real economic priorities. They should not be the basis for deciding if a project "pays its way" and therefore is good for a loan. After all, a government that borrows money would pay back from other revenues, even if the calculated rate of return for a certain project happened to be zero.[16]

It would seem desirable that the same social considerations should be taken for Bank and for IDA projects. If this takes some time to achieve for Bank projects, then there is an argument for some division of labor between the two. It is necessary to break the still existing dominance of banking views and change them towards more development-oriented views. It does seem imperative that the IDA resources, taxpayers' money, go to projects that will give the biggest social and economic benefits to the low-poverty areas. It would be highly undesirable if IDA projects lead to substantially increased benefits only for the small groups in developing countries that are already much better off than the average taxpayer.

Unemployment and underemployment are among the most urgent problems of developing countries. Many rich countries consider a 3 to 4 percent unemployment level unacceptable; the U.S. is suffering at a 6 percent level. It is difficult to measure unemployment in the developing countries, especially in the rural areas, where the largest sections of the population tend to live. In many countries the levels have, however, been estimated at 15 to 20 percent. Such figures indicate the size of the problem. And the problems increase in many countries where the labor force is growing at excessive rates. It therefore seems that measures against unemployment must be given the very highest priority by the Bank. The employment impact, direct and indirect, should be taken into account when choosing among countries, among regions, among projects, and among methods to create and use the projects. Adequate methods must be used to estimate the *real* labor costs or lack of costs, when unemployment is high.

Income distribution is, naturally, closely related to employment. Certain economists have held that an uneven income and wealth distribution is necessary to create sufficient amounts of savings for development. The experience in developing countries does not, however, generally speaking, seem to correspond with that theory. The rich have tended to invest their savings abroad or in relatively unproductive ways. The sophisticated consumption demand by the fortunate few has been directed to expensive imported goods, often of a luxury type, or to certain goods to some extent produced locally but at excessive cost because of the small quantities involved. Apart from the moral argument, there would therefore seem to be a clear economic argument for a more equitable income and wealth distribution in the developing countries. More demand would be created for unsophisticated consumer goods to be produced locally, whether in factories or by farmers. This in turn would create employment and income and allow the multiplier effect to work. Adequate tax structrues to enable governments to obtain development resources from those groups who can best spare them would seem necessary. It should be possible for the Bank to contribute more towards those goals.

There is always a temptation for a specialist to try to make "his" project technically perfect. It is easier for an engineer to try to be on the safe side in calculations—and often wiser. Few are criticized if a project is "too perfect," whereas it must be very uncomfortable to be confronted with a project that is considered substandard. This bias in favor of the technically perfect is strengthened by the fact that most of the specialists and consultants come from industrialized countries and have a natural tendency to favor techniques with which they are familiar, often of an uneconomically complicated kind. The IDA-Bank has an important responsibility to transfer know-how and technology. But it is most important to transfer *suitable* technology in the right cases and, where possible, to merge outside experience with locally existing techniques. The Bank should try, with all its projects in the poor countries, to contribute to necessary "capital stretching." Not enough is known in this field, at least not systematically, and support for research therefore seems vital.

In line with the general suggestions indicated before, the Bank Group should lay relatively less stress on short-term, purely production-oriented policies based on present concepts in the industrialized countries. The longer-term, overall, real economic benefits must be stressed. New methods for production and management must be found for the poor developing countries, where the ratios of production factors generally are the reverse of those in the industrialized countries: less capital and more labor. Not enough is known about how to achieve this, and the Bank is not alone in not having found suitable methods. Therefore, a concerted research effort should be launched with the support of the Bank Group. Possibly a consultative group of a similar kind as the one to be organized for agricultural research should be created, consisting of the UNDP, UNIDO, ILO, and IBRD together with interested countries (and foundations). The aim should be to finance research on an international scale on new, imaginative production and management techniques with the basic aim of saving on scarce capital. The group might wish to set up a technical committee to suggest suitable research projects for financing. Such a committee should try to attract as many experts as possible from the developing countries themselves. Their first task would be to screen existing knowledge of "adaptive technology," looking especially for already existing research results in developing countries. Then, support should be given to research programs in institutes, existing and new ones to be created, as far as possible in the developing countries to assure the most realistic surroundings.

In the meantime, the Bank should make efforts to concentrate on the employment aspects of investment. The needs for regional development should be kept in mind. Suitable on-the-job training must be embarked upon on a large scale. Industries should be encouraged to work as continuously as possible; it is amazing that multiple-shift work is more frequent in capital-rich industrialized countries than in labor-rich developing countries. More stress should be laid on repair and maintenance to avoid premature replacement of equipment. When loans are given to industrial finance companies, one should try to ensure that only the minimum of capital is used per job created, taking into account, of course, both direct and indirect job creation. Finally, the Bank Group should support improved marketing—including packing, quality control, etc.—in cooperation with existing international bodies already active in this field. One of them is the International Trade Centre in Geneva, specializing in trade promotion aid for developing countries.

In its agricultural projects, the Bank should take into account the fact that, for many products, small production units are the most efficient per area used. And in very many of the developing countries, land (at least really productive land) is the scarce factor. In most developing countries, improved results for all products would be obtained by land redistribution and/or land consolidation. At least the projects for general land improvement, for example irrigation, should be used to stimulate the achievement of a more even distribution of productive factors.

For some types of production, it seems that relatively big units—although often much smaller than the existing ones—are more economic. Cattle breeding might be a case in point. In that case, one must keep in mind that relatively large-scale production does not necessarily mean large-scale ownership. Here the concept of cooperatives comes in, used with excellent results in various forms in a number of the richer countries. Clearly, cooperatives need motivation and sufficient expertise. The Bank could make a great contribution by encouraging the gradual build-up of cooperatives, starting with the cooperative efforts most suitable in each case, and by supporting training of suitable personnel to manage and advise the cooperatives.

In this connection, a balance must be found between the need to push currency earning exports and the need to improve nutritional standards of the population in the producing countries. The pricing policy is important. Apart from the overwhelming humanitarian arguments for improved nutrition standards (e.g., more protein) there are clearly real economic long-term arguments.[17] Export of protein-rich products at low prices for relatively uneconomic purposes at the expense of an undernourished population does not seem a rational solution. Improved diets in the developing countries would, in many cases, lead to increased labor productivity.

The Bank would seem to have an important role in helping the developing countries to avoid the same obvious, costly misallocations in the transport sectors that have occurred in most of the richer countries. Similar results would be disastrous in the capital-poor developing countries. It is important to ensure optimal use of real resources at an early stage of development before strong pressure groups with vested interests in the auto-beltway-sector have emerged. Some solutions: proper taxing of private cars and trucks; tariffs for mass transportation and railway transport at such levels as to ensure the best, socioeconomic results, regardless of bookkeeping figures; a creative approach to village roads, feeder roads, roads aimed at opening up new development, etc., even if this approach is more difficult to use than the traditional methods for calculating short-term economic returns on savings for existing traffic.

It is unnecessary to stress the need for rapid population control; without it, other development efforts might become relatively futile. This has so far proved to be a difficult field. It seems, however, that the Bank could and should have an important role to play. By holding out substantial financial resources as a carrot, the needed coordination among existing specialized organizations in this field as well as the needed stepping-up of research, should be, if not enforced, at least strongly encouraged. Possibly a coordinating body or consultative group combining willing financiers with suitable knowledge and experience should be set up.

Education is a cornerstone of development and must be a priority field for a development institution. Many developing countries have inherited educational systems from abroad and are producing surpluses of educated persons in certain fields and too few in others. The answer to this, of course, is an increased effort to adjust education to the foreseen needs for development in each country. The Bank should have an important role in encouraging nontraditional education: suitable courses for adults; mobile education units; TV education; methods to reach out and motivate people to go to—and stay in—schools. An interesting experiment in the education field seems to have taken place in Botswana, where the emphasis is on development studies, teaching the pupils to be in close, constant contact with their future working environment. This might be worthy of support and duplication.

This paper has turned out to be more a list of suggestions for the activities of the Bank Group than an analysis of its possible role in the future. But then, the difference may not be all that big. There seems to be an international consensus, at least in principle, about the future importance and increased role of multilateralism in the field of development aid. There is a case, of course, for the creation of other bodies to replace some of the functions of the Bank Group as multilateralism spreads. Some development goals might be better achieved that way.

In many cases the Bank has been criticized—and rightly so—for its activities. However, any new multilateral organization aiming at transferring the large resources involved would, at least for the very near future, have to rely more or less on capital from similar sources as those upon which the Bank Group now draws. The technical knowledge, experience, and organizational talent that now characterize the Bank all make a strong case for achieving at least many of the development-assistance reforms needed for the seventies by encouraging changes within the IDA and the Bank rather than via *de novo* institutions. If the Bank Group can live up to the goals indicated by President McNamara, for example during the annual meetings, there seems to be a promising possibility for them to play a very meaningful role within the UN strategy for development during the 1970s.

**Notes**

1. For an excellent historical analysis of the beginnings of the Bretton Woods System, see Robert W. Oliver, *Early Plans for a World Bank*, Studies in International Finance, No. 29, Princeton University, September 1971; see also British Information Services, *Parliamentary Debates on an International Clearing Union*, July 1943 (reprinted partially in Seymour E. Harris [ed.], *The New Economics*, New York: Alfred A. Knopf, 1948) for Keynes' Clearing Union proposals, which were the seminal ideas behind the creation of a world bank; and also Roy Harrod, *The Life of John Maynard Keynes*, London: Macmillan, 1951.

2. International Bank for Reconstruction and Development, *Articles of Agreement*, as amended December 17, 1965, articles I and III.

3. Alec Cairncross, *The International Bank for Reconstruction and Development*, Essays in International Finance, No. 33, Princeton University, March 1959, has a slightly dated but illuminating discussion of these two conditions imposed on the Bank by its charter (pp. 16-22).

4. What eventually became the Articles of Agreement of the Bank originated in the work of Harry Dexter White at the Division of Monetary Research, United States Treasury, for which see Oliver, op. cit.; also the private papers of Dr. Harry White in the Princeton University Library; and John H. Williams, "Currency Stabilization: The Keynes and White Plans." *Foreign Affairs*, Vol. 21, pp. 645-658, July 1943.

5. International Bank for Reconstruction and Development, *Articles of Agreement*, article II, section 5 and 6; also article III.

6. Ibid., article V, sections 4 and 5.

7. Ibid., article V, section 8(a).

8. Ibid., article I (iii).

9. Ibid., article IX.

10. For a discussion of IDA's creation prior to the fact, see Alec Cairncross, op. cit., pp. 24-25.

11. International Development Association, Washington, D.C., Press Release, No. 2, November 9, 1960:

IDA will provide financing to the less developed areas. . . . on terms which bear less heavily on the balance of payments of these countries than conventional loans. A considerable degree of flexibility is permitted by the IDA Articles both in terms of lending and in the purpose for which loans may be made. IDA loans may carry lenient terms of repayment (for example, loans may be payable in foreign exchange with long maturities or long periods of grace, or both, or repayable wholly or partly in local currency), or the loans may be made free of interest or at a low rate of interest, or they may incorporate some combination of these terms. IDA may finance a wider range of projects than the Bank, *including projects that are not revenue-producing or directly productive; the only stipulation of the Articles is that projects shall be of "high developmental priority."* (Italics inserted.)

12. The internal organization of the Bank (not extensively discussed in this volume) was reorganized in October 1972. As a result of recommendations by the consulting firm of McKinsey and Company, the Bank was divided up into five regional departments, each with its own projects staff. In addition, there is now an overall projects department as well as four other functional departments under the categories of Development Policy, Finance, General Counsel, and Organization Planning and Personnel Management.

13. Mr. Asher acknowledges: "In making these comments, I have felt free to borrow without attribution from various chapters of a book Edward S. Mason and I were then writing. It has since been completed and will be published by Brookings in the summer of 1973 under the title *The World Bank Since Bretton Woods*. While taking full responsibility for all my comments, I wish to acknowledge my indebtedness to Mr. Mason for very much more than the single quotation attributed to him. *The World Bank Since Bretton Woods*, © The Brookings Institution, 1973."

14. International Bank for Reconstruction and Development, *Sixth Annual Report, 1950-51*, p. 14.

15. See papers by Cargill and Jha in Chapter 5 and Knapp in Chapter 2 of this volume.

16. For the orthodox IBRD approach to project appraisal, see John A. King, Jr., *Economic Development Projects and Their Appraisal: Cases and Principles from the Experience of the World Bank*, Baltimore: John Hopkins Press, 1967;

also Peter Engleman, "Sector Surveys and Feasibility Studies: Preparatory Steps in World Bank Practice," IBRD, July 1969.

17. See Alan D. Berg, "Nutrition as a National Priority: Lessons from the India Experiment," *The American Journal of Clinical Nutrition*, vol. 23, no. 11, November 1970.

# 3

## Determination of Priorities and the Allocation of Resources

**J. Burke Knapp***

The first priority in an institution such as the World Bank Group is to raise money. We cannot lend money until we raise it, and here the Bank and IDA have two quite different tasks before them.

The World Bank was established initially with a contributed capital from governments which in terms of usable currencies comes to something like $1700 million; capital increases have brought this figure up to about $2000 million, which is equivalent to about 2200 million "Smithsonian" dollars.[a] We have added to that equity base, over a period of years, another $1700 million in the form of earned surplus derived out of our earnings and plowed back into our lending operations. So we have an equity capital of something like $4 billion. But from here on out, barring a possible future increase in our capital contributed by governments, we look to the raising of our funds through the sale of bonds in the international capital markets.

The sale of bonds is a very important activity but an activity for a limited group of people. The whole institution has to be geared to operate in such a way as to command the confidence of those that provide the money, and in this case that means the bondholders. We have outstanding at the present time about $7.4 billion in bonds, which is nearly twice our equity base, and in future that proportion is bound to increase in the direction of selling more bonds.

Out of this $7.4 billion outstanding, about two-thirds has been sold in private capital markets to private purchasers of bonds, and about one-third of it has been supplied by governments, government official agencies, central banks, and so on. About one-half of the amount derived from capital markets (from sales to private bondholders) has been sold in the United States capital markets, thereby resulting in a total US contribution of about one-third of the funded debt of the World Bank. Official bonds have never been sold in the US, but we have obtained important official contributions from Germany and Japan. It is interesting commentary on the twenty-five years after the close of World War II that, after the US, which has the richest economy in the world and which has supplied almost one-third of the Bank's total resources, the second and third

*Senior Vice-President, International Bank for Reconstruction and Development, Washington, D.C.

[a]Data for lending and the Bank's capital base are cumulative through December 31, 1972; all figures are in terms of "Smithsonian" dollars at a parity of US$ 1.086 per SDR.

largest contributors have been Germany and Japan. There has been invested in Bank securities some $700 million of official German capital plus some very important funds derived from the German capital markets. In the case of Japan, so far the bulk of our borrowings have been official funds, as we only started selling bonds on the Japanese capital market in 1971. Thus, while the World Bank is deriving funds through the sale of bonds all over the world, the great bulk of it is concentrated in these principal capital markets.[1]

IDA is in a totally different situation, since it depends upon contributions from governments. It uses only soft money that cannot be raised in the capital markets. IDA started with $1000 million of resources for the four years 1961 through 1964, of which $250 million were inconvertible. The first replenishment was in the form of supplementary contributions (about $750 million from Part I countries only) to cover three years.[2] The effect was to enable annual commitments to rise from about $190 million to $300 million. The second replenishment of $1170 million for three years should have become effective in November 1968. Due to delays by the United States Government in its allocation, this amount did not come through until the middle of 1969, but enough countries made advance payments to prevent a complete hiatus in commitments.[3] By 1969 the commitment potential of IDA was about $450 million a year plus $100 million from the Bank. Additional and special contributions were made by Canada, Denmark, Finland, Norway, Sweden, and New Zealand; also, a special Swiss loan was negotiated. The third replenishment of $2.4 billion (in terms of pre-Smithsonian dollars) was negotiated in 1970, and it should raise the annual commitment level to over $1 billion a year if the Bank should continue to allocate about $100 million a year to IDA.

This, given an annual volume of straight Bank lending of about $2 billion, is going to mean a proportion between hard and soft lending of about two to one. I think if you asked any of us to put our hand on our heart and answer the question "Is that the right proportion?" we would say "No." With the state of the world as it is and as it appears to be developing, with the building up of external debt, with foreign exchange shortages, and repayment burdens in the developing countries, hard lending imposes a pretty oppressive burden. We would be a lot happier if that proportion were, say, one to one rather than two to one. But the IDA funding is building up; it is increasing all the time with each replenishment, and we hope to see it increase very substantially in the future.

As far as the area distribution is concerned, with regard to disbursement of funds, we have no quotas for countries or preconceptions with respect to geographical areas. In fact we think that for this purpose the concept of geographic regions is almost by definition nonsense. Individual countries are the clients of the World Bank, and the fact that you have a certain number of Latin American countries and that adds up to so much for Latin America as a whole or for so many countries altogether is sheer accident. There are no preconceived ideas that $x$ percent of the total ought to go to a particular area. We are a reasonably mature institution in the sense that we have had a lot of loans paid back; its borrowers have paid something of the order of $6 billion to the Bank, half in amortization and half in interest. In terms of what is actually receivable at the present time in the distribution of our portfolio, Asia has about $3.6 billion and Latin America has about $4.1 billion. This is out of a total of $11 billion, the rest going to Africa and Europe. But it should be noted that there is considerable concentration within regions. Out of the $3.6 billion in Asia, for example, four countries alone account for $2 billion: Japan, India, Pakistan, and Iran, with each of them getting around half a billion dollars, plus or minus.

In Latin America, though geographically and in terms of population not nearly so large an area, there is $4.1 billion outstanding in Bank loans, out of which the Big Three (Mexico, Brazil, and Colombia) get the bulk of the total. Brazil is the largest outstanding borrower. Argentina is missing from that list because of the very difficult and precarious state of that country now. A country that thirty years ago, before the War, was regarded virtually as a European country transplanted into Latin America, today it is one of the weakest and one of the most difficult in terms of its political and economic stability.

The Bank has $1500 million outstanding in Africa, and $1700 million in Europe. As far as Europe is concerned, much of that is a hangover from the earlier days of the Bank when it was lending to the Scandinavian countries and Austria. Today, Europe means pretty much the Mediterranean belt, that is, Spain, Greece, Turkey, and Yugoslavia; the latter, until the end of 1972 the only Communist member of the World Bank, ranks about fifth or sixth in our list of borrowers. The distribution of the Bank's portfolio has depended very largely on the credit ratings of the countries and on their ability to service debt.

The IDA picture is very different, since over 90 percent of IDA money is in Asia and Africa. There is very little funding in Latin America, simply because we regard most of the Latin American countries as creditworthy for Bank loans. As far as Europe is concerned, there is no IDA funding except in Turkey. In Asia and Africa, the Big Four in terms of clients for IDA are India (by far the largest), Pakistan, Bangladesh, and Indonesia. We have not been operating in Indonesia long enough to have built up a big portfolio there, but in terms of the Bank's current activities out of its IDA funds, something like 40 percent go to India, around 5 percent to Pakistan, 6 percent to Bangladesh and 11 percent to Indonesia, making a total of nearly two-thirds of IDA's funds going to those four countries. The balance is largely distributed among the African and smaller peripheral Asian countries. (See Table 3-3.)

In the case of the Bank, the distribution of funds is determined largely by where there are banking opportunities to earn money at the rates we lend. When it comes to IDA, on the other hand, we have to contend very actively with an allocation problem. As the two-to-one ratio between hard and soft money implies, soft money is scarce, and there are many claimants for it. The allocation

**Table 3-1**

**Foreign and International Bond Issues by Market and Country of Borrower, 1967-71[a] (Millions of US Dollars)**

| Borrowing Country | Year and Market | | | | | |
|---|---|---|---|---|---|---|
| | 1967 | | | 1968 | | |
| | North America | Europe[b] | Total | North America | Europe[b] | Total |
| **Industrialized Countries** | | | | | | |
| **Europe** | | | | | | |
| Austria | – | 85.1 | 85.1 | – | 93.3 | 93.3 |
| Belgium | – | 74.1 | 74.1 | – | 31.0 | 31.0 |
| Denmark | – | 72.0 | 72.0 | – | 105.8 | 105.8 |
| Finland | 15.0 | 25.0 | 40.0 | – | 87.4 | 87.4 |
| France | – | 157.2 | 157.2 | – | 123.8 | 123.8 |
| Germany | – | 58.2 | 58.2 | – | 8.6 | 8.6 |
| Iceland | – | 18.0 | 18.0 | – | 4.8 | 4.8 |
| Ireland | – | – | – | – | – | – |
| Italy | – | 73.1 | 73.1 | – | 84.2 | 84.2 |
| Netherlands | – | 44.4 | 44.4 | – | 183.5 | 183.5 |
| Norway | 12.0 | 83.5 | 95.5 | – | 40.7 | 40.7 |
| Sweden | – | 30.0 | 30.0 | – | 11.6 | 11.6 |
| Switzerland | – | – | – | – | – | – |
| United Kingdom | – | 74.2 | 74.2 | – | 148.9 | 148.9 |
| Multinational Corps.[c] | – | 125.0 | 125.0 | – | 33.9 | 33.9 |
| Subtotal | 27.0 | 919.8 | 946.8 | – | 957.5 | 957.5 |
| **Others** | | | | | | |
| Australia | – | 120.8 | 120.8 | – | 88.9 | 88.9 |
| Canada | 1.344.4 | 16.0 | 1,360.4 | 1,259.1 | 486.0 | 1,745.1 |
| Japan | 15.0 | – | 15.0 | – | 178.9 | 178.9 |
| New Zealand | – | 82.2 | 82.2 | – | 34.4 | 34.4 |
| South Africa | – | 62.5 | 62.5 | – | 55.0 | 55.0 |
| United States | – | 597.8 | 597.8 | 3.2 | 2,433.1 | 2,436.3 |
| Subtotal | 1,359.4 | 879.3 | 2,238.7 | 1,262.3 | 3,276.3 | 4,538.6 |
| TOTAL | 1,386.4 | 1,799.1 | 3.185.5 | 1.262.3 | 4.233.8 | 5.496.1 |
| **Multilateral European Institutions** | | | | | | |
| Council of Europe | – | – | – | – | – | – |
| Eurofima[d] | – | 42.0 | 42.0 | – | 31.1 | 31.1 |
| European Coal & Steel Community | – | 52.5 | 52.5 | – | 78.0 | 78.0 |
| European Investment Bank | – | 179.5 | 179.5 | – | 100.0 | 100.0 |
| Interfrigo[e] | – | – | – | – | – | – |
| TOTAL | – | 274.0 | 274.0 | – | 209.1 | 209.1 |
| **International Development Institutions** | | | | | | |
| Asian Development Bank | – | – | – | – | – | – |
| Inter-American Development Bank | 110.0 | 36.0 | 146.0 | 70.0 | 96.0 | 166.0 |
| World Bank | 400.0 | 308.9 | 708.9 | 413.9 | 811.7[f] | 1,225.6 |
| TOTAL | 510.0 | 344.9 | 854.9 | 483.9 | 907.7 | 1,391.6 |

[a]Includes issues both publicly offered and privately placed.

[b]Includes London, Continental Europe and the Eurobond market.

| | 1969 | | | 1970 (Year and Market) | | | 1971 | | |
|---|---|---|---|---|---|---|---|---|---|
| | North America | Europe[b] | Total | North America | Europe[b] | Total | North America | Europe[b] | Total |
| | – | 70.5 | 70.5 | – | 14.3 | 14.3 | – | 37.0 | 37.0 |
| | – | 189.5 | 189.5 | – | 18.9 | 18.9 | – | – | – |
| | – | 143.9 | 143.9 | – | 92.3 | 92.3 | – | 143.4 | 143.4 |
| | – | 70.4 | 70.4 | – | 48.9 | 48.9 | – | 98.4 | 98.4 |
| | – | 186.5 | 186.5 | – | 266.6 | 266.6 | – | 345.8 | 345.8 |
| | – | 229.4 | 229.4 | – | 126.6 | 126.6 | – | 79.0 | 79.0 |
| | 0.5 | 6.3 | 6.8 | – | – | – | – | 10.0 | 10.0 |
| | – | 57.5 | 57.5 | – | 42.3 | 42.3 | – | 101.1 | 101.1 |
| | – | 118.9 | 118.9 | – | 433.3 | 433.3 | – | 150.0 | 150.0 |
| | – | 210.5 | 210.5 | – | 291.6 | 291.6 | – | 222.0 | 222.0 |
| | – | 24.0 | 24.0 | – | 93.6 | 93.6 | – | 100.6 | 100.6 |
| | – | – | – | – | 65.0 | 65.0 | – | 87.7 | 87.7 |
| | – | 60.0 | 60.0 | – | – | – | – | 51.6 | 51.6 |
| | – | 283.5 | 283.5 | – | 257.8 | 257.8 | – | 665.3 | 665.3 |
| | – | 20.0 | 20.0 | – | 15.0 | 15.0 | – | 122.8 | 122.8 |
| | 0.5 | 1,670.9 | 1,671.4 | – | 1,766.2 | 1,766.2 | – | 2,214.7 | 2,214.7 |
| | – | 146.0 | 146.0 | – | 106.7 | 106.7 | – | 120.9 | 120.9 |
| | 1,091.1 | 334.8 | 1,425.9 | 795.2 | 177.5 | 972.7 | 634.7 | 224.9 | 859.6 |
| | 9.0 | 261.0 | 270.0 | – | 119.9 | 119.9 | – | 124.9 | 124.9 |
| | – | 25.0 | 25.0 | – | 11.6 | 11.6 | – | 95.2 | 95.2 |
| | – | 38.8 | 38.8 | – | 98.6 | 98.6 | – | 218.1 | 218.1 |
| | 1.2 | 1,257.3 | 1,258.5 | – | 1,091.8 | 1,091.8 | – | 1,381.3 | 1,381.3 |
| | 1,101.3 | 2,062.9 | 3,164.2 | 795.2 | 1,606.1 | 2,401.3 | 634.7 | 2,165.3 | 2,800.0 |
| | 1,101.8 | 3,733.8 | 4,835.6 | 795.2 | 3,372.3 | 4,167.5 | 634.7 | 4,380.0 | 5,014.7 |
| | – | – | – | – | – | – | – | – | – |
| | – | – | – | – | 17.0 | 17.0 | – | 71.1 | 71.1 |
| | – | 13.8 | 13.8 | – | 60.0 | 60.0 | – | 105.1 | 105.1 |
| | – | 82.3 | 82.3 | – | 138.9 | 138.9 | – | 255.9 | 255.9 |
| | – | 9.2 | 9.2 | – | – | – | – | 10.0 | 10.0 |
| | – | 105.3 | 105.3 | – | 215.9 | 215.9 | – | 442.1 | 442.1 |
| | – | 15.0 | 15.0 | – | 21.7[g] | 21.7 | 80.4 | 44.4 | 124.8 |
| | – | 137.2 | 137.2 | 100.0 | 65.6 | 165.6 | – | 119.2 | 119.2 |
| | – | 712.8 | 712.8 | 200.0 | 873.5[h] | 1,073.5 | 844.9 | 739.2 | 1,584.1 |
| | – | 865.0 | 865.0 | 300.0 | 960.8 | 1,260.8 | 925.3 | 902.8 | 1,828.1 |

cIncludes the following corporations: Acieries Réuniés de Burbach-Eich-Dudelange, Ameribas Holding S.A., BEC Finance N.V., N.V. Rotterdam-Rijn Pijpleiding, Shell Finance Company N.V., Shell International Finance N.V., Société Financiére Européenne, and Transalpine Finance Holdings.

## Table 3-1 (cont.)

| Borrowing Country | Year and Market | | | | | |
| | 1967 | | | 1968 | | |
| | North America | Europe[b] | Total | North America | Europe[b] | Total |
|---|---|---|---|---|---|---|
| Developing Countries | | | | | | |
| Algeria | – | – | – | – | – | – |
| Argentina | – | 25.0 | 25.0 | 26.0 | 50.0 | 76.0 |
| Bahamas | – | – | – | – | – | – |
| Brazil | – | – | – | 0.8 | 10.0 | 10.8 |
| Colombia | 0.5 | 7.0 | 7.5 | – | – | – |
| Costa Rica | – | – | – | – | – | – |
| Dominican Republic | – | – | – | 0.2 | – | 0.2 |
| EAC[i] | – | – | – | – | 16.8 | 16.8 |
| Gabon | – | – | – | – | – | – |
| Greece | – | – | – | – | 25.0 | 25.0 |
| Hungary | – | – | – | – | – | – |
| Iran | – | – | – | – | 20.0 | 20.0 |
| Israel | 203.1 | 15.0 | 218.1 | 174.0 | – | 174.0 |
| Ivory Coast | – | – | – | – | 16.1 | 16.1 |
| Jamaica | – | – | – | – | 7.2 | 7.2 |
| Malagasy Republic | – | – | – | – | 4.1 | 4.1 |
| Malaysia | – | 21.0 | 21.0 | – | 6.3 | 6.3 |
| Mexico | 39.6 | 85.0 | 124.6 | 9.0 | 138.6 | 147.6 |
| Netherlands Antilles | – | 13.8 | 13.8 | – | – | – |
| Nicaragua | 1.5 | – | 1.5 | – | – | – |
| Panama | 7.5 | – | 7.5 | – | – | – |
| Peru | 11.3 | 5.8 | 17.1 | – | – | – |
| Philippines | 8.0 | – | 8.0 | 15.0 | – | 15.0 |
| Portugal | – | 34.0 | 34.0 | – | 15.0 | 15.0 |
| Senegal | – | – | – | – | 6.1 | 6.1 |
| Spain | – | 53.0 | 53.0 | 60.0 | – | 60.0 |
| Thailand | 1.0 | – | 1.0 | – | – | – |
| Trinidad & Tobago | – | – | – | – | 7.2 | 7.2 |
| Venezuela | 1.1 | – | 1.1 | – | 25.0 | 25.0 |
| Yugoslavia | – | – | – | – | – | – |
| TOTAL | 273.6 | 259.6 | 533.2 | 285.0 | 347.4 | 632.4 |
| Recapitulation | | | | | | |
| Industrialized Countries | 1,386.4 | 1.799.1 | 3,185.5 | 1.262.3 | 4,233.8 | 5,496.1 |
| Multilateral European Institutions | – | 274.0 | 274.0 | – | 209.1 | 209.1 |
| TOTAL | 1,386.4 | 2,073.1 | 3,459.5 | 1,262.3 | 4,442.9 | 5,705.2 |
| International Development Institutions | 510.0 | 344.9 | 854.9 | 483.9 | 907.7 | 1,391.6 |
| Developing Countries | 273.6 | 259.6 | 533.2 | 285.0 | 347.4 | 632.4 |
| TOTAL | 783.6 | 604.5 | 1.388.1 | 768.9 | 1,255.1 | 2,024.0 |
| GRAND TOTAL | 2,170.0 | 2,677.6 | 4,847.6 | 2,031.2 | 5,698.0 | 7,729.2 |

[d]Société Européenne pour le Financement de Matériel Ferroviaire.

[e]Société Ferroviaire Internationale de Transport Frigorifiques.

[f]Includes an issue of KD 15.0 million publicly offered in Kuwait and two issues totalling $30.0 million privately placed in Saudi Arabia.

| | 1969 | | | Year and Market 1970 | | | 1971 | | |
|---|---|---|---|---|---|---|---|---|---|
| | North America | Europe[b] | Total | North America | Europe[b] | Total | North America | Europe[b] | Total |
| | 50.6 | 35.4 | 86.0 | 8.2 | 61.6 | 69.8 | – | – | – |
| | 1.0 | 10.0 | 11.0 | – | 15.5 | 15.5 | 6.0 | – | 6.0 |
| | 1.6 | – | 1.6 | 0.7 | – | 0.7 | – | – | – |
| | – | – | – | 0.1 | – | 0.1 | 6.8 | – | 6.8 |
| | – | – | – | – | – | – | – | – | – |
| | – | – | – | – | 3.6 | 3.6 | – | – | – |
| | – | – | – | – | – | – | – | – | – |
| | – | – | – | – | – | – | – | 25.0 | 25.0 |
| | – | 8.0 | 8.0 | – | – | – | – | – | – |
| | 136.7 | 0.9 | 137.6 | 187.8 | – | 187.8 | 237.0 | – | 237.0 |
| | – | – | – | – | – | – | – | – | – |
| | – | – | – | 1.2 | – | 1.2 | – | – | – |
| | – | – | – | – | – | – | – | – | – |
| | – | 10.0 | 10.0 | – | – | – | – | – | – |
| | 26.0 | 45.0 | 71.0 | – | 20.0 | 20.0 | 20.0 | 30.0 | 50.0 |
| | – | 38.7 | 38.7 | – | – | – | – | 17.4 | 17.4 |
| | – | – | – | – | – | – | – | – | – |
| | – | – | – | – | 30.0 | 30.0 | – | 16.0 | 16.0 |
| | – | 5.8 | 5.8 | – | – | – | – | – | – |
| | 11.0 | – | 11.0 | – | – | – | – | – | – |
| | – | – | – | – | – | – | – | – | – |
| | – | 25.0 | 25.0 | – | 30.0 | 30.0 | – | 72.3 | 72.3 |
| | – | – | – | – | – | – | – | – | – |
| | 8.2 | – | 8.2 | – | 13.3 | 13.3 | – | – | – |
| | – | – | – | – | 5.0 | 5.0 | – | – | – |
| | 235.1 | 178.8 | 413.9 | 198.0 | 179.0 | 377.0 | 269.8 | 160.7 | 430.5 |
| | 1,101.8 | 3,733.8 | 4,835.6 | 795.2 | 3,372.3 | 4,167.5 | 634.7 | 4,380.0 | 5,014.7 |
| | – | 105.3 | 105.3 | – | 215.9 | 215.9 | – | 442.1 | 442.1 |
| | 1,101.8 | 3,839.1 | 4,940.9 | 795.2 | 3,588.2 | 4,383.4 | 634.7 | 4,822.1 | 5,456.8 |
| | – | 865.0 | 865.0 | 300.0 | 960.8 | 1,260.8 | 925.3 | 902.8 | 1,828.1 |
| | 235.1 | 178.8 | 413.9 | 198.0 | 179.0 | 377.0 | 269.8 | 160.7 | 430.5 |
| | 235.1 | 1,043.8 | 1,278.9 | 498.0 | 1,139.8 | 1,637.8 | 1,195.1 | 1,063.5 | 2,258.5 |
| | 1,336.9 | 4,882.9 | 6,219.8 | 1,293.2 | 4,728.0 | 6,021.2 | 1,829.8 | 5,885.6 | 7,715.3 |

[g]Includes an issue of Y6.0 billion publicly offered in Japan.

[h]Includes an issue of £ 10 million privately placed in Libya and two issues totalling Y72 billion privately placed in Japan.

[i]East African Community.

Source: IBRD *Annual Report 1972*, World Bank, Washington, D.C.: pp. 92-93.

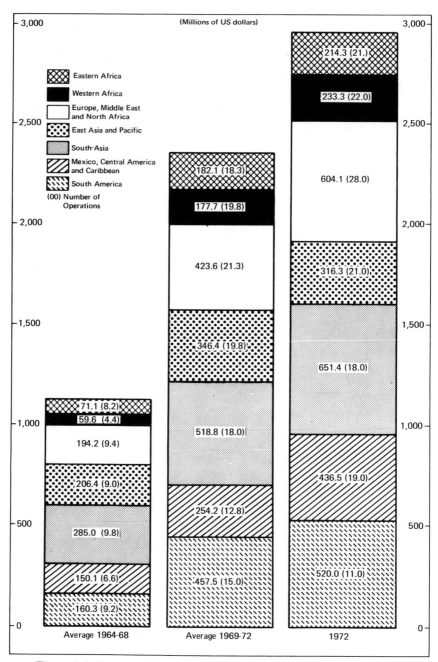

**Figure 3-1.** Bank and IDA Lending by Area, FY 1964-72. *Source:* IBRD *Annual Report 1971-72*, World Bank, Washington, D.C.

criteria for IDA funds do bring up certain interesting issues. We have written some policy papers on this and had long debates in our Board of Directors. These debates in our Board of Directors, unlike some others, have never really come to a conclusion. We have a Board of Directors that represents all the participating countries in the institution with a weighted voting power according to their capital subscriptions. On an issue like the IDA allocations it is almost literally impossible to get any two of our directors to agree on a formula. Indeed, it is probably wrong to think in terms of a slide-rule formula in any case. Thus, it devolves upon the management of the institution to make judgments based on a set of principles. And what we have with respect to this allocation problem is a series of often conflicting criteria that must, however, be reconciled eventually.

The first criterion is that IDA money is not allocated to a country unless it lacks the creditworthiness necessary for World Bank loans. This criterion derives from the very origins of the IDA fund. The Bank found, in the late fifties, that in many countries the burden of external debt, including the debt deriving from IBRD loans, was reaching a dangerous point; and yet in these countries there existed ample opportunities for productive investment towards development. IDA's basic initial purpose was to supplement Bank activities in areas where the Bank could not, under its existing regime, with existing instruments, operate. That was the basis on which the donor countries put it.

Although generally we will not allocate IDA funds if the loan meets the Bank's requirements, this is not a stringent rule. An agreement was reached a long time ago that the Bank would not drive a country to the limits of its creditworthiness before deciding to use IDA funds. If any country indicates prospective debt problems, we begin to blend in IDA funds. In fact, most IDA credits are extended to countries receiving both Bank loans and IDA funds. It could be either a hard blend or a soft blend depending upon the ratio of Bank loans to IDA credits. A hard blend would be 75 percent Bank money and 25 percent IDA funds; a medium blend would have a 50-50 ratio, and a soft blend would consist of predominantly IDA money. After that would come a straight IDA country.

There are a lot of straight IDA countries, but they are mostly very poor ones in Africa and Asia, and most of the IDA funding in fact goes to blend with Bank money. India and Pakistan have been in recent years very soft blends. There has been a great deal of Bank lending in both those countries. It is important to bear in mind that continuing amortization of loans implies that in a country like India or Pakistan, we can always do some Bank lending and yet just maintain our portfolio without increasing our exposure or risk.

The second criterion for the allocation of IDA funds is poverty. This is interesting, since the IDA Charter does not say a word about poor countries but only refers to countries whose credit risk is higher. There is, of course, a close correlation between those two factors. It has been established as a rough rule

**Table 3-2**
**India: IBRD Loans, IDA Credits and IFC Investments (Net of Cancellations) by Sectors: 1960-71 (Millions of US Dollars)**

| Sectors | 1960 | | | 1961 | | | 1962 | | | 1963 | | | 1964 | | | 1965 | | |
|---|---|---|---|---|---|---|---|---|---|---|---|---|---|---|---|---|---|---|
| | IBRD | IDA | IFC | IBRD | IDA | IFC | IBRD | IDA | IFC | IBRD | IDA | IFC | IBRD | IDA | IFC | IBRD | IDA | IFC |
| Transportation | 70.0 | – | – | – | 59.5 | – | – | 15.0 | – | – | 67.5 | – | – | 62.0 | – | – | – | – |
| Telecommunications | – | – | – | – | – | – | – | 42.0 | – | – | – | – | – | 33.0 | – | – | – | – |
| Agriculture | – | – | – | – | 27.0 | – | – | 28.0 | – | – | – | – | – | – | – | – | – | – |
| Industry (inc. DFCs & industrial imports) | 19.3 | – | 1.4 | – | – | 0.2 | 27.0 | – | – | – | 20.0 | 1.0 | – | 90.0 | 5.8 | 50.0 | 100.0 | – |
| Electric Power | – | – | – | 28.8 | – | – | – | 34.0 | – | – | – | – | – | – | – | 64.0 | – | – |
| Mining | – | – | – | – | – | – | – | – | – | – | – | – | – | – | – | – | – | – |
| Totals | 89.3 | – | 1.4 | 28.8 | 86.5 | 0.2 | 27.0 | 119.0 | – | – | 87.5 | 1.0 | – | 185.0 | 5.8 | 114.0 | 100.0 | – |
| Bank Group Totals | 90.7 | | | 184.5 | | | 138.0 | | | 115.5 | | | 190.8 | | | 214.0 | | |

| Sectors | 1966 | | | 1967 | | | 1968 | | | 1969 | | | 1970 | | | 1971 | | |
|---|---|---|---|---|---|---|---|---|---|---|---|---|---|---|---|---|---|---|
| | IBRD | IDA | IFC | IBRD | IDA | IFC | IBRD | IDA | IFC | IBRD | IDA | IFC | IBRD | IDA | IFC | IBRD | IDA | IFC |
| Transportation | – | 68.0 | – | – | – | – | – | – | – | – | 55.0 | – | – | – | – | – | – | – |
| Telecommunications | – | – | – | – | – | – | – | – | – | 27.5 | 27.5 | – | – | – | – | – | 78.0 | – |
| Agriculture | – | 23.0 | – | – | – | – | – | – | – | 13.0 | – | – | – | 97.5 | – | – | 134.4 | – |
| Industry (inc. DFCs & industrial imports) | – | 215.0 | – | 25.0 | – | 12.6 | – | – | – | – | 125.0 | – | 40.0 | 75.0 | – | 60.0 | 20.0 | – |
| Electric Power | – | – | – | – | – | – | – | – | – | – | – | 18.9 | – | – | – | – | 75.0 | – |
| Mining | – | – | – | – | – | – | – | – | – | – | – | – | – | – | – | – | – | – |
| Totals | – | 306.0 | – | 25.0 | – | 12.6 | – | – | – | 40.5 | 207.5 | 18.9 | 40.0 | 172.5 | – | 60.0 | 307.4 | – |
| Bank Group Totals | 306.0 | | | 37.6 | | | – | | | 266.9 | | | 212.5 | | | 367.4 | | |

Source: World Bank, Washington, D.C.

that IDA funds should not be used for countries with a per capita annual income higher than \$375.[4] There have been exceptions to this rule, but generally it stands. These two criteria together mean that a country may be very poor, but if its credit rating is good, then it is not eligible for IDA funding. A notable example today is Nigeria. The per capita income is very low, about \$120, but due to the rapid increase in oil revenues, Nigeria has become extremely creditworthy. No IDA funds have therefore been allocated to Nigeria since 1965. On the other side of the picture, no matter how bad a country's balance of payments and external debt situation is, if it has a per capita annual income above \$375 it does not qualify for IDA funds. The result, it should be noted, is to leave some countries without effective access to Bank funds; some have been too advanced to qualify for the "poverty test" regarding IDA funds, but the perilous state of their economic affairs has made them a bad credit risk for the World Bank.

The third criterion that is used to determine allocation of IDA funds is the economic performance of the recipient country. Generally speaking, a country that is past the \$375 level of per capita income and which has no creditworthiness is usually one that has made a mess of its affairs or which even currently is not exercising enough economic management and discipline to establish its creditworthiness. In any case, we think performance is a very important test. The members of the Bank and the donors to IDA feel strongly that a country that is assisted, especially with soft-loan funds, should be making the most effective efforts it can to mobilize its own resources for development, and to manage its economy will assure, among other things, the productive employment of the funds that we have to offer.

Performance is, of course, a relative concept, and one cannot require the same standards of performance from countries at the lower end of the income and development scale that you can from countries that are further advanced in their development. Thus, we must judge performance to some degree with an eye to the potential of the economy in question. Yet if such relativity is carried too far, it will dilute the performance criterion almost to the vanishing point. The Bank tries to maintain stringent performance standards while recognizing that these cannot be across-the-board universal standards.[5]

Two other criteria are often mentioned in terms of performance standards and fund allocations: the per capita allocation criterion and the highest rate of return criterion. Both these have obvious drawbacks in terms of equity between the poorer and the relatively more advanced LDCs.

The Pearson Commission Report was full of a lot of impressive and forward looking recommendations. One recommendation regarding IDA allocations gave us a lot of trouble. After approving the current criteria used for IDA allocations, the Commission suggested that IDA, in addition, ought to construct a model of the ideal allocation of aid funds for the world, match that against the current aid

## Table 3-3

## Cumulative Total of Bank and IDA Lending Operations Approved by Major Purpose and Area, June 30, 1972[a] (Millions of US dollars)

| Purpose[b] | Bank Loans to Current Borrowers by Area | | | | | | | |
|---|---|---|---|---|---|---|---|---|
| | Eastern Africa | Western Africa | East Asia, Pacific | South Asia | Europe, Middle East, North Africa | Mexico, Central America, Caribbean | South America | Total |
| **Agriculture, Forestry and Fishing** | | | | | | | | |
| Agricultural credit | $ – | $ 3.5 | $ 17.5 | $ 20.5 | $ 59.0 | $ 18.4 | $ 49.5 | $ 168.4 |
| Area development | 26.0 | 7.0 | 27.0 | – | 12.0 | 6.3 | 11.1 | 89.4 |
| Food and nonfood crops | 5.5 | 46.7 | – | – | 10.0 | – | – | 62.2 |
| Irrigation, flood control and drainage | 34.5 | – | 242.0 | 201.0 | 113.3 | 79.1 | 44.3 | 714.2 |
| Forestry and fishing | 7.9 | – | 30.7 | – | 4.8 | 3.4 | 5.3 | 52.1 |
| Crop-processing and storage | – | – | 14.3 | – | 3.9 | .8 | – | 19.0 |
| Livestock | 5.3 | – | 7.5 | – | 25.0 | 180.0 | 158.8 | 376.6 |
| Agricultural research | – | – | – | – | 12.7 | – | – | 12.7 |
| Other | 5.6 | – | – | 26.3 | 2.3 | 7.7 | 15.0 | 56.9 |
| Subtotal | $ 84.8 | $ 57.2 | $ 339.0 | $ 247.8 | $ 243.0 | $ 295.7 | $ 284.0 | $1,551.5 |
| Education | $ 27.5 | $ 30.1 | $ 70.2 | $ 19.0 | $ 115.2 | $ .50.5 | $ 33.7 | $ 346.2 |
| **Industry** | | | | | | | | |
| Iron and steel | $ – | $ – | $ – | $ 189.0 | $ 86.5 | $ – | $ 294.0 | $ 569.5 |
| Pulp and paper | – | – | – | 4.2 | – | – | 20.0 | 24.2 |
| Fertilizer and other chemicals | – | – | – | 32.0 | 24.0 | – | – | 56.0 |
| Mining, other extraction | 32.0 | 131.0 | – | 54.5 | 25.0 | 25.0 | 21.8 | 289.3 |
| Small industry and industrial estates | – | – | – | – | – | – | – | |
| Development finance companies | 12.0 | 17.0 | 191.5 | 666.4 | 444.0 | 37.0 | 135.5 | 1,503.4 |
| Other | – | – | – | – | 165.9 | 15.0 | 7.5 | 188.4 |
| Subtotal | $ 44.0 | $148.0 | $ 191.5 | $ 946.1 | $ 745.4 | $ 77.0 | $ 478.8 | $2,630.8 |
| Nonproject | $ 40.0 | $ 80.0 | $ – | $ 75.0 | $ 58.0 | $ – | $ 60.0 | $ 313.0 |
| Population | – | – | – | – | – | 5.0 | – | 5.0 |
| Power | 306.9 | 275.3 | 700.0 | 394.7 | 432.0 | 1,151.9 | 1,622.3 | 4,883.1 |
| Technical Assistance | – | – | – | – | – | – | – | |
| Telecommunications | 37.1 | – | 73.3 | 63.5 | 67.8 | 142.2 | 31.0 | 414.9 |
| Tourism | – | – | – | – | 44.0 | 22.0 | – | 66.0 |
| **Transportation** | | | | | | | | |
| Aviation | $ 29.0 | $ – | $ – | $ 5.6 | $ – | $ 37.0 | $ – | $ 71.6 |
| Highways | 135.7 | 150.7 | 201.8 | 212.9 | 355.7 | 391.2 | 647.8 | 2,095.8 |
| Pipelines | – | – | – | 88.2 | 57.5 | – | 23.3 | 169.0 |
| Ports, waterways and shipping | 44.8 | 96.3 | 67.7 | 138.8 | 167.3 | 34.0 | 82.1 | 631.0 |
| Railways | 207.4 | 47.2 | 234.7 | 520.2 | 368.5 | 136.0 | 278.5 | 1,792.5 |
| Other | 28.0 | 25.0 | – | – | – | – | – | 53.0 |
| Subtotal | $ 444.9 | $319.2 | $ 504.2 | $ 965.7 | $ 949.0 | $ 598.2 | $1,031.7 | $4,812.9 |
| Urbanization | $ – | $ – | $ – | $ – | $ – | $ 5.4 | $ – | $ 5.4 |
| Water supply and sewerage | 19.1 | 5.0 | 36.6 | – | 104.4 | 33.2 | 159.5 | 357.8 |
| TOTAL | $1,004.3 | $914.8 | $1,914.8 | $2,711.8 | $2,758.8 | $2,381.1 | $3,701.0 | $15,386.6 |

[a]Except for the total shown in note d, no account is taken of cancellations and refundings subsequent to original commitments. Bank loans of $260 million to IFC are excluded.

[b]Operations have been classified by the major purpose they finance. Many projects include activity in more than one sector or subsector.

| | | | | Europe, Middle East, North Africa | Mexico Central America, Caribbean | South America | Total | IDA Credits by Area | | |
| Eastern Africa | Western Africa | East Asia, Pacific | South Asia | | | | | Total Bank and IDA to Current Borrowers | Bank Loans to Past Borrowers | Total Bank and IDA |
|---|---|---|---|---|---|---|---|---|---|---|
| $ 8.6 | $ 8.8 | $ 10.5 | $ 288.9 | $ 19.0 | $ – | $ – | $ 335.8 | $ 504.2 | $ – | $ 504.2 |
| 34.9 | 34.8 | 6.5 | – | 6.0 | – | – | 82.2 | 171.6 | 4.3 | 175.9 |
| 39.1 | 8.5 | 59.0 | – | 15.0 | – | – | 121.6 | 183.8 | – | 183.8 |
| 39.9 | 14.3 | 69.2 | 276.2 | 76.0 | – | – | 475.6 | 1,189.8 | 7.0 | 1,196.8 |
| – | 1.3 | 3.5 | – | 2.0 | – | – | 6.8 | 58.9 | – | 58.9 |
| 6.3 | – | – | 38.2 | – | – | – | 44.5 | 63.5 | – | 63.5 |
| 14.0 | 6.4 | 7.0 | – | 20.5 | 9.8 | 37.1 | 94.8 | 471.4 | – | 471.4 |
| – | – | – | – | – | – | – | – | 12.7 | – | 12.7 |
| – | – | 7.5 | 8.0 | – | – | – | 15.5 | 72.4 | – | 72.4 |
| $142.8 | $ 74.1 | $163.2 | $ 611.3 | $138.5 | $ 9.8 | $ 37.1 | $1,176.8 | $ 2,728.3 | $ 11.3 | $ 2,739.6 |
| $ 84.6 | $ 63.1 | $ 25.7 | $ 37.5 | $ 42.9 | $ 6.9 | $ 5.1 | $ 265.8 | $ 612.0 | $ | $ 612.0 |
| $ – | $ – | $ – | $ – | $ – | $ – | $ – | $ – | $ 569.5 | $ 155.3 | $ 724.8 |
| – | – | – | – | – | – | – | – | 24.2 | – | 24.2 |
| – | – | 30.0 | 30.0 | – | – | – | 60.0 | 116.0 | – | 116.0 |
| 2.5 | – | – | – | – | – | – | 2.5 | 291.8 | – | 291.8 |
| – | – | – | 9.5 | – | – | – | 9.5 | 9.5 | – | 9.5 |
| 29.5 | – | 15.0 | 20.0 | 35.0 | – | – | 99.5 | 1,602.9 | 24.8 | 1,627.7 |
| – | – | – | – | – | – | – | – | 188.4 | 184.1 | 372.5 |
| $ 32.0 | $ – | $ 45.0 | $ 59.5 | $ 35.0 | $ – | $ – | $ 171.5 | $ 2,802.3 | $ 364.2 | $ 3,166.5 |
| $ – | $ – | $ – | $ 805.0 | $ – | $ – | $ – | $ 805.0 | $ 1,118.0 | $1,115.1 | $ 2,233.1 |
| – | – | 13.2 | 21.2 | 4.8 | – | – | 39.2 | 44.2 | – | 44.2 |
| 5.3 | 17.1 | 65.0 | 177.0 | 25.7 | 15.1 | 29.2 | 334.4 | 5,217.5 | 691.3 | 5,908.8 |
| – | – | 10.0 | – | – | – | – | 10.0 | 10.0 | – | 10.0 |
| – | 4.4 | 12.8 | 213.2 | – | – | – | 230.4 | 645.3 | – | 645.3 |
| – | – | – | 4.2 | 10.0 | – | – | 14.2 | 80.2 | – | 80.2 |
| $ – | $ – | $ – | $ – | $ – | $ – | $ – | $ – | $ 71.6 | $ 16.2 | $ 87.8 |
| 246.7 | 89.6 | 79.2 | 112.9 | 44.9 | 30.8 | 52.5 | 656.6 | 2,752.4 | 430.0 | 3,182.4 |
| – | – | – | – | – | – | – | – | 169.0 | – | 169.0 |
| 17.2 | 3.6 | 10.7 | 109.3 | – | – | – | 140.8 | 771.8 | 42.0 | 813.8 |
| – | 27.6 | 40.0 | 362.5 | 38.5 | – | – | 468.6 | 2,261.1 | 227.8 | 2,488.9 |
| – | – | – | – | – | – | – | – | 53.0 | – | 53.0 |
| $263.9 | $120.8 | $129.9 | $ 584.7 | $ 83.4 | $30.8 | $ 52.5 | $1,266.0 | $ 6,078.9 | $ 716.0 | $ 6,794.9 |
| $ – | $ 8.0 | $ – | $ – | $ 2.3 | $ – | $ – | $ 10.3 | $ 15.7 | $ – | $ 15.7 |
| 4.1 | 3.5 | 4.4 | 51.8 | 16.0 | 3.0 | – | 82.8 | 440.6 | – | 440.6 |
| $532.7 | $291.0 | $469.2 | $2,565.4 | $358.6 | $65.6 | $123.9 | $4,406.4 | $19.793.0 | $2,897.9 | $22,690.9[d] |

[c]Includes $497 million in European reconstruction loans made before 1952.

[d]Cancellations, terminations, and refundings total $561.5 million.

Source: IBRD *Annual Report 1972*, Appendix I, World Bank, Washington, D.C., pp. 122-23.

allocations by bilateral and other multilateral agencies, and then fill in the gaps between the two patterns out of its own funds. This in fact amounts to IDA making up for the mistakes and misallocations of various aid donors. The trouble with this suggestion is that it is these very donors who are providing the bulk of IDA funds, and they would not take very kindly to being told that IDA was seeking to remedy the deficiencies in the pattern of assistance being provided by them bilaterally.[6]

On the other hand, should IDA be operated as a microcosm of its own without regard to what the rest of the world is doing? It would be fine for us to have a perfectly logical idea of how IDA funds should be distributed as such, but to move ahead on that basis without any concern or awareness of what other people were doing would lead to some curious results. The ultimate result is a compromise of sorts which can never get reduced to an inflexible formula.

Any worldwide survey of per capita assistance will unearth the most radical differences in the amounts of development funds that countries receive from all quarters. Some are very well treated, while others are very poorly treated. When it comes down to the practical day-to-day allocations of IDA funds, it is pretty much left to the management of the institution to do it. But from time to time we do feel some pressure from interested donor countries, usually in the direction of compounding what would be regarded as errors of their own aid allocations.

The French are giving large sums of money per capita to the French African countries, and on the Pearson Test, IDA would not give anything to the French African countries, since there are many other areas with much lower per capita levels of assistance. But the French are always pressing us to slant IDA funds towards French Africa. Similarly, the Japanese, whose interest is in Southeast Asia, are persuading us to put more assistance into that area. And the United States, I need scarcely add, is always telling us that more funds should be channeled into Latin America. So, in practice, instead of asking us to make good the deficiencies in the existing pattern of allocations, the donors are in fact pressuring us to compound the already generous terms given to some countries who happen to be in their spheres of political influence and interest.

The second area of consideration regarding allocation of funds is sectors of activity. The Bank does not approach sectoral loans with any preconceptions as to the proportions in which funds should be divided between various sectors, such as agriculture, power plants, roads, railways, and so on. Countries are the units we deal with, and investment is made solely on the basis of what project will be the most productive for economic development. On the whole, Bank commitment of funds works out in the following proportions: power and transport are each responsible for close to one third of total spending; the rest goes to industry, agriculture, communications, education, water supply, population programs, urban development, and general development purposes. It was not planned that the two areas of power and transport should bulk so large in total funding, but that is the pattern that emerged from a country-by-country review of investment priorities. It is just these big, lumpy infrastructure investments which bring a country up against the need to get external assistance, since they are usually projects that cannot easily be accommodated on a year-to-year budgetary basis. In addition, such projects usually have a high foreign-exchange component and a need for technical assistance that cannot be locally provided.

In IDA the pattern of sectoral allocation is different. Industry (including import maintenance loans) and agriculture together get $2.2 billion out of the total lending of $4.6 billion, or about 45 percent of the total. These categories can be extremely misleading, however, since the interlinking between sectors makes it difficult to make a clear-cut classification of a project. A great deal of investment in transport, which is such a large part of total loans, is directly connected to agricultural development too, as well as to the industrial sector.

Robert Asher discusses the evolvement of the Bank from a financial institution in its early years into a development agency in its more recent activities. It would be a mistake to think that we function like a conventional bank. Keynes used to say that the Bank and the Fund were misnamed from the beginning, that the Bank was really a development fund and the IMF was really a bank! The Charter enjoins us to make our operations self-liquidating so that they will command the support of capital markets, and to that extent do we think as bankers do. IDA obviously uses very different concepts for its operations, and that is due to the source of its funds. In neither case do we think of projects as ends in themselves but rather as instruments for the development of the national economy. Hence, we engage in a great deal of basic institution-building along with the financing. This has manifested itself in, among other things, a growing emphasis on economic appraisals of the country, increasing depth of concentration on developmental problems, and more far-reaching projections of a country's development plans and its place in the world economy.

Lastly, the work of the Bank in directly and indirectly coordinating development assistance by others to the developing countries has important implications. It follows from this greater engagement in the developing process, as a development institution, that we become more concerned with the range of resource use, the allocation of resources and their disbursement even by agencies other than the Bank. This leads to greater concern with the overall economic policies of our member countries and to the exercise of what has been called "leverage" in support of more effective economic and financial management by the recipient country itself. It would be more accurate to think of this process as a dialogue between the Bank and a member nation with respect to its economic policies.[7] We feel that we are not really doing the job of a development institution if we do not look at the whole range of a country's development process and try to assist in solving the interlinked spectrum of problems that arise.

# Comment: High Profile, Better Target

William S. Gaud*

The World Bank Group is divided into three parts, and we have discussed only two of them so far. I am very much tempted to talk about the third, the International Finance Corporation, with which I am connected, because it poses some very interesting questions.

IFC's purpose is to promote private investment in developing countries. Has private investment got any part in development? Has private investment got any future in developing countries? What are you going to do with the sort of thing that is happening today in Latin America, the events in Chile, in Peru, and the Andean Pact? What can an institution like IFC do in the way of institution building in the developing countries?

These are some of the interesting questions that revolve around IFC's activities. Obviously, whether private enterprise can play a part in development, and how successful its future will be, will depend in large part upon whether private enterprise can simultaneously accomplish two things: one, serve the purposes of investors; two, support the objectives and plans of the developing countries. The day is long past when private investment can be judged only in terms of whether it is good for investors.

I happen to be an optimist on this. I think there is a lot that private investment can do in the underdeveloped world. But I am going to resist the temptation to talk about IFC and its problems. I prefer to carry on from where Burke Knapp left off and discuss the Bank and IDA.

Let me emphasize one part of the Bank's activities which, to me, is the most important part and one on which the Bank must concentrate if it is to discharge its leadership responsibilities. The Bank is in a difficult position and is not altogether ready to fill the large role in which it is now cast. But I think it is a great deal readier than it was a few years ago.

To begin with, the name of the game as I see it is not economic development. The name of the game is development. That is a lot broader than economic development. As Indian Prime Minister Indira Gandhi said the other day, "The goal of India is social transformation."

This includes economic development, but it also includes a lot more than

*Executive Vice-President, International Finance Corporation, Washington, D.C.; from 1962 to 1969 an executive and then Administrator of the United States Agency for International Development.

that. The Bank over the years has been gearing itself up more and more, as I see it, to support development in this broader sense. Today, for example, the Bank spends far more effort than it used to on sector studies in individual countries. It spends far more time than it used to on overall economic studies of individual countries and on trying to gauge development priorities. It has far more people working overseas on a permanent basis than it used to. It also has many more people going overseas on temporary missions not only to look into individual projects but to work on broader questions.

Another thing that the Bank is doing (as Burke Knapp indicated, lump-sum figures are apt to be a little misleading) is to concentrate far more today on agriculture than it used to. The same is true of education, of family planning, and of a number of other fields related to the type of social transformation and overall social development that are at the heart of true development. There has been a very real shift in emphasis at the Bank in this direction.

If the Bank is going to continue to do this—and I think it must—several consequences follow. One is that, having more people overseas, taking on more and more of the worldwide development job, involving itself more than it used to in policy matters, giving more advice, carrying on a dialogue on these matters, the Bank's profile is getting higher and higher. This is inevitable. This has to be if the Bank and IDA are to fulfill their development role. But it leads to a lot of problems.

As a graduate of the Agency for International Development (AID), I have had some experience with those problems, though the Bank has some advantages over AID. For example, AID's staff was and is composed entirely of Americans, whereas the Bank's staff is not. When the Bank sends a mission overseas, whether temporary or permanent, that mission does not consist solely of Americans. It contains a mixture of nationalities, some of them from developing countries. This makes economic diplomacy a good deal simpler for the Bank than it is for AID. But it still remains to be seen what the level of tolerance will be for a truly active, strong-minded multilateral institution of the kind that the Bank will be if it tries to do the job that many people think the Bank should do.

Is there any answer to this? I think it is an important question that goes to the heart of one of the Bank's major problems. If I can be parochial and refer to AID again, I think that over the years AID has done a good job in many respects. Indeed, AID has been doing for a number of years some of the things that the Bank is only now beginning to do. And it was doing some of them fairly well. But AID was cut off at the knees partly because it could not handle the profile problem. The necessary level of tolerance was not there.

AID never solved that problem. As the Bank comes to occupy a more and more prominent position on the development landscape, it will have to find ways to deal with this very practical problem. I have not got the final answer, but I think that one direction in which the Bank should and must work, in trying to find ways to soften its impact on its borrowers, is to work more extensively with and through regional organizations composed of the developing countries themselves.

I am not referring now to consortia and consultative groups. They are excellent bodies; they serve a very real, but different, purpose. Their primary function is to reach agreements on requirements and cooordinate the activities of donors. I am talking about the need to bring the LDCs more into the process of developing programs, working out priorities, reviewing performance, and so forth.

One thing that the World Bank might do would be to work much more closely than it has in the past with the Asian Development Bank, the African Development Bank, the Inter-American Development Bank, and other regional banks and institutions. All kinds of reasons—political, personal, historical and others—are brought forward as to why this has not been done. Take CIAP (Comite Interamericano de la Alianza para el Progreso or InterAmerican Committee of the Alliance for Progress) as an example. CIAP is perhaps not as effective as it might be, but at least it represents a genuine effort to bring the Latin Americans into the decision-making process. It is all very well to say that it has not been as effective as one would like, but that is not the point. The point is to do one's best to make it effective, to find the best way to bring the LDCs into the decision-making process. In my view it is essential that the Bank give this problem serious attention.

There is an almost inescapable conflict between the desire of a recipient country to decide for itself how and where aid funds are spent, and the desire of a donor country to make sure that those funds are spent reasonably and sensibly according to the donor's lights. How do you reconcile the two views and thereby avoid abrasive confrontations?

The Bank, being an international institution free of the short-term political objectives that frequently motivate individual aid-giving countries, has a better chance of success in this area than any bilateral aid donor could have.

Another problem now confronting the Bank and IDA arises out of the fact that, as they increase the volume and scope of their activities, they will lose some of their present independence and become more and more dependent upon the governments of their developed country members. This is so primarily for two reasons. First, if the Bank is to have a substantially larger lending program, it will have to raise the funds for that program in the capital markets of the developed countries, which it can do only with the consent of their governments. Second, IDA's needs are steadily increasing, and IDA funds are appropriated funds. So IDA's program, too, depends upon favorable governmental action.

The World Bank is already the biggest thing on the development horizon. In the last fiscal year its commitments exceeded those of any other government or agency in the aid field. Moreover, this trend seems likely to continue. The United States proposes to shift more of its development aid from the bilateral to the multilateral programs. The Canadians love multilateral aid. The British like it, and so do the Scandinavians, the Dutch, and a number of others. This is the golden age, you might say, of multilateral aid.

The more the Bank is dependent on governments, the more likely it is that individual governments will seek to impose their will on the Bank. In 1970, for example, when the US Congress passed the Appropriation Act for the multilateral agencies—the World Bank, the IDA, the InterAmerican Development Bank—a good many congressmen made a determined effort to subject these institutions to the audit review of the United States General Accounting Office. My guess is that this is only the first of a series of efforts that some members of the US Congress will make to impose on the multilateral institutions the same kinds of barnacles and restraints that have been imposed on the United States bilateral aid programs. In other words, as the center of gravity shifts from bilateral aid to multilateral aid, the attention of the Congress will also shift, and, I fear, some of its members will try to impose on the activities of the Bank the same kinds of restrictions, some of them political in nature, that are now imposed on AID.

This is a sure way to ruin a multilateral institution or program. If the United States succeeds in imposing its particular requirements, the Germans will want to impose theirs, the British theirs, and so on and so forth. Before you know it, there will be no multilateral program in the true sense of the word.

This could be a serious problem for the Bank. It is vital to preserve the integrity and independence of its programs. They must not be used to achieve the political, economic, or other objectives of its individual members.

To sum up, you might say that to date the Bank has been like a little girl in a nunnery, going along doing nice things, handling good projects, without too much attention being paid to her. But now she is going to have to leave the nunnery and come out into the cold cruel world with everyone's eyes fixed upon her. It will be quite a change.

# Comment: The Raising of Resources

Richard W. Richardson*

This otherwise excellent discussion tends to miss at least one basic point. Foreign aid as we practice it today in this country, or even as we conceive of it today, has only very limited relevance to the programs that we urged through the early sixties or even the late fifties, for the reason that William Gaud has more than once alluded to: mainly, we do not have enough funds. We have never really had enough funds, I think, although back in the early 1960s responsible men could disagree about this when the issue of absorptive capacity of the developing nations seemed to loom as an obstacle to increasing transfers to aid funds. Now there is consensus that aid funds are inadequate by any measure. We are squarely up against a worldwide development problem that is increasing rather than diminishing in size, at the very time when the flow of aid funds at truly concessional rates is declining, so that the gap is widening on two counts.

The World Bank, at least as much as any other lending institution, uses conventional criteria for its loans, one of which may be summed up under the concept of "bankability." A loan to the LDCs from the Bank, whether soft or hard, proceeds on the assumption that the borrower will be in an economic condition to repay the loan by its maturity date without losing any of its economic momentum. In making loans, both multilateral and bilateral programs rely on concepts of efficiency, rates of return, and rates of wastage in the use of loans that are now, and have probably always been, wholly inappropriate to the environment of the less developed country (LDC). We argued that case in the sixties when aid levels were higher than they presently are; and of course our vision of what is required to do the development job is much affected by how efficiently we think the recipient can use an aid dollar. As the number of such dollars declines, it becomes more difficult to maintain that we should liberalize our standards, in other words, expect less, in the use of aid funds. It seems certain that standards of efficiency will become stricter rather than more lenient and that the grant component of aid funds will decline rather than increase as total world availability of aid funds diminish.

The great sadness, of course, is that we have lost sight of the problem before we even made much of a dent in it. If the world of 1960 was full of impoverished countries with archaic social and economic structures, this is still

*Associate Director of Research, Twentieth Century Fund, New York; and formerly Chief Economist, U.S. Senate Banking and Currency Committee, Washington, D.C.

57

true in the 1970s. The development horizon for acceptable living conditions had to be measured in half-centuries rather than in years when viewed from 1960; it still does.

In this connection, the US did itself and the world a disservice in the past decade by tactics that probably contributed to the decline of the Agency for International Development (AID) as much as anything else. It begins to appear that the World Bank will be put to much the same kind of Congressional scrutiny that AID was, especially if the US increases its contributions to that institution. Perhaps the Bank will avoid some of the mistakes made by the bilateral program in its efforts to protect itself from the Congressional hatchet. AID outdid itself in imposing restrictions on its own operations in anticipation of Congressional criticism. The Congress, ever alert to the political implications inherent in new exposés of AID's wrongdoing, hemmed in the AID program with restraints that progressively reduced the value of an AID loan to the ultimate recipient. But the Agency itself contributed substantially to this depreciation of the AID dollar, by imposing as great a variety of administrative safeguards as probably has ever been witnessed. An enormous amount of negotiating energy was used up in the imposition of these conditions, rather than being directed, as they rightfully should have been, to the economic and social policies of the borrowing countries. By the time a negotiator managed to mollify a finance minister outraged by terms designed to insure additional US exports, he usually felt somewhat ennervated as he sought to negotiate a more rational coffee policy in the borrowing country. AID, in retrospect, would have served itself better by only imposing restrictions actually demanded by Congress—and then only after a good fight.

As it was, the relationship of the AID to the Congress reminded me very much of the way we once tried to housebreak a cat when I was very young. Every time that cat messed on the floor, my mother would rub its nose in the mess and then throw it out our window. That cat finally became so housebroken that after it messed the floor it would rub its own nose in the mess and then jump out the window! This was the tragedy of AID as an institution: the energies of its best exetutives had increasingly, and finally almost entirely, to be turned to the matter of procuring the funds from Congress, while the very large intellectual problems involved in their expenditures went unsolved or only partly solved. Great strides were made during the sixties in the conception and execution of AID lending, including significant advances in the program-lending technique, in broadening the basis for project lending, and in new techniques and new lending devices such as the sector loan. But we were consistently distracted from refinement of these techniques by the day-to-day problems generated by a hostile Congress, an indifferent public, and poor public relations.

The notion that troubles me here and now, I think, is that there is an academic quality in worrying about performance criteria in the lending process, because the leverage of the lender—as measured first and foremost by the size of the loan—has become smaller and in some cases nominal. That is certainly true of most of the bilateral programs in this country. It is probably even true, although of course less so, of consortium arrangements under World Bank or other leadership in the past few years. Through this device, I believe the World Bank has made much out of the potential in these small sums of money, but they remain small sums, and no one is so acutely aware of that fact as the recipient countries themselves. Even when AID amounts were larger, recipients quickly came to realize that they really were not as fully constrained by the terms of the original negotiation as the donor might have hoped when the loan was originally made. Brazilians and Indians alike learned after a couple of years of major AID programs that it was always possible to violate the terms of an AID program without necessarily forfeiting the AID funds associated with that program. AID officials, acutely aware of the complicated texture of economic and political circumstances associated with our aid program, were naturally reluctant to act hastily or irrevocably even when major conditions were abrogated by the recipient.

With respect to public relations, I think US officials also did a disservice out of that same zeal to win over a balky legislature. We developed or borrowed catch phrases and slogans such as "Development Decade," "Green Revolution," and "Take-off," which suggested that the business of development in these backward countries could be accomplished quickly and even automatically. Professionals always knew better; they always knew that economic and social progress could be measured only in painful decades, and they knew that there was no magic button that, if only we could find it and push it, would produce dramatic and startling changes in society or economy. But officials persisted with these fictions because they cared so much about getting on with the development efforts, and it seemed that they would be even less successful in raising funds if we did not set some politically acceptable limits on the length of the program. This approach now haunts the foreign-aid program, because the results of the past decade or more compared unfavorably with the expectations generated by the program officials themselves. Here is an application of "the revolution of rising aspirations" which was never anticipated. And this is the more ironic because the results (or at least the actual performance of LDCs generally during the 1960s) has actually been far from poor. The performance standards that they failed to meet were mainly the ones we ourselves fabricated to meet domestic political problems.

In several respects, the World Bank seems to have better possibilities of success than the bilateral program. That, at least, is the conventional wisdom, but I myself am somewhat skeptical. The main difference seems to be that bilateral programs are "political," whereas a multilateral program is apolitical and can thus provide an austere and neutral political climate within which to engage in economic policy negotiations and aid lending in accordance with objective criteria. There may be much to this advantage, but I think it is important to recognize that these multilateral institutions, including the World Bank, are not *apolitical* but rather are *multipolitical*. The Board of Directors of such institutions may be dominated by creditor countries, as in the case of the World Bank, or by debtor countries, as in the case of a regional bank. But in each instance, the Board of Directors will have its own peculiar political axes to grind, and its own particular standards to meet. They will not be the standards of the directors of a bilateral program, because many more interests are involved. But that does not make those standards *objective*; no organization of humans with diverse points of view and interests could or should be so characterized.

It has nevertheless been found convenient to regard multilateral institutions as capable of great objectivity in lending, and therefore as the proper instruments for future US lending to the LDCs. I suspect that this point of view is really only a convenient weapon in the generalized attack on bilateral aid. The truth is we have no idea how effective, how efficient, how nonpolitical the multilateral institutions would be if they became the *dominant* leaders and have to shoulder the burdens of policy reform that previously fell to the US bilateral program. It is, after all, a fact that the multilateral institutions only infrequently took the negotiating initiative or showed the program and policy inventiveness character- istic of the US bilateral program in the last decade, although they were important allies and partners in the lending process.

When and if the US Congress sees fit to amplify significantly the resources it appropriates to the World Bank, it remains to be seen whether it will continue to hold so sanguine a view of the efficiency of those institutions. My own guess is that we will witness a renewal of the suspicion, the doubt, and the bickering that hemmed in the bilateral programs in the past decade. We already see some evidence of this as the Congress experiments with language that would give the General Accounting Office (GAO) access to internal records and processes of those institutions to which we appropriate funds. We may eventually discover that the World Bank's approach to lending in Pakistan does not sit well with Congress, and it would then be interesting to discover whether or not the Congress will be willing to allow the Bank to continue such a program according to its own "objective" lights, uninfluenced by US political interests in Pakistan.

The bilateral US program of the last decade is currently criticized, on the one hand, for the political bias with which it determined its programs, but on the other hand, it is almost as frequently criticized for the single-minded pursuit of "economic" criteria in its programs, to the exclusion of political and social consequences. Both criticisms, of course, have some merit depending on the part of the world to which they refer. But it is an interesting evidence of the extreme ambivalence that nations feel—and I suspect the US is not alone in harboring such feelings—when the issue turns on the degree to which a country to whom we are lending large amounts of money chooses to pursue an independent course in its domestic and foreign affairs. I am not at all certain that this ambivalence, and the political stresses that it generates at home, will be much reduced by interpolating international institutions between the Congress and the borrower. When a serious political problem develops between the United States and a less developed country, it will quickly become a matter of concern that the World Bank, or some other multilateral institution that the US heavily supports, is pursuing a lending policy in that country which may be contrary to the bilateral interests of the United States. The multilateral institution may be better able to withstand the ensuing hue and cry, but it is hard to imagine that their internal policies will not to some extent be tempered by their concern for such problems.

As a final matter, I would like to mention another problem to which I alluded earlier: the shortage of aid funds now available to the less developed world. This was of course the point that Mr. Knapp was making in some detail. The Bank in very recent years has already become increasingly preoccupied with the matter of fund raising, both in private markets and from official sources. And while these two sources of funds are affected by different conditions, it is true that both private markets and public coffers are affected in common by attitudes in general towards foreign aid. As a result, the Bank has experienced the need to expend greater amounts of energy for progressively smaller results in raising funds from industrial member countries. It is to be hoped that the Bank will not experience a repetition of the tragedy of AID in its efforts to raise funds, to which I referred before.

It nevertheless seems to me that one major area requiring more thought and discussion is precisely the matter of how the Bank can raise additional money in larger quantities than now seems possible, given the current climate in official lending circles, especially in the US. William Gaud offers some negative prescripts here which are probably quite useful in the effort to raise additional funds for IDA: do not antagonize the Congress; stay out of the line of fire; and appear nonpolitical. As I suggested earlier, I am not at all sure that when a serious political issue crops up between a member country and the US, the Bank will be able to maintain a sufficiently low profile to be ignored by a hostile Congress, but perhaps I am too pessimistic. In any event, it seems to me that the Bank will have to turn to ways of finding additional funds to supplement what they now are able to acquire from conventional sources, public and private.

I believe that the Bank has devoted a great deal of energy to the question of securing quantum increases in resources available to it for lending to its clients, both on soft and hard terms. The Bank is an aggressive borrower in world markets. Still, it apparently will not be able to realize really significant increases in resources from private markets at least for several years to come. If this is true, they will have to seek other ways of raising additional funds, even beyond what increments of official appropriations may be forthcoming from the US and other member governments. In any event, only the Bank has the expertise and the prestige necessary to develop and implement new ideas in foreign aid as we enter the seventies, and this is as true at the fund-raising level as it is in the matter of the use of these funds with imagination and intelligence.

If, in fact, we conclude that the private markets are not sufficiently responsive to present initiatives by the multilateral lending institutions, it would seem a good idea to explore the more aggressive use of the guarantee authority possessed by the international institutions. It may be that the World Bank could take the initiative to invent more imaginative uses of that guarantee authority, perhaps in conjunction with guarantees issued individually by industrial members of the Bank in whose private markets the Bank periodically seeks funds. Several years ago, I recall, the Bank took the initiative in exploring a proposal first raised at the United Nations Conference on Trade and Development (UNCTAD) by Israel.[8] This proposal provided that industrial countries lend a guarantee to funds raised in their own markets by borrowing LDCs. With such borrowing guaranteed, LDCs would presumably be able to borrow from private sources to a degree not otherwise possible, and at interest rates comparable to the best in the market. At the same time, the industrial country would be relieved of the political and economic burden placed on its own budget by the large and increasing needs of the LDCs. That proposal further involved a subsidy of the market rate of interest to the borrowing country, which would have been financed by a budgetary appropriation. The budgetary burden on the lending country, therefore, would be confined strictly to the interest subsidy on borrowings in its capital market. This would presumably allow for a far larger volume of concessional lending than has proved possible through official lending mechanisms alone. The original proposal, if I recall correctly, dealt with guarantees by industrial country governments only. But it is not entirely impossible to conceive of the Bank itself undertaking the same kind of guarantee program to cover borrowings by less developed countries in the various capital markets of Bank member countries. Perhaps this idea, as well as the earlier plan, ought to be examined in the light of contemporary events, even though the original plan was for one or another reason laid aside several years ago.

The use of Special Drawing Rights (SDRs) as a vehicle for foreign-aid transfers has been explored recently in several forums, including the Petersen Task Force convened by President Nixon a couple of years ago.[9] The US, among other countries, has formally resisted the use of SDRs as a concessional lending device for a number of reasons, some of which relate to the novelty of this monetary experiment and the inevitable uncertainties associated with its inception as a partial solution to the liquidity problem. Perhaps, officials are understandably nervous about creating possible confusion between the world's liquidity requirements and the world's capital requirements if SDRs from the outset become available as concessional capital loans to developing countries.

Yet there is nothing inherently illogical about such use of monetary mechanisms. It is only a matter of convention that aid-giving countries have relied largely upon their fiscal (budgetary) mechanisms, and there is nothing of either a technical or economic nature that militates against the use of monetary mechanisms to achieve the same ends. Since political considerations have increasingly crippled our capacity to lend through the traditional budgetary routes, we will have to become inventive about finding other ways around this problem.

Although this is an area conventionally reserved to the International Monetary Fund, it may well be that the Bank can play a key role in shaping views in this matter both within the IMF and among member nations. The IMF itself has always proceeded on its recognition that the development problem is not merely monetary in character, but is closely linked to budgetary and fiscal questions; it would be only appropriate if the Bank, for its part, undertook an active role in fostering the use of SDRs, a monetary device, in the promotion of economic development.

## Notes

1. Alec Cairncross, *The International Bank for Reconstruction and Development*, Essays in International Finance, No. 33, Princeton University, March 1959, pp. 7-13.

2. Members whose subscriptions may be freely used or exchanged by the Association and who have participated in the replenishment of the Association's resources are included in Part I. These are Australia, Austria, Belgium, Canada, Denmark, Finland, France, Germany, Italy, Japan, Kuwait, Luxembourg, Netherlands, Norway, South Africa, Sweden, UK, and US. In 1972, Iceland became a Part I member.

3. The US is responsible for 40 percent of Part I contributions. While individual commitments by other countries can be made, it needs a two-thirds commitment of all donor countries for any replenishment to take actual effect. Otherwise, it just stays as a "potential" commitment; hence the US contribution is vital to the activation of replenishment funds. Any delaying action, such as the one conducted by the US Government in sending the 1969 replenishment up to Congress, can effectively slow down IDA funding to its members.

4. In terms of 1970 GNP at market prices and average 1967-71 exchange rates ( *World Bank Atlas*, IBRD, 1972 edition).

5. See also Andrew M. Kamarck, "Appraisal of Country Economic Performance," *Some Aspects of the Economic Philosophy of the World Bank*, Washington, D.C., September 1968.

6. Pearson et al., *Partners in Development: Report of the Commission on International Development*, Washington, D.C.: IBRD and Praeger, 1969, pp. 226-27.

7. For more radical, but often inaccurate, views of the "leverage" issue, which is also the subject of Chapter 5, see Teresa Hayter, *Aid of Imperialism*, Penguin, 1971; and Harry Magdoff, *The Age of Imperialism: The Economics of U.S. Foreign Policy*, Monthly Review Press, 1969, Chapter 4.

8. *The Horowitz Proposal, A Staff Report*, Washington, D.C., February 1965.

9. Petersen, et al., *U.S. Foreign Assistance in the 1970s: A New Approach*, Report to the President from the Task Force on International Development, Washington, D.C.: March 4, 1970; see also Edward R. Fried, "International Liquidity and Foreign Aid," *Foreign Affairs*, vol. 48, no. 1, October 1969, pp. 138-49.

# 4

## Terms and Flexibility of Bank Lending

P.D. Henderson*

This chapter is divided into three main sections. In the first, the existing terms of Bank loans and IDA credits are described and compared with the terms made available by other leading agencies. Then, in the second section consideration is given to the flexibility of these terms and the question of how far a greater degree of flexibility might be useful and could be provided. In the final section some other aspects of the flexibility of Bank transfers are briefly discussed, and in particular the interrelated issues of the purposes for which loans and credits are or might be extended and the forms in which they are made. This raises such familiar questions as the sectoral composition of Bank lending and the extent to which loans and credits should be extended in project form.

## The Terms of IBRD Loans

It is usual to specify terms of lending with respect to three parameters: the rate of interest charged; the maturity or repayment period of the loan; and the length of the grace period before repayments of principal fall due. The combined effect of these can be taken into account by calculating the grant element of a loan. This is done by discounting all receipts and payments associated with the loan at some specified rate of interest and expressing the present value of these as a percentage of the nominal amount of the loan. Although this measure is a rough one, largely but not solely because the choice of a rate of interest is bound to be rather arbitrary, the grant element is a useful indicator of the degree of softness of a loan or credit, and of the effects of a given change in one or other of the three parameters listed above. In quoting figures for the grant element of particular forms of loans, I have followed here the current practice of the OECD Development Assistance Committee in using a rate of interest for discounting of 10 percent per annum.

Let us look at the terms of IBRD loans with respect to the three parameters and see what is implied for the grant element in these loans.

---

*At the time of writing, Director, Economics Department, International Bank for Reconstruction and Development, Washington, D.C. The author notes that this chapter has been much improved by the advice and comments of three Bank staff colleagues; S. Raymond Cope, Benjamin B. King, and Jo W. Saxe.

First, the rate of interest on Bank loans is at present 7 1/4 percent per annum. The rate is determined by the Executive Directors of the Bank and is reviewed periodically. The present figure was established in August 1970 and by historical standards is high. The objective of the Bank is, and has always been, to keep the rate as low as is consistent with the maintenance of adequate earnings and a generally sound financial position. Naturally, the main single determinant of the lending rate, and the main constraining factor in the attempt to keep it low, is the rate at which the Bank is able to borrow on world markets and elsewhere. But the lending rate is influenced also by other factors, such as the rate that the Bank can itself obtain on its liquid assets. For some time now the lending rate has been below the rate at which the Bank can borrow. Interest charges are payable only on disbursements actually made, in other words, on the outstanding amount of disbursements.

All Bank loans are made at the same rate of interest. This holds good independently of the country to which the commitment is made or the type of project that is financed. Some loans are made, not to the entity which is carrying out the project, but to the government or some kind of intermediary institution, which in turn relends to the project entity. In these circumstances the intermediary may relend at a rate somewhat higher than the rate it pays to the Bank, in order to cover its own administrative expenses.

The period of repayment and the grace period of the Bank loan may take account of the economic position of the borrowing country, or the nature of the project, or both. Broadly speaking, variation on project grounds is both more common and more systematic than variation with respect to countries. Thus, the maturity of a Bank loan is likely to depend on the assumed length of life of the assets that are being financed, which may, for example, be twenty-five years for a hydroelectric plant, but fifteen or twenty years for a road improvement scheme. Similarly, the grace period, in which interest but not amortization payments are due, is decided in relation to the expected lapse of time between the date of commitment and the time at which the project concerned will come into operation and begin to yield substantial net benefits. Thus, in education loans a ten-year grace period is common, while loans for roads typically have a shorter period of perhaps four to seven years.

Under these arrangements, the hardest or least favorable terms that a borrowing country could at present expect to receive on an IBRD loan would involve a combination of a 7 1/4 percent rate of interest, a four-year grace period, and an eleven-year amortization or repayment period, giving a total term of fifteen years. Using a 10 percent rate of interest for discounting receipts and payments, this implies a grant element of approximately 16 percent. At the other end of the current spectrum of possibilities, the softest terms that might be obtained on an IBRD loan would be a combination of the same 7 1/4 percent rate of interest, a ten-year grace period, and a thirty-year maturity. This implies a grant element of about 23 percent. This is a good deal better in proportionate terms, but still not very high. The same improvement in terms (from 16 to 23 percent) that is obtained by extending the grace period from four to ten years and the repayment period from fifteen to thirty years would also result from a reduction of the lending rate from 7 1/4 percent to 6 percent.

## The Terms of IDA Credits

On IDA credits no interest is charged, but a service charge of 3/4 percent per annum is made on the principal amount of the credit withdrawn and outstanding. There is no commitment charge. (On Bank loans, a commitment charge of 3/4 percent is payable on the undisbursed amount of the loan.) All IDA credits up to now have been extended for a fifty-year term, with repayment over forty years following a ten-year grace period: unlike Bank loans, none of these periods has varied in accordance with either the situation of the borrowing country or with the purpose to which the credit has been directed.

This combination of grace period and repayment provisions, together with the service charge of 3/4 percent, implies a grant element of some 86 percent. Thus, the difference in softness between even the most favorable IBRD loan and an IDA credit of equal amount is very considerable. If we choose to make the comparison between the two on the basis adopted here, using a 10 percent rate of interest, then a dollar's worth of an IDA credit is at present worth on average some four dollars worth of an IBRD loan. This point can be illustrated by expressing the most recent commitment figures, for the fiscal year 1971, in terms of grant-equivalent as well as nominal amounts. These figures are set out in the table below. It can be seen from the table that while IDA commitments were less than one-quarter of the total when measured in nominal terms, they come to well over half of the grant-equivalent amount of Bank/IDA commitments. The average grant-equivalent of the total of commitments depends on the relative weighting of Bank loans and IDA credits in the total. For the fiscal year 1971 it was about 35 percent.

**Table 4-1**
**Bank and IDA Commitments, Financial Year 1971**

| | Actual Commitments | | Grant Equivalents | |
|---|---|---|---|---|
| | Amount ($ m.) | Percentage | Amount ($ m.) | Percentage |
| IBRD loans | 1,896 | 76.5 | 379 | 43.0 |
| IDA credits | 584 | 23.5 | 502 | 57.0 |
| Total | 2,480 | 100.0 | 881 | 100.0 |

Note: Figures for actual commitments are taken from the World Bank's *Annual Report* for 1971. An average grant-equivalent of 20 percent has been assumed for IBRD loans in this period.

## Bank and IDA Terms and Those of Other Lenders

The two sets of terms outlined above, for Bank loans and IDA credits, can be compared with the terms on which overseas development assistance is made available by the chief bilateral lenders. On this the most recent information comes from the 1971 report from the Chairman of the Development Assistance Committee, which provides information on the terms of bilateral commitments of official development assistance made in 1969 and 1970 by the sixteen D.A.C. countries.[1] With respect to the three parameters described above, the average terms of all bilateral loans from these sixteen countries for the year 1970 were as follows: interest rate, 2.8 percent; maturity period, 29.9 years; and grace period, 7.4 years. The combination of these terms implies an average grant element in bilateral loan commitments of 57 percent. These terms are less generous than the IDA figure of 86 percent, though one of the sixteen countries, Canada, provided slightly more favorable lending terms than those of IDA credits. The terms, however, are considerably more favorable than those on which Bank loans are made, and with the present composition of Bank loans and IDA credits are a good deal more favorable than those of Bank/IDA commitments as a whole.

This comparison, however, considerably underestimates the relative softness of the development-assistance terms offered by the bilateral lenders, since it takes account only of loans. It therefore omits the bilateral assistance made available in the form of grants rather than loans, for which the grant element is by definition 100 percent. In 1970, no less than 63 percent of total bilateral ODA commitments took the form of grants rather than loans. Including these has the effect of raising the grant element of bilateral assistance to 84 percent, virtually to the level of IDA credits.

This comparison also needs to be qualified, since much bilateral assistance is tied to purchases in the lending country, while procurement under Bank loans and IDA credits is undertaken on the basis of unrestricted competitive bidding. As a result, the figure of 84 percent just quoted somewhat overstates the grant element in bilateral aid. It is, however, clear that a wide gap exists between Bank loans and most other forms of official development assistance, as well as between Bank loans and IDA credits. One consequence of this gap is that a continuing expansion of Bank lending commitments, in a period when bilateral assistance is increasing at a lower rate, must imply a worsening of the average terms of official assistance for those countries not eligible for IDA credits. In this connection, however, the possibility has to be considered that at the margin Bank loans may take the place of suppliers' credits which are normally available only on less favorable terms and conditions. Where this is the case, a greater degree of reliance on the Bank may be consistent with an improvement in the average terms of a country's total external borrowing.

Should Bank lending terms be more flexible? Although as we have seen the terms of both IDA credits and (with unimportant exceptions) Bank loans are in each case uniform as between different borrowing countries, it is nevertheless possible for the Bank to achieve a certain amount of flexibility with respect to the average terms on which it lends to particular countries. This is done by what is known as "blending," providing a mixture of Bank loans and IDA credits. The average term of the mixture will clearly depend on the relative proportions of Bank loans and IDA credits in the total amount made available to each country. In practice, the relative proportions, and hence the degree of hardness or softness of the blend, vary a good deal in accordance with the degree of creditworthiness of the country concerned for borrowing in the form of Bank loans.

The number of borrowing countries to which this can be applied is necessarily limited, since in order to qualify for such a blend a country must be sufficiently creditworthy to be eligible for some Bank lending, while at the same time it must have a sufficient insufficiency of creditworthiness to qualify as a recipient of IDA credits. This double condition is not in fact as restrictive as it might appear: at present over one-quarter of the countries in which the Bank has an active lending program fall into the "blend" category, and in round terms some 30 percent of lending commitments in the fiscal year 1971 were made to these countries. (If India, which though formally a blend country is perhaps a borderline case, is classified instead as an IDA country, this proportion falls to a figure close to 20 percent.) Nevertheless, the majority of borrowing countries at any given time will be eligible for Bank loans or for IDA credits, but not both.

Thus, the extent to which the terms of Bank/IDA lending can be varied with respect to particular countries is at present rather circumscribed. Certain aspects of this limited flexibility can, I think, be usefully distinguished.

First, only two forms of lending are made available, namely Bank loans and IDA credits, which differ very widely in the softness of their terms. Under present circumstances it is not possible for us to make available a loan for which the grant element is between 25 percent and 85 percent. This gap in the spectrum of lending possibilities is only partly bridged by the fact that in some cases a blend can be made available.

A second element of inflexibility is that within each of the groups of countries eligible either for Bank loans only or for IDA credits only—the two groups for which blending is not a possibility—the terms of lending are virtually uniform despite the fact that the circumstances of particular countries within each group may differ considerably. This point applies with particular emphasis to the countries eligible only for Bank loans. At present the Bank offers exactly the same terms to countries as rich and developed as Finland, Ireland, Israel, and New Zealand as it does to a country as poor and underdeveloped as Nigeria, which because of its large and rapidly growing oil revenues is fully creditworthy for Bank lending, or to such developing countries as Ivory Coast, Peru, or Zambia, which also do not at present qualify for IDA funds. Within the group of IDA countries the differences are much less striking, but they are still noticeable: countries such as Ghana, Korea, Tunisia, and Turkey are classed together with the poorest and most disadvantaged of the developing countries. All these four countries, however, either are or have been "blend" countries.

A third and related point is that, with the limited qualifications made above in relation to Bank lending, the only ground for variations in lending terms recognized by the Bank and IDA is differences in the degree of creditworthiness of different countries. It is on this ground that Nigeria gets the same terms as Finland, and much worse terms than Ghana. This is arguably an anomalous state of affairs. It is hard not to feel that the terms of lending to different countries should be flexible enough to take more fully into account other characteristics than the degree of creditworthiness, and in particular that there should be more regard to the level of income per head as a broad indicator of the magnitude of a country's development problems.

If one accepts this prima facie case for greater flexibility with respect to degrees of poverty, then the question arises of how to provide for it.[2] Here it seems to me useful to distinguish two possible broad lines of approach, one of which appears more promising—or perhaps one should say, less unpromising— than the other. Each of them has a number of possible variants that will not be considered here.

The first approach that suggests itself is to increase the extent to which blending can be undertaken. Since *ex hypothesi* those countries eligible for IDA credits are already receiving as much in the way of Bank lending as their creditworthiness situation permits, this can be done only by action in one direction, by enlarging the number of countries that qualify as recipients of IDA funds. Thus, a certain degree of poverty would become a sufficient condition for IDA eligibility, instead of as at present a necessary condition only. Such a change could be combined, but need not be, with one or both of two additional features: a change in the income ceiling below which a country became eligible for IDA credits; and a system by which the allocation of IDA credits below this ceiling was made more sensitive to differences in income per head below the agreed ceiling level.

It is clear that if we made the reasonable assumption that the amount available to IDA is given and would not be increased by extending the list of eligible countries, then the newly eligible countries under such a scheme would benefit only at the expense of those that qualify at present. This in itself need not be a decisive objection: it simply follows from the principle that in allocating a fixed amount, relatively more weight should be given to the poverty criterion as compared with creditworthiness. A more serious problem with this approach is that, as pointed out by Mr. Knapp in Chapter 3, the principal *raison d'etre* of IDA, and the ground for its creation, was to provide a means of lending to countries that could not borrow on Bank terms because of limited credit-worthiness. The "insufficiency of creditworthiness" criterion is a basic one, and its abandonment would therefore imply a drastic change in the role and concept of IDA. Partly in order to avoid this, and also because of the difficulty in using any single instrument of lending in order to achieve a number of different objectives, my own preference would be for the introduction of some new form of intermediate loan rather than for an extension of the list of countries that could obtain IDA credits.

Such an intermediate loan would be made on terms substantially more favorable than those of Bank loans but at the same time substantially less favorable than those of IDA credits: one might think in terms of a grant element of around 50 percent. They would be made available to the poorer and needier of the countries presently eligible only for Bank loans, and in principle also to the richer and more developed of the countries at present eligible to receive IDA credits. Under such a system (assuming for the moment that it could be established) the main categories of Bank/IDA borrowing countries would become:

1. the richer, fully creditworthy countries, possibly defined as those with per capita incomes of over $500, which would as now be eligible only for standard Bank loans;
2. the poorer fully creditworthy countries, which would be eligible for the new intermediate Bank loans as well as for lending on standard terms;
3. blend countries, which might possibly then be subdivided into those receiving both types of Bank loan, standard and intermediate, as well as IDA credits; and those receiving only intermediate loans as well as IDA credits; and finally
4. countries receiving IDA credits only, which would presumably tend to be the poorest and least developed of those which qualify for such credits at present.

What form should be given to these intermediate loans? Although many possibilities exist, which need not be enumerated here, the main required properties of such an instrument are two.

1. In order to achieve a sufficiently large improvement in terms as compared with existing Bank loans, there should be provision either for a substantially lower rate of interest or for a waiver of interest payments during the grace period; and

2. In order to go some way to meeting the problems of the less creditworthy countries, the lower rate of interest but with no provision for waiver should be combined with a longer grace period and maturity period than is the case with existing Bank loans.

To give a specific illustration, one might think in terms of intermediate loans as being extended *either* on the existing Bank terms with respect to interest rates and repayment periods, but with a standard grace period of possibly five years in which interest payments could be completely waived, *or* at a lower rate of interest (perhaps 4 percent) together with a grace period and maturity period of ten years and forty years respectively. Each of these alternatives has a grant element that somewhat exceeds 50 percent. Assuming that both were acceptable and that the complications of a dual form of intermediate loan were manageable, the choice between the two could be left to the borrowing country.

Another possible element of choice, under the alternative of a subsidized rate of interest rather than an interest waiver, would be to give countries an option between two variants with the same grant element, the first with a lower rate of interest and a shorter grace period and maturity period and the second combining somewhat higher (though still subsidized) rate with a longer grace period and maturity period.

It is clear that any scheme along these lines would have to be financed on a grant basis by the richer countries. Funds would have to be made available, on the first alternative, to meet the difference between the subsidized interest rate and the rate on standard Bank loans, through what has come to be known as a multilateral interest equalization fund;[3] and on the second alternative, to meet the interest payments due to the Bank during the period of waiver. Hence, despite its apparently useful features, any system of intermediate loans is open to the objection that, with a given amount of grant assistance which the richer countries are prepared to make available in any specified period, it can confer benefits on some developing countries only at the expense of equivalent losses to others. If we further assume that a given amount of grant funds at the disposal of the Bank and IDA, then the losers would again be the countries that at present qualify for IDA credits. There is no escape from this dilemma unless it becomes clear that the creation of a new instrument of lending, such as the form of intermediate loans described here, would in itself lead to a net increase in the total amount of grant funds available to the Bank and IDA for lending on easier terms. At present this possibility seems a remote one.

Thus, despite the arguments for softer forms of Bank lending, in the interests of greater flexibility, such a development is unlikely to be practicable for at any rate some time to come. Unless and until the future growth of IDA lending becomes more firmly assured, it would be premature to think in terms of using scarce grant financing for this new purpose. It is, however, to be hoped that over time there will be larger and more assured flow of grant funds to the Bank and IDA. As and when this takes place, the possibility might arise of using some part of the increase for the purpose of instituting intermediate loans, rather than reserving the whole amount for IDA only.

Even granted the necessary increase in funds and a readiness in principle to use a portion of them in this way, there would still be difficult problems to be faced in devising and operating a scheme for intermediate loans. The division of funds, between IDA on the one hand and the fund for providing softer Bank loans on the other, would inevitably be an awkward and contentious matter. There would also be hard decisions to be taken about the criteria of eligibility for countries to receive intermediate loans, and the basis for allocating these loans among the countries declared eligible for them. But given the necessary growth over time of the funds available, and the will to use them for the purpose of creating a new instrument of concessional lending, these issues could no doubt be resolved.

It is perhaps worth noting that the optimum degree of flexibility falls well below the maximum. Although to be flexible is generally accounted a virtue in an institution, it is also and rightly thought to be a sound principle not to attempt to do too much, and to have regard for the interests and responsibilities of others and the advantages of specialization. What it makes sense for the Bank to do or to attempt must therefore depend to a large extent on the actions and policies of the bilateral lenders, and on the established roles of other international agencies.

A second point to bear in mind is that even within the constraints just referred to, the Bank is far from being a free agent. Although for a number of reasons it has a greater degree of autonomy than some other international agencies, the broad lines of policy are determined by its member governments. What these governments are prepared to permit or to encourage will depend on their perception of their own interests, of the needs of the developing world, and of the role of the Bank in relation to other agencies and institutions. This again sets limits to what is practicable, though these limits are neither immutable nor precisely defined.

## The Composition of Bank and IDA Project Lending

It is well known that the distribution of lending commitments among different sectors has changed over time, with a decreasing relative (though not absolute) emphasis on major infrastructure projects in the fields of power, transport, and irrigation, and a corresponding shift towards projects in industry, education, agriculture other than irrigation, and such relatively new areas of activity as population and tourism (see Figure 2-1). This, however, does not adequately describe the process of broadening and diversification that has occurred and is continuing. Changes in emphasis have taken place not just between sectors and subsectors, but within them. Thus, for example, within the public utilities sectors relatively more is now going to water supply and telecommunications lending as compared with power, while in both power and water supply increasing attention is now being given to the problems of supplying rural areas. In transport there has been a natural shift from railway to highway lending, and within the highway sector increasing attention to feeder roads as compared to major intercity highways.

Another aspect of change is the development of what are sometimes called "multidimensional" projects, which combine various elements from different sectors or subsectors. It has long been recognized that a successful agricultural project may require a great deal more than the provision of adequate infrastructure, and that project planning may have to extend to such aspects as the availability of inputs such as fertilizers and seeds, credit, transport and marketing arrangements, and price incentives. This broadening of the scope of projects has increasingly gone beyond the bounds of traditional sectors. Thus, some of the Bank's more recent agricultural projects, for example, the Lilongwe project in Malawi, have included health, education, and transport elements and are more in the nature of integrated rural development projects. A similar extension beyond the boundaries of traditional sectors is likely to become increasingly common in the financing of major urban developments, where the Bank's involvement has been growing.

In my view this process of broadening and diversification will continue. The Bank and IDA will increasingly provide finance for shelter (where there have already been loans for "sites and services" schemes) and health (which has already been an element in water supply and population loans), largely but not necessarily exclusively as elements of multidimensional projects. Lending for rural works programs is another step that can be foreseen; and more generally there will be an increase in the number of projects that attempt to tackle the problems of the rural sector through a set of interrelated measures, rather than by concentrating exclusive attention on the increase of agricultural production (which, however, will doubtless remain the most important single aspect).

Despite this evidence of flexibility, the Bank is often regarded as too narrow and restrictive in its choice of projects for financing. One reason for this is a belief that both the Bank and IDA have too strong a bias towards projects with a high foreign-exchange component, as distinct from those in which the local expenditure content is high. It is therefore necessary to consider how flexible the Bank and IDA are prepared to be with respect to the form in which loans and credits are made available, which brings us to the familiar issues of local expenditure financing and program lending.

## Local Expenditure Financing

The Articles of Agreement of the Bank allow it to make foreign exchange available for local expenditures "in exceptional circumstances." In the case of IDA, the corresponding clause in the Articles refers to "special cases," a form of words which was deliberately made less restrictive. In practice these clauses have been interpreted in a fairly liberal spirit, and the Bank and IDA have been able to expand their lending into such areas as agriculture and education, where the local expenditure element is often high, without running into obvious difficulties. The position was last reviewed by the Executive Directors earlier in 1971, in connection with one of the recommendations made by the Pearson Commission, and it was then concluded that existing guidelines permitted local expenditure financing where it was needed. On present evidence no great problem seems to exist.

Nevertheless, my own feeling is that this particular restriction on the Bank's freedom of action may need to be reconsidered before long. Three factors have a bearing on this view:

1. There is no advantage to the borrowing country, and possibly some disadvantage, if a lending agency is inhibited from financing local expenditures.

2. If the predictions made above are correct, the Bank and IDA will in future be lending more both in absolute and in relative terms for projects where foreign exchange component tends to be low.

3. Even if no projects are rejected or amended at the final stage because of restrictions on the permissible extent of local expenditure financing, the knowledge or belief that projects with a high local expenditure content will run into trouble may affect the initial identification and selection of projects to be financed.

Taken together, these considerations suggest that there is a case for establishing more clearly, possibly through a formal amendment to the Articles of Agreement, that the Bank and IDA will finance local expenditures whenever this is judged necessary in order for them to take an appropriate share in the costs of the projects that they wish to finance.

## Program Lending

This leaves open the question of how far the Bank should confine itself to project lending. On this point, the Articles of Agreement of the Bank (and similarly in the case of IDA) provide that, "loans made or guaranteed by the Bank shall, except in special circumstances, be made for the purpose of specific projects of reconstruction or development."[4] Although the Bank and IDA have made a number of program loans or credits, starting as early as 1947 with loans to European countries for purposes of reconstruction, no clear specification of the prerequisite "special circumstances" has ever been laid down. The question of how far the Bank should be prepared to undertake program lending was considered by the Executive Directors early in 1971. It was then concluded that it was appropriate for the Bank and IDA to make program loans available to a country that had a satisfactory development program and supporting economic and financial policies, and where project lending alone would not provide an adequate amount of external finance at the time when it was needed. This decision in my judgment gives program lending a more securely established role in Bank/IDA operations: in future, such lending is likely to be more readily taken for granted, as a regular though not very frequent practice.

The respective advantages of program and project lending are a large and controversial topic that cannot be pursued in this chapter.[5] In relation to the particular role of the Bank, three points should, I think, be mentioned here.

First, the degree of flexibility which can be built into project lending depends on the extent and variety of the projects that can be financed. It has already been noted that in its choice of sectors the Bank has shown a readiness to innovate and to extend its operations, and that (though perhaps some reservation is called for here) it has been both willing and able to undertake the financing of local expenditures in appropriate cases. To these two elements of flexibility should be added a third, namely, the wide range of interpretations that can be, and has been, given to the notion of a "specific project," which now, for example, embraces indirect loans to development banks and credit institutions, sector loans comprising a variety of related projects, and packages such as the proposed rehabilitation program for what was then East Pakistan following the cyclone damage of 1970. For these reasons a general adherence to project lending is less restrictive than might appear.

Second, it is clear that project lending is not very flexible with respect to timing. Disbursements are normally made only over a substantial period, and often begin to be significant only some time after the loan commitment has been made; while because of the need to take time in identifying and preparing projects, commitments themselves may only become possible long after what may appear to be urgent needs for external financing have been established. Hence, if a country's dependence on external finance increases suddenly or if the opportunities for putting aid to good use are enlarged, there may be no way in which a timely response can be made through the medium of project lending. It follows that the strength of the general case for nonproject lending depends in part on how far unforeseen changes in the value to a country of longer-term external finance are felt to be a typical and important feature of the development process, for which special provision needs to be made.

Third, for the Bank and IDA in particular the case for nonproject lending partly depends on the policies pursued by other lending agencies, and the balance they choose to strike between various forms of official development assistance.

My own guess as to the future is that program lending by the Bank and IDA will become a growing, though still small, proportion of total lending commitments, and that an expansion of this kind will not be a matter of serious controversy. This still leaves open, however, some difficult and contentious issues, such as the criteria by which countries are to be regarded as eligible for these program loans and what conditions should be attached to them. It is also open to question whether this prospective balance of project and nonproject lending will confer the degree of flexibility that is likely to be needed in the Second Development Decade.

# Comment: Grants, Loans, and Local-Cost Financing

John P. Lewis*

David Henderson has provided an able review of the terms and flexibility of World Bank lending that requires very little supplementing by me. However, there are two rather simple yet fundamental background points that it may be useful to underscore. The first is that if one is thinking about a spectrum of financial vehicles for transferring resources from rich to poor countries graded by the softness of the concessional terms they offer the recipient, the range of instruments presently available to the World Bank Group leaves out the softest end of the spectrum altogether. The other point concerns the alternative means available, in a development-assistance effort already committed (as the World Bank Group presently is) to a dominant format of project funding, for injecting additional degrees of flexibility into the aid flow. It is as alternative devices for this purpose that program or nonproject lending on the one hand, and, on the other, "local-cost financing" (or, as Mr. Henderson calls it, "local expenditure financing") should, at least in part, be viewed.

The World Bank Group, as it is now conceived and operated, does not make grants. This, to my way of thinking, is a severe handicap. It is one reason why the familiar comment about the Bank being misnamed, about its being more nearly a "fund" than a "bank," is wrong. The IBRD is indeed a bank in its assumption that all of its transfers sooner or later must be paid back, and this is one of its deep-seated limitations as a rounded development-assistance agency.

Among donor governments, and among some recipient governments as well, there is a pervasive mystique, strengthened over the years by the example and at times the rhetoric of the World Bank itself, that outright grants to poor countries are not just the softest-term vehicles available: they are also soft-headed, sloppy, conducive to mismanagement of resources on the part of the recipients. This is, or in a rational world would be, largely nonsense. If the simplest rationale for international concessional transfers, especially via multilateral agencies, is also the most cogent; if, that is to say, the strongest reason for aid is to attack the unprecedented international income inequalities that have grown up among the countries of this planet mostly in the past century, then the most logical mode for conveying assistance is one that effects a once-for-all transfer of resources. It is true that both suppliers and recipients of transfers

*At time of writing, Dean, Woodrow Wilson School, and Professor of Economics and International Affairs, Princeton University.

have an interest in seeing that such international redistributions of income as can be managed are used in the recipient countries to accelerate indigenous output- and income-generating capabilities, and not just for adding to current consumption. This priority follows, for one thing, from the paucity of the total transfers that it is yet feasible to organize in a world that is still so nation-state dominated.

But although the objective may be, therefore, to promote *rates* of improving material welfare in the poor countries that are higher than those in the rich countries, even this on average has not yet been achieved. And even if and when such a convergence between the per capita growth paths of rich and poor countries does become reliably established, there is nothing to suggest that, within the time frame of the softest, most concessional international loans now available, it will be either sensible or just to expect a reverse flow of net resource transfers from the poor countries to the rich.

Such being the case, the only way that an international transfer system that relies primarily on loans can maintain its aggregative rationality is by such strategems, discussed elsewhere in this volume, as debt adjustment and/or continuing expansions of fresh loans that stay sufficiently ahead of the reflows from old loans to keep the net transfers flowing in the right directions in the right volumes. These are inherently clumsy devices. In many donor countries the political pain associated with aid giving is a function, not mainly of the donor's volume of net aid, but of the size and frequency of its fresh or "gross" aid provisions. Thus, the loan's mode of transfer over time maximizes the political difficulties of maintaining adequate net flows. It would be much cleaner, simpler, and, indeed, "businesslike" to make more extensive use of outright grants in the first place.

A developing country government would have to be foolish, moreover, to require the extra stimulus of prospective repayment in order to allocate and use its external resources efficiently. The basic incentive for efficiency inheres in the scarcity of those resources themselves, not in the financial vehicle via which they come. It is sufficient proof of this to remember that if a developing country is allocating resources rationally, the price at which external capital should be priced into the domestic economy should in any event reflect capital's internal scarcity, not its external cost. If the economic cost of capital domestically is, say, 12 percent, then that figure is the social return that an investment should earn, whether it is deployed in the private or public sector, whether or not it comes from abroad and regardless of the external interest and repayment obligations it bears. Admittedly, it takes some sophistication for governments consistently to behave this way, and all on occasions fall short. Yet the problem of not undervaluing in-transfers of capital inheres in all foreign aid, not just in its grant component, for wherever recipient governments are getting concessional terms, they are, in a market sense, getting something for nothing. Increasingly, governments are evolving and employing responsible practices in this regard, and

I would argue that there is nothing, either in the mind-sets of the recipient governments themselves or in the experience of bilateral donors who have made extensive use of grants as well as loans, to suggest that grants need be less conducive than loans to the efficient deployment and management of capital inflows.

It may be asked whether these virtues of grants over loans would not be clearest in a bipolar world where there were just two classes of countries, rich and poor, with the former making grant transfers to the latter. Does not the issue become more complex in a world where, as Mr. Henderson indicates, there is in fact a gradation of countries with different levels of income and creditworthiness and therefore different degrees of need for international transfers? Under such circumstances, is there not a strong case also for a soft-hard spectrum of transfer terms, perhaps extended to embrace a substantial volume of outright grants to the poorest countries but then also including a hardening array of loan mixes for those better off? As a practical matter I would not object to this interpretation. No one in his wildest imagining expects that development assistance, including that being channeled via the World Bank Group, is all going to be converted to grant terms within the foreseeable future; and if only a fraction of the concessional transfers can be grants, they should, indeed, as the foregoing interpretation suggests, be concentrated on the poorest, neediest countries.

As a conceptual matter, however, it is worth noting that it is not necessary in order equitably to accommodate a distribution to different degrees of need, to attach different per-dollar discounts to the allocations to different recipients. It is also quite possible to graduate the *amounts* of the distributions of concessional dollars going to different recipients in accordance with some measure of need. This, of course, is what many internal grants-in-aid formulas do, and if a grants-only system of development assistance were conceivable, it could do the same, with recipient countries being left free to borrow on nonconcessional terms internationally to the extent of their ability.

The point of all this, once again, is not seriously to propose that the World Bank should be fully recast into a grants-dispensing organ. If, however, the Bank Group is in fact to solidify its role as the world's leading and pivotal development-assistance institution, there is a strong case for endowing it with substantial grants-making capacity. Otherwise, unless some alternative channels for the distribution of nonreturnable resources, such as the UNDP, nonrepayable SDR distributions, and seabed royalties, acquire considerable scale and effectiveness, the transition from bilateral to multilateral assistance will be, in this regard, retrogressive.

My second point is less significant, but unfortunately (since no one, as far as I know, is thinking seriously just now about converting the IBRD into a grants-making institution) it has more near-term relevance to Bank operations. It is that the justification for international and, more particularly, IBRD funding of the local costs or expenditures as well as the external (import) costs of particular projects is less than commonly meets the eye. There is great enthusiasm just now for such funding, particularly in connection with ventures such as family planning, public-works attacks on mass poverty and underemployment, and educational reform that have limited direct import content and yet are judged to have high priority. At the same time, by definition, development assistance never can do more than provide a recipient with imports.

Thus, "local-cost financing" by an aid donor is, in a sense, a contradiction in terms. It involves an element of playacting. What happens is that the donor, in the guise of funding those inputs to a project which in fact are supplied out of indigenous resources, provides the recipient government with some free foreign exchange. In return the donor may get the opportunity to claim responsibility for a bigger proportion of a favored activity, or to influence the conduct of that activity more than otherwise would be acceptable, or to skew indigenous resource allocations in its favor.

There can, therefore, be a "leverage"—or to use an even nastier word, a bribery—motivation for local-cost financing. Such, indeed, has been the principal purpose of bilateral aid donors in using the approach from time to time (e.g., of USAID in providing foreign-exchange offsets to host governments' expanded population control budgets). The same motivation probably explains in part the readiness now of the World Bank Group to do more local-cost funding in developmental fields in which the Bank has newly heightened interests.

But such influence-buying or allocations-tilting is not, in the case of the IBRD and IDA, the principal motivation for local-cost funding. The main purpose, rather, is to escape the strictures that the Bank's traditional commitment to project assistance would otherwise place on the ability of the institution to respond to some developing countries' aggregative needs for net imports. Like Mr. Henderson, I shall not take the space here to attempt a proper explanation or evaluation of the Bank's long-standing emphasis on project assistance. The policy has a number of merits. Yet it is also undeniable that some developing countries have urgent needs for net imports that exceed and differ from the import content of particular foreign-assisted development projects. In the past, India and Pakistan have been outstanding in this regard, but as industrialization proceeds in the developing world, the incidence of the need for aid funding of "nonprojectizable" imports is spreading. Failure to meet the need spells distortions of the development process that favor new over existing productive capacity, imported over domestic capital goods, and inappropriately capital-intensive technologies.

Until now aided countries' requirements for a miscellany of merchandise that is necessary to expansion but can be neither project-related nor financed by export earnings have been ones that certain bilateral donors (most notably the United States, which in many cases has played the role of residual donor) have been readier to meet than has the World Bank Group. The means they mainly have used is the general-purpose, nonproject, or program loan. Bilateral program loans have had their infirmities; they usually have been tied to country-of-origin purchases and typically have been somewhat restricted as to categories of eligible items. Yet as responses to recipients' needs for nonproject net imports, they are comparatively straightforward. Of all conventional forms of development assistance, program lending is the least glamorous; it is reputed to be the most subject to diversion and abuse (although its comparative vulnerability in this regard, and the comparative invulnerability of project lending, both tend to be exaggerated); and in the hands of a recipient government of some competence, it is the most useful.

As the scope of the Bank's assistance rises relative to that of bilateral donors, so does its need to serve as a residual funder of net imports. But the Bank, as Mr. Henderson notes, has had a doctrinal allergy to program lending. Theoretically, it also has one to local-cost financing, but two or three years ago the latter within the institution was regarded as the lesser of two evils. Hence the push toward local expenditure funding. Unhappily, for reasons that Mr. Henderson also indicates, local-cost financing is a much less satisfactory solution than program lending to the principal problem to which it is meant to respond: the former typically is committed in smaller amounts than the latter, and it takes much longer to disburse. Thus, local-cost financing provides a residual donor with a far less flexible instrument with which to meet those short-run, partly unpredictable changes in a country's balance of payments needs that donors decide merit a response.

One can only hope, therefore, that the canons of anti-program-lending orthodoxy within IBRD and IDA, first trespassed upon in the early 1960s and further relaxed in 1971, will continue to lose adherents in the Bank. Some local-cost financing of projects no doubt will and should continue, both for the purposes of leverage and in order to allow recipient country contractors a chance to bid on multilateral contracts being let for projects in their own countries (an issue bypassed in these brief comments). But it is hard to see how the Bank Group can operate as the world's key development assistance agency without frequent and normal resort to program lending.

Finally, to recall once again the theme of my first comment, it should be noted that, except for custom, the preceding sentence could better end with the words "program transfers." If the World Bank Group passed out grants instead of loans, exactly the same issue would arise: the need for supplementing conventional project grants with program grants and/or grants covering the local content as well as the import content of projects.

# Comment: The Transfer of Resources

Mahbub ul Haq*

Mr. Henderson has presented the existing Bank practices in regard to terms and conditions of its lending with great lucidity and clarity. He has also referred to a number of proposals to impart more flexibility to Bank Group lending practices and procedures. Instead of commenting directly on his paper, much of which I agree with, it would be more useful to review the Bank's terms of lending from the point of view of a recipient country.

In Pakistan what we constantly worried about was not gross inflow of foreign assistance but net transfer of resources from abroad after principal and interest on past debt were repaid. After all, this was what was most relevant to our investment effort and our balance of payments position. The current and projected gap between gross inflows and net transfers also brought out, more vividly than anything else, the nature of terms and conditions on our loans that we had accepted in the past or were likely to get in the future. If the difference between gross inflows and net transfers was rather small, it showed the predominance of grants and soft loans; if it was very large, it showed how tough the terms on loans had been.

So when I arrived in the Bank in 1970, I tried to find out what the net transfer of resources had been from the Bank Group to the developing countries in the past and how it was likely to move in the future. This was not as easy to discover as I had expected, for the simple reason that attention was very largely concentrated on gross lending commitments. This brought home to me my first major piece of education: the interest of the donors in gross lending figures and targets—in *future* operations—as against the interest of the developing countries in monitoring net transfer of resources which reflects past borrowing as well as current and future disbursements.

When I pieced together whatever data were available to obtain a picture of the net transfers from the Bank Group to the LDCs in the 1960s, certain impressions seemed to emerge which were not quite reassuring:[a]

1. It appears that while the total Bank Group lending has expanded rather rapidly in recent years, the net transfer of resources has in fact declined. From

---

*Director, Policy Planning and Program Review Department, International Bank for Reconstruction and Development, Washington, D.C.
[a]This was the picture in 1970 when the article was written: it has changed dramatically since then.

financial year 1967 to financial year 1970, the total commitments from the
Bank Group increased from about $1.1 billion to $2.2 billion. During the same
period, the net transfer of resources steadily declined from $514 million in FY
1967 to $467 million in FY 1968, $375 million in FY 1969 and $283 million in
FY 1970.

2. In certain cases, the net transfer of resources has declined so sharply that
much of the Bank Group's fresh lending is merely covering repayments of
principal and interest due to the Bank. An extreme case is that of India, where
about $270 million of new lending is proposed in FY 1970 by the Bank Group,
but the net transfer of resources is expected to be minus $20 million.

I must immediately make two points to clarify the perspective within which
these figures should be interpreted:

First FY 1967-70 is not a very representative period for comparison. In
particular, FY 1970 appears to be affected by a number of special circumstances. What is more important, the net transfer of resources during this period
reflects the impact of lending patterns in the early 1960s; it does not yet reflect
the major spurt in gross lending in the last four years, which was mainly in
project form and has not fully disbursed yet. Thus, the decline in net transfer of
resources in the last four years does not indicate a trend: net transfers are bound
to go up sharply in the 1970s as a result of considerable recent expansion in the
Bank Group's lending.[b]

Second, some of these figures reflect policy actions outside the control of the
Bank Group. For instance, the net transfers to India fell so dramatically during
FY 1970 because of the earlier pause in IDA replenishment during 1966-67.[c] In
fact, this delay in IDA replenishment affects the entire picture in FY 1967-70
and particularly the situation in FY 1970. The level at which IDA funds are
being replenished and pressures for a diversified allocation pattern also influence
what can be reasonably done for the poorer LDCs, which generally receive
limited IDA funds, as against the richer LDCs which receive Bank money that is
subject to fewer rationing problems. Thus, the Bank Group is not a free agent
and works within definite constraints.

But the point I wish to emphasize is that many of the policy options become
clearer only if we focus on the concept of the net transfer of resources rather
than gross lending, whether it is a question of program lending or terms and
conditions of loans or debt burden. More emphasis on the concept of net
transfer of resources invariably means that the Bank has to acquire additional
flexibility in fixing terms and conditions of its loans and in its techniques of
lending. In this connection, I agree with Mr. Henderson's proposal to introduce

[b]This has already happened (May 1973). According to the latest available estimates, net
transfer of resources has jumped up from $283 million in FY 1970 to $750 million in FY
73 and is projected to increase further to $1340 million by FY 1975.

[c]Net transfer of resources to India has already increased to about $100 million in FY 1973
and is projected at $230 million in FY 1975.

an intermediate type of lending in-between the present Bank and IDA terms and his emphasis on program lending. In fact, if I may, I would like to make some further observations on the question of program lending.

I have been trying to discover for sometime now what the real reasons are for a prejudice against program lending, which should have been regarded merely as a technique of transferring resources rather than as something inherently good or evil. This is another area where the attitudes of the donors and the recipients seem to be quite different.

It appears to me that many of the arguments against program lending, in the last analysis, reflect a certain lack of confidence in the economic management of the developing countries. Project lending is supposed to promote investment by creating assets, and it can be easily monitored by establishing project conditions. But who knows about program lending? It may well encourage consumption. It is not easy to trace in the system. Fertilizer gets consumed, but a fertilizer factory stands as a testimonial to foreign aid. There is something disgraceful about developing countries depending on foreign assistance even for their current needs. It is surprising how far this kind of reasoning is responsible for much of the prejudice against program lending, even though it may often be dressed up in fairly sophisticated arguments.

And yet is it really correct? To begin with, resources are fungible, and by transferring resources in one form or another one may only be cherishing illusions that one is controlling the end-use of resources. Again, there is a sad confusion here about what is productive. If plants are not working to full capacity for lack of raw materials, it makes more sense to supply current inputs under program aid so that the economy can get moving rather than to insist on setting up yet more plants. One should not be mesmerized by misplaced concreteness. The timely supply of adequate raw materials may make a greater contribution to future saving and export effort of the system by getting the production going than the supply of pieces of capital machinery. Finally, what is really sad about the whole thing is the apparent willingness of donors to aid countries through project lending even when they have so little confidence in their overall economic policies that they will not consider giving them any flexible money through program lending. What sense does this make? Why undertake projects in such cases, because they are dependent on the same overall framework of economic policies for their efficiency and productivity? Why get involved in a country through project loans on a longer-term basis when there is little confidence in its economic framework even in the short run?

One of the amusing aspects of a refusal to do program lending is the consequent inability of donors to help the government in power. Program lending disburses rather fast, in one to two years, while project loans take considerably longer to disburse, about four to five years. Since the average lifetime of many governments in the developing world is not more than three to four years, project loans may often help not the current government but the next one about which the donors may know nothing. So let me add one more practical argument in favor of program lending: program loans often enable donors to transfer resources to governments they are actually dealing with, rather than to their successors whose policies or programs they can not foresee or monitor.

But to be serious, most of the controversy around program lending will tend to disappear if we focus on the concept of net transfer of resources and treat project or program lending as alternative ways of arranging such a transfer. Of course, we should satisfy ourselves about the need or level of such a transfer by reviewing the policies of the recipient, but once a decision is taken, the form of transfer should be dictated entirely by the exigencies of the situation. If the country concerned has considerable underutilized capacity, or is manufacturing a large part of its own machinery, or struggling under a huge debt burden that leaves little free foreign exchange out of its own earnings, or faced with a sudden need for a quick transfer of resources for reconstruction or development, there is no reason why it should not be given intermediate goods and raw materials through program lending. If the country concerned is financing extensive public works programs or social sectors with a large local currency expenditure, there is no reason why it should not be provided foreign exchange cover for such expenditure through local-cost financing. In other words, judgments about whether or not to transfer resources should be divorced from the *form* of such a transfer.

I realize that this is more easily said than done. A number of vested interests, both in donor and recipient countries, would prefer project loans accompanied by consultants. But this is where the advantage of multilateral institutions comes in—or, at least, should come in. I have often wondered why it is that bilateral donors are more liberal about program loans when they are considering their own lending but take rather a restrictive view about them as Part I members of the Bank. Why is it that the DAC countries themselves give 22 percent of their total assistance in the form of program loans while the World Bank does about 7 percent? The answer may well be that much of the bilateral assistance is tied and comes back to the donor, whether given in project or program loans. But the Bank money is untied, and there is less assurance of its coming back, especially to certain major donors, unless it is tied down to projects.

I simply do not believe that the Bank can go through the 1970s with its program lending restricted to 7 to 10 percent of the total. This will neither be in line with the Bank's emerging role as a dominant lender nor with the expanding requirements of the developing countries for program-type assistance. When the Bank was small, it could easily be argued that its comparative advantage lay in project lending while other large donors could do program lending: it cannot take this stand now and has to assume the burdens of leadership. The requirements of some of the LDCs for program lending are likely to increase fast as they develop their own capital goods sectors, as their debt payments increase, and as more is spent in social sectors on programs that are difficult to projectize. In these circumstances, the Bank can adequately help the LDCs if it is willing to accept program lending as a normal form of assistance and if it is prepared to make about 20 to 25 percent of its total lending in the form of program loans.

Let me also say that one of the things that has greatly impressed me about the Bank is its ability to absorb change. There is a vigorous dialogue that goes on continuously within the Bank about the future role and responsibilities of the Bank Group. What I had to say here was no more than a small element in such a dialogue. I have every hope that the Bank has the ability and dynamism to adjust to new challenges as they arise during the 1970s.

## Notes

1. *Development Assistance Review*, Report of the Chairman of the Development Assistance Committee, Paris: OECD, 1971.

2. See International Bank for Reconstruction and Development, *Possible Improvements in Techniques of Lending*, A Study by the Staff of the World Bank for UNCTAD, Washington D.C., April 1970.

3. International Bank for Reconstruction and Development, *The Horowitz Proposal, A Staff Report*, Washington, D.C.: February 1965, especially pp. 25-30.

4. International Bank for Reconstruction and Development, *Articles of Agreement*, article III, section 4, clause (vii).

5. See Raymond F. Mikesell, *The Economics of Foreign Aid*, Chicago: Aldine Publishing Co., 1968, pp. 167-84; also Hans W. Singer, "External Aid: For Plans or Projects?" *Economic Journal*, vol. 76, 1965, pp. 539-45, reprinted in Bhagwati and Eckhaus (eds.), *Foreign Aid*, Penguins, 1970.

# 5

## Efforts to Influence Recipient Performance: Case Study of India

I.P.M. Cargill*

The role of the World Bank in influencing the economic policies of the less developed countries, and especially the policies of India, is a large and complex subject with a number of facets. Obviously there are many ways in which attempts can be made to influence development policies, and there are many levels, both governmental and functional, at which influence can be exerted. There is also the question, in cases where influence might be attempted, of just how effective it actually is in shifting the direction of policies from where they might otherwise go. Finally, there is the question of the propriety of attempts by an external agency to influence the economic policies of a sovereign country.

It is indeed appropriate to consider this whole matter of external policy influence in the context of India. In the first place, the World Bank has had long associations with India going back to the late 1940s. Furthermore, India has been for a long time the largest recipient of foreign financial assistance for development in the world. It certainly is by far the largest customer of the World Bank and the International Development Association. In June 1970 there were outstanding in India over $600 million of World Bank loans and well over $1.6 billion of total financing in India, including IDA credits, by the World Bank Group. Obviously the magnitudes we are talking about in India are extremely large, and their size is hardly irrelevant to the subject of the exercise of influence on economic policies.

I might briefly describe the procedural arrangment for international consideration of India's foreign-aid requirements and their financing, not only by the World Bank and IDA but also by the various governmental donors and by other international agencies. This arrangement is called the Aid-India Consortium. It is a loosely organized body, made up of the different bilateral and multilateral sources of external official development assistance for India. It meets at least once each year, usually twice, and sometimes more often. The Indian Government is also represented at the consortium meeting, reviews the economy of India and its problems, policies, and requirements. The World Bank presides over these meetings and also serves the Consortium as a secretariat. It provides the Consortium each year with a report on the Indian economy, its basic development problems, and makes an assessment of India's external financing require-

*Regional Vice President, Asia, International Bank for Reconstruction and Development, Washington, D.C. Formerly, Director, South Asia Area Department from 1968 to 1972.

ments for the forthcoming year and in the medium term. The Bank also prepares special papers on matters chosen by the group for particular consideration; such as the progress of Indian agriculture, trade problems and policies, family planning programs, external debt problems, and debt relief requirements.

The Aid-India Consortium first arose out of the requirements of India's acute foreign-exchange difficulties during the Second Five-Year Plan period. It was found in the course of the period that balance of payments problems were far more difficult and exchange shortages more severe than the planners had contemplated. This situation confronted India with the problem of either obtaining greater financial support from abroad or curbing its development efforts and related investment programs. In these circumstances the then President of the World Bank, Eugene Black, called, in October 1958, a meeting of the main aid-giving countries and suggested that a special effort be made to assist India. The immediate response was not very enthusiastic, but it did serve to stimulate international interest in India's economic problems and development needs, and it was only shortly thereafter, at the beginning of the 1960s, that the Consortium became an important factor in mobilizing resources for assistance to India. At this time India was launching its Third Five-Year Plan, aimed at much more ambitious development efforts with particular emphasis on industrialization. An appeal was made, within the Consortium framework and largely on the initiative of the United States, for much greater international financial support for the Indian economy, and this included some assurances, not only of immediate aid, but also continuing aid on the scale necessary to carry out the Plan.

The case for this international support for India was based on studies made by a large World Bank mission which analyzed India's plans, made assessments of the external funds required, and recommended international financing of these requirements in a report to the Consortium. In fact, the Third Plan was drawn up on the assumption that nearly 40 percent of the foreign exchange required would indeed be supplied by foreign sources of aid, including the World Bank. At that time, in order to facilitate the planning tasks of policy-makers in the Government of India, pledges of aid for India were made for a two-year period. The magnitudes involved were large indeed, and for the first two-year period a total of $2365 million was pledged to India by Consortium members. This is exclusive of bilateral PL 480 commodity shipments by the U.S.

This is the early history of the Consortium and how it was operated. Let me add one more aspect of the Consortium as it relates to the question of influence on economic policies. In theory at least there was an implicit expectation on the part of the Consortium members that their aid to India would be put to good use, and this involved a kind of tacit understanding among the members and India that policies would be followed which were deemed effective in promoting the development of the Indian economy. From the Indian side, there was also reason to presume that so long as reasonably effective policies were pursued, the international community would continue with financial support of India's development program. With these implied understandings underlying the Consortium concept, the World Bank in its capacity, not only as a source of funds, but also as a convener, chairman, and secretariat of the Consortium, fell into a kind of role of middleman, evaluating for donors the effectiveness of Indian development policies on the one hand and acting for India in the mobilization of adequate amounts and forms of aid from the donors on the other hand. It can easily be seen that, with this role and with direct financing by the World Bank of Indian programs, it would have been surprising if the matter of World Bank influence on Indian economic policy did not arise.

In fact, in the beginning of the Third Five-Year Plan this question of influence was not of real significance at major policy levels and was confined to the technical, economic, and organizational aspects of particular World Bank Projects in India. As more sophisticated social scientists might say, it was a micro-oriented exercise of influence. It was not until toward the middle of the Plan period in 1963 and 1964 that questions about broader Indian economic policies began to arise. The reason for this was concern about the slow pace of progress in India's economic development, especially a lack of improvement in Indian agriculture and the sluggish trend of Indian exports. Both contributed to very difficult balance of payments problem. It was becoming clear that, as things were going, either aid needs would outrun plan calculations or efforts to develop the Indian economy would have to be curbed.

Obviously the disappointing course of the Third Plan was at least as evident to people in India as it was to outside observers. In these circumstances, in 1964 the President of the Bank, George Woods, agreed with the Indian Prime Minister that a special mission should undertake a critical examination of economic policies in India and submit its recommendations to the Indian Government and to the World Bank. The Mission was led by Bernard Bell and was known as the Bell Mission. It spent about six months in India in 1965, and its report was ready in the beginning of 1966. It is important to emphasize that this report was prepared primarily for the consideration of the Government of India. The interest of the World Bank in India from the standpoint of the Bank's portfolio was quite secondary, and it was only much later that the report was circulated to members of the Consortium. This was done with the knowledge and approval of the Government of India.

The report was voluminous, with more than a dozen volumes, and in some respects it was critical of Indian policies. The important policies on which criticism focused were mainly in the fields of agriculture and of trade and foreign-exchange administration. Policy alternatives were considered in the report, and these were the subject of extensive discussions between the Indian Government and the World Bank. I doubt, however, that there was any policy suggested in the report which had not already been formulated and seriously considered within the Indian Government itself.

In this respect I might comment specifically on the devaluation of the Indian rupee and related changes in trade and exchange policies which took place in mid-1966. It has been sometimes contended that India was pressured into these measures by the World Bank and the International Monetary Fund. Such was not the case. All of these measures had been well aired within the Indian Government and their advantages and disadvantages thoroughly considered before the Bell Mission report. Subsequent discussions with the Bank and the Fund contributed something further to these considerations, mainly in the form of ways to minimize the risks of foreign-exchange loss involved in a devaluation accompanied by trade liberalization. The suggested means for facing these risks with confidence was by mobilizing additional fast-disbursing foreign assistance through the Consortium. By undertaking to initiate this effort by the Consortium, the Bank certainly eased the difficulties of the Indian decision to devalue. Hence, I suppose it can be said that the Bank had some influence on the decision. But to think of that decision as a result of leverage or threat or any other kind of exercise of pressure is quite misleading. As a matter of fact, the actual timing of devaluation came as a surprise to the World Bank, and it was only thereafter that the task was undertaken of obtaining the necessary financial support from the Consortium countries for the devaluation package.

Now let me deal briefly with any influence the World Bank or the Bell Mission might have had on agricultural policy. The Bell Mission report rightly pointed out that agricultural development had only a secondary emphasis in India's development plans. This was not great revelation; it was well known, both within India and outside, that first priority was given to industrial development. In hindsight, there may have been good reason within the limits of known agricultural techniques at that time for this subordinate emphasis on agriculture. Nevertheless, more could certainly have been done for the Indian farmer, and this was emphasized by the Bell Mission. However, the influence of the Bell Mission report was not so much in reshaping agricultural policy but rather in dramatizing the need, technologically, administratively, and financially, for finding a way to help India produce more of its large and increasing food requirements.

The Bell Mission included an outstanding group of experts dealing with agriculture. They were led by an Australian, Sir John Crawford, one of the great public servants of the world and a highly intelligent man of great experience and graciousness. The achievement of this group was to draw attention to the need, and to create a receptive climate in India, for measures of agricultural improvement which greatly facilitated the subsequent profound changes in agricultural technology, broadly characterized as the "Green Revolution." But these changes resulted primarily from scientific advances achieved elsewhere with new high-yielding grain varieties, and the adaptation of these to Indian conditions. The adaptation was a momentous achievement in Indian agriculture, and if it can be credited to any particular influence, the credit is due to three outstanding Indian officials. One was Subramaniam, who was Minister for Food and Agriculture and certainly one of the ablest ministers India has had. He was supported by an unusually outstanding Secretary of Agriculture, Sivaraman, and an equally able and imaginative scientist, Swaminathan, who was the director of India's agricultural research program.

Despite what I have said, I would not wish to give the impression that the Bank has had no part in the changing patterns of Indian agriculture. My focus so far has been on economic policy at the highest levels, affecting the economy as a whole or broad sectors thereof. It is at these levels that I question whether any important redirections of policy have been brought about through the influence or advice of the Bank or the Consortium that would not have been brought about anyway by the Government of India. Nevertheless, I do think we can claim some part in facilitating the agricultural changes that have taken place in India in recent years. And this brings me to some consideration of the Bank's role at less exalted policy levels. The lending programs of the Bank and IDA have reflected our own, as well as the Government of India's, sense of urgency about Indian food problems, and in agreement with the Government we have given special emphasis in our operations to the funding of various activities that formed part of the "Green Revolution." These have included loans and technical assistance for a variety of agricultural purposes including fertilizer plants, irrigation projects, high-yielding hybrid seed programs, and financing of agricultural credit.

The approach to such projects by the World Bank in India, as elsewhere, is never one of passive acceptance of project plans designed by the borrowing country. In financing projects we are always concerned to ensure insofar as possible that the technical, organizational, and financial plans for the project are such that it can be carried out with reasonable efficiency and that it will produce an economic return high enough to justify the cost. This approach can, of course, result in disagreements with the borrowing countries over particular project plans. Such disagreements may arise out of divergent views of technical specialists. Differences may also occur at times over project organization and management because of problems of administrative limitation or inertia or other reasons for resistance to change. Or they may reflect other differences in Bank and country interests which are often quite understandable but which may also run counter to the effort to achieve a return as favorable as possible in relation to cost. For example, the country may wish to purchase project equipment from local suppliers even though it may be more expensive than equipment obtained through imports. We have had disagreements of this kind, at the project level, with India, and such disagreements have sometimes led the Bank or the Government of India to drop projects that were under consideration. But there have also been changes in position, sometimes on the part of the Bank but also sometimes on the part of the Government of India, in order to resolve these disagreements. In this way it can be said that there are cases in which the Bank has influenced the technology or the financial or institutional nature of particular projects in ways that otherwise might not have happened. This has been the case not only with some of the agricultural projects, but also with some projects in other sectors.

In noting this kind of exercise of influence at the project level, I should also add that, in those project cases in which we have not been able to reach agreement, this has not affected the overall level of World Bank and IDA financing in India. India's needs are so large and project possibilities are so many that we have been able and willing to redirect our financing to other projects when such disagreements have obstructed a particular project. Hence, one cannot say that the weight of overall financial influence has been exercised on policies or performance even at the project level.

Nevertheless, when it seemed necessary, we have attempted at this level through persuasion and negotiation to improve projects in ways that we thought were technically, economically, and institutionally preferable. It is in this way and at the project level that it is fair to say that we have tried to exercise influence on the economic policies of India. We can also claim, in this respect, that such exercise of influence has been effective in the sense that we believe that particular projects have been improved. Finally, it seems that at this level and with no other objective than project improvement, the propriety of such exercise of influence is hardly in question on the part of an institution attempting to use international resources to the best advantage of developing countries.

Before closing, I should like to comment on one further aspect of India's development problems in which the Bank and the Consortium have been involved. India carries a very heavy external debt burden, in part because of the large amount of foreign borrowing that India has needed for its development programs. It is also because the terms of such borrowing have been wholly inappropriate to the development of the Indian economy. As a result of this heavy debt and the large annual debt-service requirements, many foreign lenders to India have been taking out in debt service almost as much as they have been putting in as new capital. Sometimes they have even taken out more. This happened with World Bank operations in 1963 and 1964 and again in 1969, although financing from IDA has much more than offset any adverse balance for India in net World Bank transactions. Rising debt service has eaten increasingly into the new aid for India and this, in combination with the declining levels of new aid in recent years, has meant that the net transfers of capital into India from external sources have steadily gone down. In the peak years of assistance during the mid-sixties, gross Consortium aid reached annually nearly $1500 million and net aid after debt service was over $1100 million a year in the years 1964 to 1967. This included food aid from the US, which was very large in that period of poor Indian harvests. In 1971 gross Consortium aid was down to about $1000 million, and debt service offset nearly half of that amount. Thus, in the five years between 1966 and 1971 the net transfers of Consortium aid will have dropped by more than 50 percent. In these declining net aid circumstances, the Bank undertook to organize a rescheduling of some of the Indian debt, and an agreement was reached within the Consortium to relieve India of $100 million a year of debt service during three years, 1968-70, and again in 1971. In addition the Bank as well as the Development Assistance Committee of the OECD have also pressed members of the Consortium to improve the terms of aid. This has been at least partly responsible for steady improvements in the terms of aid by important Consortium countries such as Japan and Germany. I note these aspects of the Indian debt problem in order to point out that Bank influence has been exercised not only on India in the ways indicated, but also on the Consortium members to increase their aid, to improve the terms, and to reduce the debt service.

The Consortium has been valuable and effective in helping India. Its achievements have been significant, though much more limited than is sometimes suggested. It has been a useful forum for providing India with the views of friendly countries on problems and policies, and in general it has been helpful to aid-donors in preparing and deciding on their aid programs for India in the context of this cooperative effort. I have not doubt at all that in the United Kingdom, perhaps in the United States, certainly in Germany, France, and the smaller Consortium countries, the ability of the administration to obtain support of legislators and the general public for development assistance to India has been facilitated by the fact that they can point to a concerted international effort to help economic development in India.

# Comment:  Leaning Against Open Doors?

L.K. Jha*

The remarks made so far have carefully skirted around the main issue of how the Bank tries to exert its influence on aid recipients. The discussion should take place at two levels. In the first place, the World Bank acts not merely as a lender but also as a coordinator of aid for many countries. Thus, it is necessary to make a distinction between the Bank acting in its capacity as a lender and the role it plays as the coordinator of aid in the Consortium countries. Second, it is useful to separate the World Bank's concern about overall economic performance from its concern in those specific sectors of the economy where its lending activities are concentrated.

Peter Cargill has dealt primarily with the World Bank's role in the Aid-India Consortium. The analysis he gives of the idealist conception and actual practice, and the limitations that face the World Bank, would be generally accepted. That the World Bank can play a positive and useful role cannot be denied, since it is through its efforts that members of the Consortium are able to take a coordinated view of India's problems and India's needs of external assistance.

The exercise of the Consortium, however, has been very much of a joint endeavor, in a sense, between the Bank and the Government of India. Both of us have really not tried to state our needs in the sense of what could be done if we had the resources, but only to project such minimum requirements that would enable at least limited progress to continue to be made within the framework of any realistic assumption of how much aid would be available. In fact, that is one of the inhibitions with which we start out planning. We take the view that aid is likely to be available, at best, of a certain order. We feel that to put forth a larger plan with more ambitious targets would only be an exercise in frustration, because the external resources will not be available. We know that they will not, and as a result there will be a series of disappointed people all over the country asserting that we set out to do too much with too little. It does not ameliorate matters to say that this occurred because we did not get aid; that is not a very convincing answer for any government to give to its own people. So the plans themselves get cramped and curtailed for that reason, and in actual fact, when it comes to making a prediction to the Consortium, every year a review has to be made of the climate in different donor countries. It would be difficult either for

*Former Ambassador for India to the United States, 1969 to 1973, and former Governor, Reserve Bank of India. Currently Governor of the Indian State of Jammu and Kashmir.

the Bank or for India to feel that the performance of the Indian economy has been a particularly relevant factor in determining the level of aid.[1]

When Mr. Cargill argues against the Bank having a "heady role" and urges "that the Bank could play its role more realistically if it were to concede the limitations of the role," one can agree with him fully. One would also endorse his observation that the best course on which to direct the economy is not very clear, and even if it were clear, it may not be practical to implement it easily in such a large, varied, and complex economy.

However, the sum total of the Bank's efforts to influence recipient performance in India is not to be found in the presentation the Bank makes to the Consortium and such recommendations as it embodies in its report. The Bank itself and its associate IDA are major providers of aid to India, aid of a quality that no bilateral aid quite matches[2] (see Table 3-2). The Bank's technicians, who are involved in individual negotiations of loans as well as assessments of the performance of the economy as a whole, have often gone far beyond the limits presented in Mr. Cargill's paper.

There is a well-established (and by now well-known) principle within the Bank that, with each loan, it should make an attempt to secure some reform in economic policies or institution building. Thus, the Bank seeks "rational" financial and pricing policies to ensure that reasonable rates of return are earned by the enterprises it finances. Similarly, concern is expressed about interest rate structure, simplification of administrative procedures, and so on. Stated in a general way, such advice appears reasonable and often in accord with the general direction of policy in India. But when it comes to details, it is not uncommon to find the Bank's technicians taking an unrealistic view about the pace of change. In addition, there is, perhaps, a general tendency to favor market mechanisms and disfavor administrative regulation. There are also occasions when the advice rendered by the Bank is not consistent with its own past judgments. On some occasions the enthusiasm of the Bank's experts carries them away to the extent of requiring a change in a sector totally unconnected with the one to which the loan is being given.

Let me turn to the specific point of the role of the World Bank in influencing performance in India. Obviously there are some very good examples of excellent influence, and Peter Cargill, on behalf of the Bank and IDA, has been careful enough to select them. In the agricultural case, I think the statement "leaning against open doors" was very true. In fact, if I could go a little into the history of the sixties, it should be emphasized that the basic principles of the new agricultural policy had been accepted and approved within the Government of India before the Crawford Report[a] came out, and the fact that two successive droughts occurred at that time meant that its effects were not felt for two years after the initial decisions. Second, a large part of the success of the agricultural

[a]World Bank Economic Mission to India, 1964, led by Bernard Bell. The agricultural section of the Mission's report was written by Sir John Crawford.

policy was due to the technical breakthrough that came about at a very opportune moment as a result of indigenous research on the new seeds. This could not have been anticipated no matter what the policies were within the Government. These facts are important balancing factors to bear in mind. Then again, I would accept Peter Cargill's point fully that many projects have benefited in their structure and in their orientation because of the advice of the Bank. But in this matter it is more technical advice and the use of technology that is the area of influence rather than economic policy or economic performance.

Development is not a purely economic phenomenon, and it cannot therefore pursue what Milton Friedman would regard as "the ideal targets." First, it entails the transformation of a society and includes such things as health and education. Above all, it is an effort to make the country self-reliant, aid being used as an instrument to end the need for aid. The moment you go beyond that you come to this thought: the targets of development are those that the country itself finds acceptable for filling its own aspirations. Any attempt that starts deflecting from that may indeed be causing a setback rather than a fulfillment. In other words, a distinction should, to my mind, be made between giving support (which can be very desirable and helpful as in the case of the Bank's assistance to Indian agriculture) to what are obviously sound policies the country wants to implement, and the policies it needs endorsement and advice to put through.

Second, many of the judgments even in the economic sphere must take into account noneconomic factors relevant to local conditions. Measures to ensure popular participation and support for the developmental effort play a vital but not visible role in achieving progress. When you are really trying to get at loggerheads with what the country is trying to or wants to do, there is one more point to keep in mind: if the World Bank's influence gets beyond a certain point, if it begins to look like pressure, even for something desirable in itself or something desired by the country itself, pressure by the Bank to achieve it can be a very deadly political weapon. The World Bank is a source of external finance to India, and it is very easy, when an unpopular measure is taken, for its critics to argue that the country has either been bribed or blackmailed into a policy measure. Unless there is a degree of political sensitivity, one may get a situation where the whole relationship between the World Bank and the recipient country can get awkward.[3]

I am strongly in favor of influence, and essentially it is a two-way influence. If asked what we have done to influence the World Bank, I would say quite a great deal: If one looks at the birth of the Consortium approach, financing projects in the public sector, and giving nonproject aid, all these have come to be the accepted thinking of the World Bank, even before this very symposium. It is as much a case of India converting the World Bank to these views as the World Bank influencing the policies towards agriculture in India. This two-way traffic, to my mind, is a very healthy thing indeed. The thing to guard against is the role of the World Bank as an agent for pressurizing rather than leaning at the infant open door.

Two points of detail need emphasizing. When the Bank is functioning as a lender, not as a reporter to the Consortium, and trying to bring about certain changes in the structure of a project being financed, it occasionally tends to ask for technical standards that may be extravagantly high for the poor country. If roads are to be constructed, there have been occasions when the Bank experts wanted a very high international standard of road quality because the project was being financed internationally. This is the kind of thing one has to guard against. If a country is setting up a factory that is going to compete in the world markets, it is desirable for it to be an efficient and competitive producer of its product. But the roads of India are not ready to compete with the roads of the United States or Germany. Therefore, it may well be advisable to accept lower standards rather than aim at unnecessarily high ones.

Second, the development of technical abilities is a very important part of the development process. Too often the World Bank insists on a foreign consultant, and this is a damper on the growth of technical self-reliance. The opportunity and the right to make mistakes is a very essential ingredient, to my mind, in the development process. While the Bank could and should be trying to make a better road, it should also have the flexibility to let an experiment be made. A problem arises when one attempts to let the tail wag the dog.

Not very long ago, for instance, the Bank was considering large-scale financing of tube wells in India. Of course, it wanted the tube well project to be viable, and if the tube well had to pay too high a price for power it would have been uneconomic. However, too low a power price would have made the power plants uneconomic. The World Bank's suggestion was that the power rates should be raised. It was trying to apply a corrective to the power policy of the state which, to my mind, was unnecessary internal interference. Their question was: How can you expect the power plant to be viable if you sell your power at such low rates? When you are financing a tube well project, you can easily say that the power was being supplied too cheaply. That, I think, is a case of the tail wagging the dog. The whole issue put the state government concerned in a very awkward situation; critics said that because they wanted money for the tube well project, they raised the price of power for everybody else. The state government depressurized the problem ultimately. But when the World Bank does act in that manner, it is tearing into very sensitive areas.

In conclusion, the World Bank should recognize that its judgments and opinions can be wrong and sometimes very contradictory. In 1960-61, a World Bank team was in India and I was talking to them about the Bank's operations. The leader of the team said to me: "Next year the states are having their local elections. The politicians want to see electric lights in the villages to get more votes. But that kind of investment has no relevance to development." This was the kind of response I received. Again, when the Bank was financing the Indian

Railways, they said, "Well, the competition from the roads is too intense. The railways are very important for development. All the road services have the right load factor, and you might see that the roadways do not get too active to undermine the viability of the railways." Sometime later, when the roadways become the object of an economic study of the Bank, the argument went that railway policy was such that the roadways could not develop. This kind of a thing can happen in sectoral dealings. The basic point is that there is every possibility and opportunity for good economic advice to be originating within the country and creating a climate of better policies. Whether the World Bank comes in then as a gentle supporter of a door about to open and gives it a push, or whether the Government says "No" because this is something coming from outside in the form of pressure or leverage, that is something which has an extremely significant and rather delicate balance.

# Comment: A Bilateral Viewpoint

Maurice J. Williams*

The crisis that arose in 1957-58 in India's foreign exchange position was of great concern to the United States, which for some years has sustained a major interest in the success of India's economic development program. Illustrative of this interest is the fact that the U.S. Government has provided almost $10 billion in economic assistance to India, over $8 billion after India's 1957-58 foreign-exchange crisis.[4]

The philosophy underlying the reorganization of the American economic assistance program in 1960-61 was ideal from the standpoint of helping with India's economic development problems. Indeed, many people believe that the US foreign-assistance reorganization of 1961 was primarily directed to the Indian development case. This is not surprising when you consider the size of India and the importance that the success of its development program has assumed for the World Bank and the India Consortium of Western contributing countries. The principal architects of the new American aid policy in 1961 were men who knew the Indian subcontinent and who were deeply committed to the importance of economic development. Chester Bowles had been Ambassador to India and in 1961 he was Under Secretary of State. David Bell, who had helped to set up the Planning Commission in Pakistan, was Director of the Budget Bureau. John O. Bell, who coordinated assistance programs for the State Department and knew the subcontinent well, also played an important part in the new aid policy.

The main emphasis of the 1961 reorganization was to provide major economic assistance to countries that had an overall plan for development and were prepared to take the hard policy decisions for its realization. Economic development criteria were to play a more important role than in the past in US decisions affecting aid allocations. In particular, the US would make multiyear commitments of assistance to countries that demonstrated that they could effectively use capital resources, both domestic and external.

India appeared to meet the new US assistance criteria exceedingly well. India had a well-articulated plan for development. Its leadership was dedicated to the development program as a major national objective and appeared prepared to carry out the program to the extent of the resources available. Equally important, India had an experienced senior civil service which could identify and

*Deputy Administrator, U.S. Agency for International Development, Washington, D.C.

promote appropriate changes in the development program to achieve the mutually desired results. There was no need to question India's economic judgment, which appeared to be as good or better than any foreigner's. These widely accepted considerations led the US to make a major commitment of economic assistance to India.

The US pledge to India Consortium was announced at $1 billion to cover a period of two years. Additionally, the US agreed with the Government of India that PL 480 agricultural commodities in support of India's development needs would be available for an enlarged—almost open-ended—four-year commitment. The expectations were that India would be able to make rapid progress in economic growth with the lessening of the major constraint of foreign-exchange shortage and with assured supply of food, the major constraint to an expanded investment program.

Despite the longer-term commitment and higher aid level, by 1964, there was widespread dissatisfaction with India's economic performance, as articulated at the time by IBRD President George Woods. Economic performance was sluggish. Major development problems were not being addressed, a conclusion highlighted by the thirteen-volume Bank Mission report of 1964. The suspicion was growing among development economists, both in India and other countries, that the high level of foreign assistance might become a disincentive to India's development effort. Some concluded that a measure of "performance bargaining," in relation to the continued high level of foreign assistance, was indicated.

Relating economic assistance levels to performance, as it was conceived in the aid doctrine of the early 1960s, involved important issues of timing, in relation to the balance between possible incentives and disincentives. What appeared to be the more obviously logical aid doctrine held that the time to reach understanding over the essential policy framework for accelerated development was before, not after, major multiyear commitments of economic assistance. But there was a school of thought that advocated high levels of foreign aid as an essential early step in order to change traditional attitudes, which in turn would lead to policy changes for accelerated economic growth at a later stage. Understandably, there was a great deal of imprecision in the doctrine of "performance bargaining" or relating foreign assistance to development performance. In the case of India, none of these issues was seriously discussed in the early 1960s, since it was assumed that India knew its requirements for development and could be expected to pursue them without outside prodding or inducements. When this assumption appeared wrong, as it did by 1964, it proved exceedingly difficult to discuss the need to improve India's economic policies with the Government of India.

Perhaps the most serious issue relating to performance was whether the high levels of aid already committed to India constituted a strong disincentive to India's own policy efforts. The theory adopted in the Indian case in the early 1960s had been that increased aid would release an increased effort and increased internal mobilization of resources by the developing country. If the increased level of aid had the opposite effect—that of delaying essential policy and structural changes—the whole rationale of a stepped up "big push" in foreign assistance would be called into question. It was in this broad context that questions concerning India's performance were considered by officials of the Indian Government and aid contributors.

There is some indication that major PL 480 food assistance from the United States delayed policy changes in India favoring its own agricultural development. This is not entirely surprising, since India's early development strategy was the development of an industrial base, with its corollary of transferring resources for investment in industry from an impoverished agricultural sector. In large part, American economic assistance made realization of this strategy possible, both directly by assistance to industry and indirectly by large food aid that permitted the delay of adjustments in favor of India's agriculture, which otherwise probably would have been made sooner. It is in this sense that American food aid was a disincentive to Indian agriculture and played a part in facilitating India's strategy of industrial development. The two successive years of drought, 1965-67, confirmed and strengthened the growing realization by the Government of India, and the Government of the United States, of the necessity for according higher priority to Indian agricultural development.

It has been argued that Indian policy emphasizing industry over agriculture was desirable because of the relatively lower returns on agriculture prior to the "Green Revolution," the tendency then to overemphasize expensive and low-yielding irrigation projects, and the availability of large low real cost US food resources which were not available for any other purpose. This is a complex question which cannot be answered categorically. But given the importance of agricultural progress to consumption and growth prospects, and the low returns on public-sector industrial investment, it appears unfortunate that the necessary policy reforms were postponed, and that the availability of PL 480 assistance apparently contributed to this postponement.

Agricultural policy reforms recommended by the Bank Mission of 1964-65 found an "open door" of acceptance by the Government of India. But other important recommendations have been accepted much more slowly. The need was clear for policy changes in the public industrial sector, effective changes in the pricing of imports of capital goods and raw materials, and better export incentives, but the pressures for reform in these areas have been less compelling.

It is not possible from the data available to establish empirically a correlation between levels of aid and India's performance, although it does appear that when net aid was higher (in the first half of the 1960s), industrial production was also higher. The Bank annual assessments of aid need and the difficulties in Indian performance have already been fully described. One conclusion from the experience is that no matter what happened to the Indian economy during the 1960s, the Bank's annual assessment of need always came out about the same.

Despite drought, the war of 1965, and annual changes in output, the Consortium year after year accepted essentially the same target for aid requirements. In practical terms, the World Bank and the Government of India tended to decide in advance what the contributors would be likely to make available. There was no sense in setting a target so high that it was going to discourage everybody, India as well as the contributing countries. I do not mean to imply that the targets were beyond the bounds of actual need. On the contrary, the Bank assessments consistently understated India's need for external help. This facet of assessing need and performance in relation to aid prospects is an essential part of the Bank's Consortium role. An unusual dilemma has arisen since the late 1960s in that India, driven by legitimate interests in reaching self-sufficiency and the political imperative to strive in that direction, has consistently proposed less foreign assistance than the Bank has concluded was needed.

Perhaps a major reason that no meaningful relationship could be established between aid level and India's development performance was that the aid doctrine of the early 1960s overemphasized purely economic performance. As we have already mentioned, India does not show up well on the purely economic performance scale. In growth of GNP, return on investment, marginal savings, exports, and other strictly economic indicators, India has been well down the performance scale over the past decade relative to other developing countries that also received major foreign assistance. Dissatisfaction with India's development performance was because expectations were unrealistically high and falsely based on an oversimplified view of the development process.

In retrospect we see that the earlier economic criteria for evaluating performance were too narrow. The Western tradition of economic analysis I learned as a student at the University of Chicago was carefully to exclude social and political factors from economic assessment. Our training was to assess economic policy in terms of factors governing efficiency and maximizing production, and to set aside the question of distribution and social welfare as not amenable to rigorous analysis.

Today we recognize the need for a broader basis for evaluation of development performance, a basis that takes into account political and social factors. We see more clearly that growth in production in overall terms has to be related to policies for distributive justice. We know that if we compartmentalize our consideration of growth economics, without regarding social and distributive problems, we cannot realistically appreciate the problems facing leaders who are charged with making policy in India and in other developing countries. Today we know that the traditional economic tools are too narrow and provide a false precision in measuring development performance.

Performance assessments by aid contributors have not given sufficient weight to the relation of growth to issues of income distribution. Income disparity in India is large and probably still widening. India's democratic system of government and political philosophy brings this problem to the political forefront. Consequently, the social and political problems arising from the growing disparity of incomes, as India achieved more rapid development, were important imperatives governing Indian development policy. In the historical perspective, the income disparity in India today is about what it was in the United States in 1890 and in the United Kingdom in about 1860, but the margin of resources relative to population pressures are much slimmer for India, and income distribution has become a more salient political question than it was in the United Kingdom and the United States in those periods. The World Bank and the Consortium countries were neither sensitive to nor able to assess these factors adequately in the early part of the 1960s, a failure that contributed to their disillusionment with India's performance.

On the social and political side, India's development performance has been better than that of many countries that rank better on economic indicators alone. India has maintained and strengthened its democratic political structure, a considerable accomplishment when one considers the performance of other aid recipients or when one considers India's problems of regional and linguistic diversity, traditional social structure, and continuing poverty in the face of rising expectations. India has maintained a concern for income distribution during the years when many Western economists were proposing policies based on a single-minded concentration on growth.

Today, with the increased emphasis on income distribution and employment in the development community, India's economic and political concerns in this area are better understood. In the last election, Indira Gandhi led her Congress (Reform) Party to an overwhelming victory on a platform that included as a major plank the aim of " *Garibi Hatao* "–"Poverty, eliminate it." Nevertheless, some of the policies India followed, particularly in the industry sector, may have been less efficient in accomplishing its income distribution and employment objectives than policies advocated by the Bank Mission and many Indians. John Lewis has written persuasively on this point, arguing for a growth-oriented "relevant radicalism."[5]

In a broader frame of reference, the aid contributors can be fairly optimistic about India's development performance. The process of economic assistance in terms of the transfer of technology is largely completed. Major industrial technologies have been transferred and basic industry established in manufactured steel, chemical processing, electronics manufacture, and fertilizer production and even in atomic power production and its ancillary aspects. Agricultural prospects are promising, both in terms of technology and supportive policies. Trained manpower is available in larger quantities than in any other less developed country, although quantitative expansion has been at some qualitative loss, on the average. A large part of the population does not match up to adequate standards of literacy or possess technical training, but there is a large pool of highly trained and talented scientists, economists, engineers, and administrators. Natural resources are fairly ample, the leadership is strong, and there is a measure of political stability. There is every reason to expect that India can take a strong lead in setting its own policy framework and developing a politically workable standard of judgment of its own development performance for the 1970s.

The question of the level of aid as a possible disincentive to performance remains a persistent one for India and aid-contributing countries. The US looks back to the apparent disincentive to Indian agriculture of its food assistance prior to the droughts of 1966 and 1967 and seeks to reassure itself that its aid programs do not implicitly provide other types of disincentives.

Related to the potential disincentive effect of high aid levels is the concern that the return on public-sector industrial investments in India has not been good. Yet industrial development has been India's major objective for the past years. In a real sense, if the large investments in industry do not yield a high rate of return, India will have greater difficulty in maintaining an adequately high rate of growth without sustained foreign aid, good intentions to the contrary. A major question today is whether a sustained high level of net foreign aid, in terms of supporting the industrial sector, would discourage India from undertaking the kinds of policy reforms for the industry sector as a whole and management reforms in the public sector that would increase exports, industrial production, employment, and exports. I do not believe we know the answer. A related problem for India in resource mobilization is that as more and more investment goes into agriculture, and as PL 480 food assistance is phased out, the easy mobilization of resources from the sale of American surplus agricultural commodities has disappeared. India's own agricultural production has compensated for imports, but the ability to tax the agricultural sector has not kept pace. These are two problem areas that India faces today. I hope that someone finds "open doors" for acceptance of relevant reforms and we fall through them!

In the first half of the 1960s, growth of the economy was sharply constrained by the low growth in agriculture. In the past several years things have changed to the extent that agriculture has been growing faster than industry. With the technological progress in agriculture, industry should be able to grow faster, not slower, than it had before. Raising the growth rate of industry and of other nonagricultural sectors is important in achieving India's employment and distributive justice objectives. With a 2.4 percent rate of population increase, a further 1 percent increase in GNP growth (which has recently been in the 4 to 5 percent range) would mean an increase of about half in the growth rate of per capita income. With the higher growth rate, the scope for any consideration of distributive justice becomes much wider and the welfare implications much better. This is an important point to remember as we continue in the future to struggle with relevant issues of development performance using the imprecise tools of our knowledge.

## Notes

1. See, for example, K.N. Raj, *Indian Economic Growth: Performance and Prospects*, New Delhi: George Allen and Unwin and Allied Publishers, 1965.

2. See International Bank for Reconstruction and Development, "Activities of the World Bank Group in India," Washington, D.C., December 1970 (mimeo).

3. See, for example, the dispatch by J. Anthony Lukas in *The New York Times*, June 6, 1966, implying pressure was exerted by the World Bank and the IMF for India to devalue the rupee.

4. Actually US$ 9.2 billion between 1946 and 1972, of which loans are $ 6.7 billion, grants are $ 2 billion, and other items are $ 0.5 billion.

5. John P. Lewis, "Wanted in India: A Relevant Radicalism," Policy Memorandum No. 36, Center for International Studies, Princeton University, December 1969.

# 6

# The External Debt Problem

John H. Adler*

That the World Bank has taken an interest in the problem of world indebtedness is another indication that the Bank indeed has gone a long way from being just a development *financing* institution to a development institution, concerned not only with financial aspects, but involved in the full range of relations between the developed and the developing countries.

The Bank has a direct financial interest in the problem of indebtedness of the developing countries because a large proportion of the debt of the developing countries is owed to the Bank; the World Bank is the second largest creditor of the public and publicly guaranteed debts of the developing countries; only the debt owed to the United States Government and its agencies (such as the Export-Import Bank) is larger. But even when its share in the debt of the developing countries was smaller, the Bank concerned itself with the indebtedness of its member countries; its loan agreements provide that governments that obtain or guarantee loans given by the Bank must regularly submit information about their external public debt. The Bank is now working with OECD on an expanded external-debt reporting system that will combine the debt information provided by the debtor countries with the information on lending and the resulting indebtedness which the donors provide to the OECD. This is an example of useful cooperation, with its full contingent of technical problems and headaches, and therefore inevitable delays.

The external public debt of the developing countries has increased tremendously over the last ten or fifteen years. The annual rate of increase from 1956 to 1969 was 14 percent. This means it has doubled every five years. The amount of debt outstanding at the beginning of 1970 was approximately $59 billion, including an undisbursed amount of $13 billion; $46 billion is outstanding and disbursed. Service payments also have grown rapidly, though at a somewhat slower pace than debt, at 9 percent per annum in the 1960s, compared with 14 percent in the late fifties.[1]

As a result of the rapid growth of debt and the much slower growth of exports (goods and services) the debt-service ratios, the ratio of debt to exports, have grown considerably, but for most countries they still do not exceed 15

*Director, Programming and Budgeting Department, International Bank for Reconstruction and Development, Washington, D.C.

percent. But on looking closer one finds that there is a large number of important countries with debt-service ratios of the order of 16 to 18 percent and several are in the range of 20 to 25 percent. These figures pertain to public debt and public-guaranteed debt of a maturity of more than one year; they do not include the very substantial "float" of short-term commercial debt, mostly to exporters and commercial banks, with repayment periods of two to four months. Also excluded is all purely private debt of longer maturity. It is very difficult to tell how large this debt is, but by and large it is not considered likely to be substantial, because a large portion of the debt which is private on the creditor's side is guaranteed by the government of the recipient country and

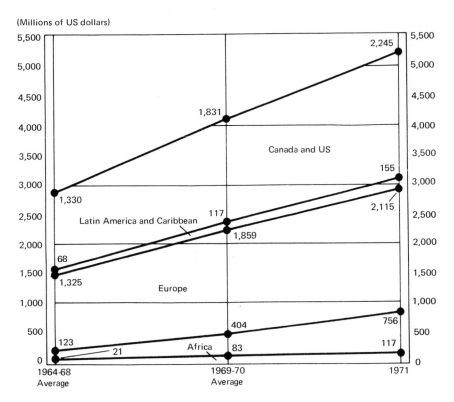

*Holdings of Bank bonds by international organizations, not shown in the chart, totaled approximately $37 million at June 30, 1971.*

**Figure 6-1.** World Bank: Outstanding Debt. Estimated Geographical Distribution, Averages 1964-68, 1969-70 and 1971*. *Source:* IBRD *Annual Report 1970-71*, World Bank, Washington, D.C.

therefore included. But even leaving aside private, nonguaranteed debts, in the case of quite a number of countries, debt-service payments constitute a major claim against export earnings and thereby endanger the debtor country's ability to use foreign-exchange earnings for development purposes. The heavy debt service also makes creditors uneasy and therefore may prevent creditors from providing credit as generously as if there were not already a first mortgage on export earnings in the form of service payments obligations on the existing debt.

The concern with the level of external debt and the amount of debt-service payments is of course not confined to the IBRD, but widespread among people concerned, intellectually or professionally, with the progress of the developing countries. In order to put this concern into proper perspective, it must be realized that the inflow of loans from abroad has always been considered an essential part of development strategy because it provides additions to the investable resources available in the developing country. In some of the earlier development theories or strategies, it was emphasized that not only was borrowing from abroad a great help to development, but it was also claimed that this was the only way in which poor countries could overcome stagnation or slow growth. The theory and strategy of the Big Push put great emphasis upon attaining the momentum and the resource base for a more satisfactory rate of development.[2]

It must be realized, however, that any theory or strategy of development that relies on new inflows of additional resources from abroad must somehow relate the benefits of the addition of resources to the cost of servicing the debt. Although all aspects of the inflow of resources, their utilization, and the outflow of resources arising out of the resulting debt service are interrelated, for purposes of exposition it is useful to distinguish three criteria that must be fulfilled if foreign debt is to make a lasting contribution to development: efficiency, transformation, and liquidity.

The efficiency criterion simply asserts that the cost of borrowing from abroad must not be larger than the increase in output resulting from the inflow of resources. It is a virtually self-evident proposition: the additional output, the "yield" of the investment financed through borrowing abroad, must be at least equal to the cost, in other words, the rate of interest. In practical application it is somewhat more difficult to determine whether the criterion is being met, because what matters—for each piece of investment financed by borrowing from abroad—is the social yield to which the simple financial return has to be adjusted in order to take account of those increases in the net national product not included in the return to the value of the foreign-financed investment. The adjustment includes such things as the difference between market wages and the opportunity cost of labor, and the benefits to the economy that cannot be "internalized" because they accrue as external economies to some other productive unit or some consumer elsewhere in the economy, and thus are not included in the return to capital. For the economy as a whole the application of the concept is simple: borrowing from abroad pays as long as the rate of interest on all foreign loans does not exceed the rate of growth of the net national product. At the margin, borrowing from abroad pays as long as the social yield of the additional investment exceeds the interest rate on the additional foreign-financed investment.

Second, the transformation criterion is met if the addition to the net national product resulting from borrowing abroad produces or sets free enough foreign-exchange earnings to pay the foreign debt. The difference between the efficiency and transformation criteria arises because of the difference between internal and external demand, or more generally, equilibrium conditions. The difference reflects, of course, some sort of "imperfection," or "friction," or discontinuity that can be readily assumed away in the theoretical models. Alternatively, the net internal product estimates and the estimates of the growth of the net national product can be adjusted *à la* Little and Mirrlees,[3] to reflect world prices, and the adjustment makes everything "correct." But in the real world, the difference between producing more and selling more abroad is real, just as there is a difference, which Chenery has brought out, between a resources gap and a balance of payments gap.[4] In practice, the transformation criterion simply says: It is not enough to get a return, however large, on foreign-financed investment; at least part of the return must be transferred abroad. In other words, part of the increased output associated with the foreign-financed investment must generate additional exports or replace imports large enough to service the foreign debt; or somewhere else in the economy additional foreign exchange must be generated or set aside to service the debt.

The liquidity criterion can be stated simply: Debt-service obligations, that is, interest and amortization, must not at any point exceed the increase in output associated with the foreign-financed investment. The significance of the liquidity criterion may best be explained by an example.

Suppose a foreign loan has been obtained for a power-generating plant, at an annual rate of interest of 7 percent and the rate of return, or the net earnings of the power company, amount to 12 percent, so the efficiency criterion is met. Moreover, because of the great contribution that the power plant makes to the efficiency of the economy as a whole, foreign-exchange earnings increase by an amount equivalent to 12 percent of the foreign-financed cost of the plant. A debt-service liquidity problem arises if, in addition to the 7 percent interest, amortization of, say, 10 percent of the loan has to be met, so at that point of time debt payments amount to some 15 percent, while transferable earnings are only 12 percent.

For the economy as a whole, the liquidity criterion implies that even if foreign borrowings, together with domestic resources, are invested so as to bring about a high rate of growth (and thus the efficiency criterion is met) and if foreign-exchange earnings grow at a satisfactory rate (so that transformation criterion is met), a debtor country still may run into debt-service difficulties if it has obtained loans or credits with short maturities—frequently the case with suppliers' credits or with credits from commercial banks—or it is faced with a "bulge" in its debt-service schedule. Whether or not this kind of debt-service difficulty can be overcome depends, of course, on the country's ability and willingness to compress the demand for imports—and thereby investment and consumption—sufficiently, and on its ability to obtain additional resources from abroad to tide it over the temporary liquidity crisis, and the willingness of its creditors, or aid-givers, to provide such resources.

The preceding reference to a debtor country's ability to compress its imports in order to meet its debt-service obligations illustrates one major, and at times apparently overwhelming, difficulty of distinguishing the problem of indebtedness from the broad and intricate problems of the economics and politics of development. Whether or not a country is able and willing to meet the service on its external debt by foregoing the use of foreign-exchange resources for some other purpose, such as the financing of development expenditures or of consumption or of armaments, depends on a whole range of considerations not amenable to economic analysis or susceptible to meaningful quantification. It is impossible to determine and decide in general terms under what circumstances a country will be able to pay its debts and under what conditions it will not. And it is ludicrous to attempt to develop general rules under which a country should be made to pay its debts or be given debt relief.

The same observation applies to the two other criteria of efficiency and transformation. Efficiency in the use of external resources is obviously only a minor aspect of a country's efficiency in the use of all its resources. The efficient mobilization and use of resources is the basic subject matter of development theory and development policy or strategy. Similarly, the transformation criterion is only a special application to debt-service obligations of the much broader concern with a country's balance of payments and balance of payments prospects, which in turn are of course only one specific, though crucial, aspect of the still broader problem of resource allocation. Thus, there is no way of dealing with the problem of external indebtedness, except in the general framework of an evaluation of a country's economic policies, its balance of payments prospects, its adaptability to changing internal and external conditions—in other words, through an analysis of its economic performance.[5]

In the last few years the Bank has become more and more concerned about the increase in the external debt of the developing countries in general and some of its major borrowers in particular. It could not help being aware of the debt problem and the danger of defaults. Several countries in all parts of the world, including Argentina, Brazil, Chile, and Peru in Latin America, and India, Indonesia, Ghana, and Turkey elsewhere, had found it necessary to enter into multilateral negotiations with their bilateral creditors to ask for a postponement of part of their debt-service payments; in some cases, debt service was renegotiated several times.[6] Although the Bank was never asked to participate in accepting deferments and was granted *de facto* a preferred creditor position (and it volunteered a postponement of debt payments only once), the growing share of debt owed to the Bank in the total external debt of a number of countries made it necessary, in its assessment of the creditworthiness of its borrowers, to pay special attention to the terms and conditions at which debtor countries contract external debt and, more broadly, how effective they are in the management of this external debt. Moreover, for some time the Bank, together with several other organizations such as the Development Assistance Committee (DAC) of OECD, has been concerned about the worsening terms at which the developing countries were obtaining capital assistance from official sources and loans and credits from private lenders. The share of grant aid in official development assistance was declining, the interest rate on private capital inflows was rising, and the composition of total flows to developing countries was deteriorating because of a decline in the proportion of official development assistance.

The advent of debt renegotiations by a number of countries and, at the same time, a hardening of the terms of capital flows to developing countries in turn led to recommendations for wholesale debt renegotiations on the one hand, and to predictions of widespread defaults and, as a consequence, of a cessation of capital flows, on the other. The equip that the Second Development Decade would turn out to be a Decade of Defaults was widely repeated. It was in this atmosphere of predictions of doom that Robert McNamara announced at the IMF-IBRD Annual Meeting in Copenhagen, in September 1970, that the Bank would undertake a study of the debt problem and report to the member countries at the next meeting.[7]

In line with the earlier comment about the need to evaluate a country's indebtedness and its ability to service its debt within the broad framework of a general evaluation of its development effort, its performance and its prospects, the Bank staff undertook an analysis of some thirty major countries. These countries account for close to 80 percent of the population of developing countries and some 60 percent of all capital flows from rich to poor countries; the difference in coverage is due to the large private flows to those oil countries not included in our sample, and the omission of a large number of small countries, especially in Africa, which receive a disproportionately large share of bilateral aid. On the basis of all available data, supplemented by estimates that were sometimes daring but I believe never unreasonable, projections were made of domestic savings, gross investment, capital inflows including direct investments, exports and imports of goods and services, debt-service payments, and dividend transfers on direct investments. For the next five to ten years the projections distinguished between capital receipts, including aid disbursements, from various sources and on various terms; the balance of payments projections took account of the prospects of the country's major export commodities, its dependence on "essential" imports (of foodstuffs, fuels, investment goods), and so on. The domestic parameters were derived wherever possible from development plans, frequently adjusted to reflect the Bank staff's view of their feasibility and realism. For the more distant years, the projection became inevitably more aggregative and schematic.

But irrespective of the degree of refinement or crudeness, the projections have to meet the tests of internal consistency and plausibility: the flow of resources into investment had to be consistent with the level of savings and net transfers from abroad, and the latter had to be a reasonable assessment of prospects for the future with regard to the volume of capital inflows and their terms. As the term "reasonable" in the preceding sentence suggests, the preparation of the projections involved the exercise of judgment, individual and collective, of economic forces and, beyond them, of political factors, both internal—with regard to the feasibility of policy alternatives—and external—regarding export prospects and the size and direction of the flow of aid and of private capital.

The outcome of the exercise has been a better understanding of the debt problem; the recognition that the causes and the cures of the debt problem must be sought in the wider context of economic policies, and not on the basis of specific mechanical rules of contuct; and the overall conclusions that the high level of external debt and its heavy concentration in a number of countries does not necessarily lead to a global crisis of indebtedness, as some observers had indicated, and that therefore there was no need for new institutional or organizational arrangements to take charge of debt renegotiations and debt reschedulings. The study also concluded that given a reasonable degree of understanding and cooperation between debtor and creditor countries, there was no reason why the flow of public and private capital, including loans from the World Bank and the regional banks, should not be continued and in the case of many countries expanded.

As to the causes of past debt crises (which it was believed could provide some clues for the future), the IBRD study did not break new ground but relied heavily on a series of studies of the events leading to multilateral debt renegotiations in the 1950s and 1960s undertaken by the International Monetary Fund. On the basis of these studies and the evaluation and judgment of the Bank's own staff, it appears that three constellations of causal factors may be distinguished.

In the Latin American countries that had gone through multilateral debt renegotiations (Argentina, Brazil, Chile, and Peru) and in Turkey, the common characteristics of developments leading up to debt renegotiations were: budget deficits financed by domestic credit expansion and through the accumulation of short-term external debt; inflation and reluctance to adjust the exchange rate in spite of growing disparities between internal and external prices; and a decline in export earnings, either as a consequence of faulty exchange policies or as a result of declining export prices.

The same factors were at work in Ghana and Indonesia, but they were compounded by the misdirection of investment, in part brought about by corruption, and by inefficiency in the operations of new industrial plants. Although this deterioration of the economic situation was obvious, short-term supplier credits backed by export credit guarantees and insurance facilities continued to pour in.

The debt problem in India did not manifest itself in the form of a sudden crisis. The pressures of balance of payments difficulties built up gradually over a number of years, when exports expanded much more slowly than planned. The situation was compounded by two successive harvest failures at a time when the inflow of capital on concessionary terms was reduced. Debt relief thus became, and was recognized as, an alternative to new aid.

On the basis of the study of the causes of debt-service difficulties in recent years, of the analysis of the role of capital inflows in the development process, and, above all, of a rather painstaking evaluation of the growth prospects, the likelihood of capital inflows at various times, and of the competence and effectiveness of economic management that may be reasonably expected, the Bank's debt study distinguished between three groups or categories of countries, with regard to their external debt.

The first category includes the great majority of all developing countries. With regard to the countries included in this group it appears safe to say that the danger of debt service difficulties is remote, either because their external debt is small in relation to their national income, their export earnings, their public revenues, or whatever other standard of reference one might choose; or, in countries with large amounts of debt, government has shown ability and efficiency in the handling of its external debt and is likely to react promptly and effectively to developments that may threaten its creditworthiness.

This group includes a large number of small countries in Africa which have obtained the bulk of foreign aid (mostly from France) in the form of grants, and therefore have foreign debts in negligible amounts only. Their growth and their ability to avoid debt problems depends however on the continued inflow of resources from abroad on highly concessionary terms. Their balance of payments prospects and their ability to adjust to adverse external or internal developments are limited, and the extent of their creditworthiness for loans on commercial terms is narrowly circumscribed.

Examples of countries with sizable external debt but considered safe from the point of view of creditworthiness are Malaysia, Singapore, Mexico, a number of smaller Latin American countries, and, on somewhat different grounds, Israel. Malaysia's economy has grown at a steady rate of about 6 percent a year, despite the price pressures on its most important export commodity, rubber. Its continued creditworthiness is the result of limited reliance in the past on short- and medium-term credits and its cautious (according to some observers, too conservative) management of economic affairs. In the case of Singapore, substantial capital inflows have supplemented a high rate of capital formation and paid off handsomely in the form of high rates of GNP and export growth. Mexico has relied on external borrowings over a long period to great advantage; the growth and modernization of the economy have progressed at a satisfactory rate, although major problems, mostly of income distribution and regional balance, remain. In the late sixties, Mexico's debt-service ratio was of the order of 20 to 25 percent, uncomfortably high in comparison with most other countries. Nevertheless, foreign creditors, favorably impressed by the management of the Mexican economy and the Mexican authorities' awareness of the country's economic problems, have maintained their confidence in the country. This, together with its success in placing public bond issues abroad, should go a long way toward assuring Mexico's continued ability to meet its debt-service obligations, notwithstanding the large amounts involved. Also included in this group of countries with unimpaired creditworthiness is Israel, which has a debt-service ratio even higher than that of Mexico but can rely on access to private loans on highly favorable terms motivated by noneconomic considerations.[8]

The second group of countries includes those that may find themselves in a liquidity crisis because of developments beyond their control or because of their inability to cope with problems besetting their economy. Although these countries have fundamentally sound growth prospects, they are vulnerable to sudden and unexpected shortfalls in foreign-exchange earnings or sudden increases in imports, caused by such things as crop failures or inflationary pressures. This group, which together accounts for perhaps as much as one-third of the external debt of developing countries, includes several Latin-American countries, such as Argentina and Chile (which are already engaged in seeking balance of payments relief through new borrowings and rescheduling of debt-service payments), Turkey, Tunisia, and the Philippines. This is not to say that these countries and others that find themselves in similar conditions are likely to get into debt-servicing difficulties; presumably most of them will not. It only means they must pay particular attention to their external debt in framing their development programs, and debt management must be a key element in the formulation of their economic policies.

The characteristic these countries have in common is that a large part of their debt is concentrated in short maturities and that debt-service payments are high in relation to their foreign-exchange earnings. Because of the latter, they are likely to find it difficult to adjust quickly to shortfalls of foreign-exchange resources and to obtain increases in net capital inflows to tide them over such periods of shortfalls. Under these conditions they may find it desirable to obtain a temporary respite in their debt-service payments until measures to relieve balance of payments pressures become effective. In some cases this can be accomplished through bilateral negotiations to reschedule debt-service payments. In cases involving concerted action by most or all external creditors, arrangements for a temporary deferment of part of the debt service are usually combined with agreements to provide additional medium- and long-term loans and, in many instances, short-term accommodation through access to the resources of the International Monetary Fund or through credits from commercial banks.

The Bank study came to the conclusion that with a proper understanding of the temporary nature of the problem for both the creditors and debtors there was no need to use aid on concessionary terms, the scarcest of all capital resources, in connection with this kind of debt relief operation. But to assure the success of these arrangements it was essential to reach an understanding regarding the assumption of additional debt in the future. Remedial action regarding the existing debt should not be regarded just as a means of making room for additional borrowings and additional service obligations, which in due course would lead to another debt crisis. Thus, the acceptance of a reasonable degree of discipline by debtor countries and potential sources of credits, with regard to the amounts and terms of further lending, becomes a prerequisite for avoiding the occurrence of a debt crisis. The exercise of restraint on borrowing and lending must be recognized as a means of maintaining, or resuming, the economic growth of the debtor country at a socially and politically tolerable and sustainable rate. Debt settlements depriving the debtor country of the resources essential for continued growth are just as detrimental to the interest of creditors as the temporary forcing of growth or the raising of consumption by means of capital inflows at a level that cannot be sustained; in either case, the interests of debtors and creditors are harmed.

The need to maintain the long-run pace of development at a tolerable rate becomes an even more important consideration with regard to the third group of countries. This group at present includes only six countries—Bangladesh, Ceylon, Ghana, India, Indonesia, and Pakistan—which taken together account for about one-fifth of the debt of the developing countries, but it is possible that some other countries (for example, Afghanistan and Egypt) will be added to this list. These countries have experienced debt-service difficulties and can be considered creditworthy for only marginal additions to their external debt on commercial terms. Several of the countries have already received debt relief as a result of multilateral renegotiations; some of them have indicated the need for a further reduction of their debt-service burden or an extension of existing relief arrangements. Others have suspended the transfer of debt-service payments until negotiations can take place. Although the debt-service difficulties of these countries have arisen for a variety of different reasons, they have one characteristic in common: a lasting solution appears impossible unless debt relief is granted on highly concessionary terms and extended over a prolonged period, and unless the reduction of debt-service payments is combined with an undertaking to provide additional external resources, again on concessionary terms. This assertion is based on an analysis of the prospects of the countries regarding their ability to mobilize domestic resources and to expand exports. It also reflects a judgment regarding the likely size of gross capital inflows on concessionary terms and the constraints that lenders are likely to impose on the use of resources they are willing to provide. It recognizes by implication that the flexibility of the countries' economic policies is limited by the flow per capita income, which rules out policies aiming at a reduction of the level of consumption of a large proportion of the population even temporarily; and that for that reason it is likely to take a prolonged period until their dependence on aid on concessionary terms will come to an end.

Whether or not a lasting solution of the debt problems of these countries (and of others in a similar position or likely to get into a similar position) can be found depends to a considerable extent on the flow of concessionary aid over the next few years. A combination of the countries' own efforts, a sustained flow of aid on concessionary terms (supplemented by a gross flow of capital on conventional terms large enough to offset amortization payments due on debt contracted on conventional terms), and a limitation of the burden of debt service should make it possible to achieve a satisfactory rate of economic advancement and in due course enhance their creditworthiness. But over the next five or ten years help through more aid and relief through debt rescheduling are essential.[9]

The most important conclusion, which has major policy implications, is that the present level of indebtedness of the developing countries is not likely to result in widespread defaults and does not require wholesale debt renegotiations. Except for a small group of countries that find themselves already in debt-servicing difficulties, the developing countries should be able to service their external debt and to assume additional obligations, although in the case of some countries the possibility of intermittent debt-service problems, which may require deferment or refinancing of some payments, must be faced.

This generally optimistic conclusion implies that debtor and creditor countries will cooperate in devising and monitoring policies designed to avoid breakdowns of debtor-creditor relations. On the side of debtor countries that means vigorous efforts to avoid excessive reliance on external resources to finance development expenditures. It also implies that creditor countries will be willing to provide loans and credits in amounts and at terms appropriate to the growth and balance of payments prospects of the various borrowing countries.

If it is generally understood that the most effective way of dealing with debt problems is to avoid them, the need for special institutional arrangements for renegotiating and refinancing external debts does not arise. It is, however, clearly in the interest of creditors and debtors alike to support the IBRD and IMF in their efforts to monitor the performance, and especially the debt management, of the debtor countries. Since avoidable debt-service difficulties generally arise because of the use of external resources for undesirable purposes, such as projects with low returns, armaments, ostentation or conspicuous public consumption, or because debts are contracted at terms incompatible with the debtor country's balance of payments prospects, it is essential for creditor countries to help the debtor countries to be selective in the acceptance of offers of credits and loans.

The IBRD and IMF can play an important role in strengthening the debtor-creditor relations between the developing countries and their sources of external finance. First, in cooperation with each other, and with other organizations such as CIAP and the regional banks, they can monitor the debt management of the borrowing countries and advise them with respect to measures for controlling the volume and the terms of capital inflows. Second, through their periodic reports and with the help of such institutional arrangements as consultative groups and consortia, they can advise the creditor countries on the need for external resources and on the appropriateness of terms of lending. And finally, if the need for debt renegotiations does arise, they can provide support from their own financial resources for the countries whose debts require rescheduling and refinancing.

# Comment: Debt Adjustment: The Tyranny of Bankers, Brokers, and Bondholders

Charles R. Frank, Jr.*

John Adler has supplied us with an excellent assessment of the external debt position of the less developed countries. His analysis leads him to be optimistic. Widespread default and debt renegotiations are not regarded as very likely. He views the main role of the IBRD as a monitor of the debt situation of the less developed countries and as an advisor in helping these countries devise policies that will enable them to avoid serious debt-servicing difficulties. He does not deal with two important issues. First, is the rapid increase in World Bank lending on commercial terms, relative to bilateral government lending on soft terms, a possible contributory factor to present and future debt-servicing problems? Second, what should be the role of the World Bank in specific debt-rescheduling exercises when they occur? Since the latter question is more specific and involves less complex issues, we will examine it first.

The role of the Bank in debt rescheduling has been very limited. On no occasion has it rescheduled its own loans, although it has provided staff and support to a number of rescheduling operations. The Bank can and does make fresh loans in a rescheduling situation. However, these loans usually are made on a project basis and are therefore subject to disbursement delays. In addition, fresh loans extended by the Bank do not involve free foreign exchange. Thus, they are not as useful in solving a country's balance of payments problem as would be a simple debt rollover. I do not think one can criticize the Bank for its cautious attitude. In fact, caution is wholly appropriate and crucial to the Bank's continued success as a unique and useful financial intermediary that has been an important source of relatively low-cost capital to the less developed world.

Most less developed countries have limited access to international capital markets. Given the insubstantial flow of funds on concessionary terms to the LDCs, as an alternative to the World Bank as a source of capital, they would either have to settle for a much lower level of borrowing from abroad or would find themselves increasingly dependent on short- and medium-term, high-cost suppliers credits and commercial bank loans. The World Bank provides these countries with substantial indirect access to international bond markets on a relatively low-cost basis. The Bank provides this access because of its prestige, its ability as a very large intermediary to pool risks, and its excellent financial performance.

*Professor of Economics and International Affairs, Princeton University.

123

**Table 6-1**

**External Public Debt Outstanding of Selected Developing Countries by Country and Type of Creditor, December 31, 1970 (Millions of U.S. Dollars)**

| Area Country | Including undisbursed | | | | | | | Service Payments on External Public Debt as Percentage of Exports of Goods and Services, 1965-1970 | | | | | |
|---|---|---|---|---|---|---|---|---|---|---|---|---|---|
| | Disbursed Only | Total | Bilateral Official | Multi-lateral | Suppliers | Private Private Banks | Other | 1965 | 1966 | 1967 | 1968 | 1969 | 1970 |
| **AFRICA** | | | | | | | | | | | | | |
| Botswana[a] | 12.4 | 13.3 | 5.7 | 6.1 | 0.6 | — | 1.0 | 3.5 | 3.3 | 5.4 | 6.7 | 3.3 | 2.7 |
| Burundi | 7.3 | 9.5 | 1.4 | 6.7 | 1.3 | — | 0.2 | 2.3 | 2.2 | 2.5 | 3.0 | 3.6 | 1.9 |
| Cameroon | 114.7 | 218.3 | 126.5 | 85.6 | 5.7 | — | 0.5 | 3.2 | 4.0 | 4.0 | 3.5 | 3.3 | 3.8 |
| Central African Republic | — | — | | | | | | | | | | | |
| Chad | 20.4 | 29.4 | 18.9 | 8.7 | 1.8 | — | — | n.a. | n.a. | n.a. | 4.2 | 5.5 | 5.9 |
| Congo, Democratic Republic | 40.9 | 50.7 | 34.3 | 7.1 | 8.0 | — | 1.4 | n.a. | n.a. | 2.9 | 11.5 | 9.9 | 6.6 |
| Dahomey | 39.5 | 54.8 | 36.6 | 8.1 | 9.0 | 1.0 | 0.2 | 1.4 | 1.8 | 1.9 | 2.9 | 3.1 | — |
| Ethiopa | 169.0 | 270.2 | 112.8 | 113.7 | 9.5 | 34.2 | — | 4.9 | 6.3 | 5.2 | 7.0 | 3.8 | 4.8 |
| Gabon | 95.3 | 115.4 | 40.4 | 39.2 | 27.9 | — | 7.8 | 4.9 | 7.6 | 9.5 | 9.2 | 10.6 | 11.3 |
| Ghana | 498.8 | 571.5 | 277.6 | 73.5 | 220.4 | — | — | 5.0 | 5.4 | 5.8 | 8.0 | 8.2 | 6.2 |
| Guinea | 283.6 | 378.4 | 246.5 | 64.5 | 51.3 | 16.1 | — | 18.8 | 6.5 | 7.2 | 12.3 | 9.9 | 4.9 |
| Ivory Coast | (1) | (1) | (1) | (1) | (1) | (1) | (1) | n.a. | n.a. | n.a. | 8.9 | n.a. | n.a. |
| Kenya | 282.3 | 393.8 | 237.9 | 102.0 | 7.7 | 4.1 | 42.0 | 4.2 | 4.7 | 7.0 | 5.8 | 4.9 | 6.2 |
| Lesotho[a] | 7.1 | 7.5 | 2.7 | 4.1 | — | 0.7 | — | 5.5 | 5.7 | 6.8 | 6.9 | 5.8 | 5.3 |
| Liberia | 157.5 | 176.8 | 123.5 | 16.5 | 28.0 | 8.8 | — | 1.4 | 2.4 | 1.2 | n.a. | n.a. | 2.8 |
| Malagasy Republic | 95.4 | 137.7 | 80.9 | 42.1 | 4.3 | 6.2 | 4.3 | 8.6 | 6.0 | 6.0 | 6.8 | 6.4 | 7.5 |
| Malawi | 121.1 | 155.8 | 103.3 | 32.8 | 2.5 | 0.9 | 16.4 | n.a. | 3.8 | 8.7 | 6.1 | 5.8 | 4.8 |
| Mali | 236.2 | 287.7 | 265.2 | 17.3 | 4.5 | 0.7 | — | 5.5 | 5.6 | 5.7 | 6.3 | 3.3 | 7.4 |
| Mauritius | 27.9 | 43.0 | 30.8 | 5.6 | — | 1.9 | 4.6 | 11.8 | 11.8 | 16.1 | 14.5 | 23.2 | 2.9 |
| Morocco | 636.4 | 854.7 | 589.7 | 159.3 | 53.5 | 20.2 | 32.1 | 2.3 | 3.2 | 3.5 | 6.6 | 3.1 | 3.5 |
| Nigeria | 463.6 | 683.4 | 321.1 | 266.0 | 63.6 | 18.1 | 14.6 | 4.7 | 6.8 | 6.6 | 7.2 | 8.5 | 7.6 |
| Rhodesia | — | — | — | — | — | — | — | 3.3 | 5.4 | 5.1 | 6.2 | 6.2 | 4.1 |
| Rwanda | 1.9 | 11.6 | 1.9 | 9.3 | 0.4 | — | — | 4.4 | 1.9 | 6.8 | 3.7 | 2.7 | 1.2 |

| | | | | | | | | | | | | | |
|---|---|---|---|---|---|---|---|---|---|---|---|---|---|
| Senegal | 84.1 | 114.4 | 82.4 | 26.8 | — | — | 5.2 | 1.9 | 2.1 | 2.3 | 2.3 | 3.4 | 3.6 |
| Sierra Leone | 66.0 | 84.5 | 33.9 | 17.3 | 26.1 | 0.7 | 6.5 | 6.1 | 7.6 | 8.7 | 6.1 | 7.0 | 8.9 |
| Somalia | 74.0 | 105.2 | 96.2 | 9.1 | — | — | — | 1.4 | 2.1 | 2.1 | 1.9 | 1.4 | 1.9 |
| Sudan | 285.5 | 339.0 | 167.3 | 126.1 | 7.7 | 36.4 | 1.6 | 5.7 | 6.5 | 5.4 | 7.1 | 9.3 | 8.7 |
| Swaziland | 27.9 | 27.9 | 8.6 | 8.9 | 8.6 | 1.8 | — | 3.9 | 3.4 | 3.4 | 3.3 | 2.7 | 3.1 |
| Tanzania | 220.7 | 575.7 | 390.8 | 99.6 | 0.9 | 23.2 | 61.2 | 4.4 | 3.7 | 4.8 | 6.7 | 6.3 | 7.0 |
| Togo | 35.7 | 39.9 | 32.2 | 3.7 | 4.0 | — | — | 2.3 | 1.3 | 2.4 | 4.0 | n.a. | 5.6 |
| Tunisia | 522.7 | 787.3 | 472.8 | 111.3 | 88.4 | 103.9 | 10.8 | 7.4 | 14.2 | 20.1 | 22.4 | 20.4 | 18.2 |
| Uganda | 122.5 | 183.6 | 115.9 | 46.2 | — | 0.3 | 21.2 | n.a. | 4.4 | 5.5 | 8.4 | 9.7 | 4.5 |
| Upper Volta | 20.4 | 30.7 | 21.8 | 7.5 | 1.3 | 0.1 | — | 3.4 | 3.7 | 4.5 | 7.5 | 8.7 | 12.0 |
| Zambia | 491.6 | 615.8 | 92.4 | 137.7 | 9.2 | 9.7 | 366.9 | 4.2 | 2.1 | 2.3 | 2.7 | 2.0 | 5.0 |
| EAST ASIA | | | | | | | | | | | | | |
| China, Republic of | 616.5 | 985.1 | 352.6 | 303.3 | 298.7 | 27.4 | 3.2 | 2.9 | 3.6 | 3.2 | 3.3 | 4.3 | 4.4 |
| Indonesia | 2,934.8 | 3,462.8 | 2,960.4 | 187.0 | 140.0 | — | 175.0 | 11.0 | 9.1 | 7.0 | 9.1 | 5.9 | 6.8 |
| Korea, Republic of | 1,750.3 | 2,636.8 | 856.9 | 219.6 | 1,211.8 | 183.6 | 164.9 | 2.7 | 3.6 | 5.6 | 7.5 | 12.4 | 16.9 |
| Malaysia | 364.0 | 549.3 | 163.8 | 269.7 | 19.7 | 14.1 | 82.0 | 1.2 | 1.4 | 2.1 | 2.1 | 2.2 | 2.6 |
| Philippines[b] | 641.3 | 822.4 | 266.8 | 224.3 | 53.6 | 266.5 | 11.3 | 5.3 | 6.3 | 7.2 | 5.3 | 5.5 | 7.3 |
| Singapore | 128.2 | 283.3 | 91.0 | 156.7 | 28.4 | — | 7.2 | 0.1 | 0.1 | 0.1 | 0.3 | 0.4 | 0.6 |
| Thailand | 303.1 | 455.6 | 128.9 | 325.5 | 1.3 | — | — | 3.2 | 2.9 | 3.7 | 3.2 | 3.3 | 3.7 |
| MIDDLE EAST | | | | | | | | | | | | | |
| Iran | 1,339.0 | 3,021.5 | 1,235.9 | 469.7 | 775.3 | 505.1 | 35.6 | 8.6 | 7.6 | 7.8 | 10.5 | 13.8 | 10.0 |
| Iraq | 229.1 | 275.8 | 231.2 | 18.7 | 25.9 | — | — | 0.5 | 0.8 | 0.8 | 1.4 | 1.9 | 3.0 |
| Israel[c] | 2,022.2 | 2,022.2 | 362.1 | 84.1 | 42.1 | 462.9 | 1,071.1 | 21.4 | 20.3 | 14.5 | 16.2 | 16.5 | 17.0 |
| Jordan | 105.7 | 169.5 | 159.5 | 10.0 | — | — | — | 1.0 | 1.4 | 1.5 | 1.8 | 2.8 | 3.5 |
| Syrian Arab Republic | 213.1 | 243.8 | 191.0 | 8.5 | 44.3 | — | — | n.a. | n.a. | 6.8 | 7.5 | 8.8 | 11.2 |
| SOUTH ASIA | | | | | | | | | | | | | |
| Afghanistan | 526.9 | 688.6 | 664.1 | 15.4 | 7.6 | 1.5 | — | 7.9 | 8.9 | 16.6 | 16.6 | 20.0 | 28.4 |
| Ceylon | 313.0 | 515.8 | 333.5 | 116.7 | 54.0 | 4.7 | 6.9 | 2.0 | 2.8 | 3.4 | 7.1 | 8.3 | 9.9 |
| India | 7,792.7 | 9,235.1 | 6,816.3 | 1,884.6 | 457.6 | 74.2 | 2.4 | 16.5 | 19.8 | 22.6 | 20.3 | 22.0 | 23.2 |
| Pakistan[d] | 3,215.4 | 4,302.1 | 2,952.3 | 996.1 | 268.5 | 85.3 | — | 11.0 | 12.9 | 16.8 | 19.4 | 21.7 | 25.4 |

**Table 6-1 (cont.)**

| Area Country | Disbursed Only | Total | Including undisbursed | | | | | Service Payments on External Public Debt as Percentage of Exports of Goods and Services, 1965-1970 | | | | | |
|---|---|---|---|---|---|---|---|---|---|---|---|---|---|
| | | | Bilateral Official | Multi-lateral | Suppliers | Private Private Banks | Other | 1965 | 1966 | 1967 | 1968 | 1969 | 1970 |
| SOUTHERN EUROPE | | | | | | | | | | | | | |
| Cyprus | 32.1 | 49.1 | 7.6 | 31.8 | 9.2 | — | 0.5 | 1.5 | 1.4 | 2.3 | 2.0 | 1.9 | 2.1 |
| Greece | 808.2 | 1,003.6 | 261.2 | 113.8 | 94.1 | 329.7 | 204.8 | 3.1 | 3.5 | 4.6 | 4.4 | 4.6 | 5.1 |
| Malta | 25.0 | 25.0 | 20.4 | 4.6 | — | — | — | 0.5 | 0.8 | 1.2 | 1.2 | 1.4 | 1.7 |
| Spain | 1,217.9 | 1,530.0 | 692.6 | 135.5 | 122.3 | 359.9 | 119.7 | 2.1 | 1.8 | 1.8 | 2.4 | 3.1 | 3.9 |
| Turkey | 1,862.2 | 2,626.1 | 1,939.3 | 578.2 | 40.5 | 49.1 | 18.9 | 24.5 | 17.6 | 14.7 | 13.9 | 16.7 | 17.8 |
| Yugoslavia e | 1,220.2 | 1,729.5 | 895.0 | 426.4 | 218.3 | 136.6 | 53.3 | 14.0 | 13.1 | 12.1 | 13.0 | 14.6 | 8.1 |
| WESTERN HEMISPHERE | | | | | | | | | | | | | |
| Argentina | 2,108.2 | 2,457.3 | 484.6 | 534.8 | 838.1 | 111.4 | 488.4 | 20.1 | 25.3 | 26.8 | 27.2 | 23.9 | 20.9 |
| Bolivia | 459.3 | 529.2 | 273.3 | 54.5 | 49.4 | 1.5 | 150.5 | 4.7 | 4.7 | 5.8 | 5.5 | 5.6 | 10.3 |
| Brazil f | 2,982.3 | 3,808.5 | 1,926.5 | 934.1 | 621.9 | — | 326.0 | n.a. | n.a. | n.a. | 20.9 | 17.9 | 16.6 |
| Chile | 2,004.6 | 2,503.4 | 1,101.6 | 243.1 | 534.5 | 366.3 | 257.9 | 15.3 | 13.2 | 12.4 | 16.0 | 15.9 | n.a. |
| Colombia | 1,229.5 | 1,720.4 | 778.0 | 713.2 | 111.0 | 63.7 | 54.5 | 14.4 | 16.5 | 14.0 | 12.8 | 11.2 | 11.4 |
| Costa Rica | 124.3 | 216.8 | 76.2 | a105.2 | 5.4 | 18.0 | 11.9 | 10.3 | 12.0 | 11.9 | 12.1 | 10.5 | 9.8 |
| Dominican Republic | 226.8 | 281.6 | 224.3 | 28.4 | 19.7 | 9.3 | — | 19.3 | 12.6 | 7.2 | 7.8 | 8.7 | 5.1 |
| Ecuador | 199.5 | 337.1 | 117.2 | 80.9 | 107.2 | 12.7 | 19.0 | 6.3 | 6.4 | 6.3 | 8.3 | 10.4 | 9.3 |
| El Salvador | 86.1 | 119.7 | 43.7 | 60.6 | | 14.4 | 1.0 | 3.6 | 3.6 | 2.6 | 2.6 | 3.2 | 3.7 |
| Guatemala | 109.0 | 176.1 | 63.3 | 50.4 | 3.6 | 42.7 | 16.0 | 5.0 | 5.5 | 9.8 | 8.5 | 8.7 | 8.8 |
| Guyana | 70.2 | 113.0 | 93.0 | 13.0 | | | 6.9 | 4.1 | 3.9 | 4.3 | 3.5 | 3.5 | 3.1 |
| Honduras | 85.6 | 138.9 | 38.3 | 96.9 | 3.8 | | | 2.4 | 2.1 | 2.0 | 1.7 | 2.3 | 2.8 |
| Jamaica | 136.0 | 179.6 | 45.5 | 45.6 | | 24.0 | 64.6 | 1.9 | 2.0 | 2.5 | 3.3 | 3.1 | 3.1 |
| Mexico | 3,252.1 | 3,791.2 | 538.6 | 1,116.7 | 486.7 | 830.7 | 818.6 | 24.7 | 21.2 | 21.5 | 25.1 | 22.4 | 22.7 |
| Nicaragua | 146.0 | 223.8 | 74.0 | 80.1 | 23.6 | 44.0 | 2.1 | 4.3 | 5.3 | 6.1 | 6.7 | 9.1 | 10.6 |
| Panama a | 156.3 | 234.4 | 89.8 | 52.1 | 17.2 | 5.8 | 69.5 | 2.5 | 2.3 | 2.3 | 2.5 | 2.5 | 7.4 |
| Paraguay | 96.8 | 142.4 | 63.1 | 44.7 | 32.1 | 0.6 | 1.8 | 6.6 | 5.4 | 7.2 | 9.4 | 8.8 | 10.4 |
| Peru | 871.9 | 1,184.4 | 267.8 | 214.1 | 362.3 | 125.8 | 214.5 | 6.8 | 9.7 | 10.6 | 22.0 | 13.8 | 14.5 |
| Trinidad and Tobago | 67.8 | 90.0 | 24.6 | 41.4 | 4.4 | 5.9 | 13.6 | 1.9 | 2.0 | 1.9 | 1.5 | 2.1 | 2.1 |
| Uruguay | 239.4 | 318.1 | 112.4 | 104.5 | 23.9 | 60.8 | 16.6 | 6.7 | 12.3 | 20.3 | 19.2 | 18.8 | 22.5 |
| Venezuela | 680.0 | 806.1 | 176.8 | 322.8 | 26.3 | 240.1 | 40.1 | 1.6 | 2.7 | 2.0 | 2.0 | 2.0 | 2.8 |

[a]Because of special monetary arrangements peculiar to countries such as these, the debt-service ratio must be regarded with more than usual caution in considering the country's external financial situation.

[b]Does not include publicly guaranteed private debt estimated at $600 million.

[c]Does not include undisbursed.

[d]Refers to debt contracted prior to December 31, 1970 by Pakistan, which at that time included East Pakistan, now Bangladesh.

[e]Does not include nonguaranteed debt of the "social sector" contracted after March 31, 1966.

[f]Includes some nonguaranteed debt of the private sector to suppliers and excludes the undisbursed portion of suppliers' credits and of bilateral official loans except for those owed to the US Government. Also excludes financial credits, mostly to the private sector.

Note: The debt service ratio is, by itself, a rather inadequate indicator of the seriousness of a country's debt problem. Many other factors must also be considered, such as the stability and diversification of the country's export structure, the prospects for future growth, the extent to which imports can be reduced without adversely affecting current production, the time-profile of the country's outstanding debt, the size of foreign-exchange reserves and available compensatory financing facilities, and the debt-service record of the country. For this reason, international comparisons of debt-service ratios have only limited meaning.

Source: World Bank, *Annual Report 1971-72*, World Bank, Washington, D.C.: pp. 82-83.

In order to continue to perform its functions as a useful social and economic institution, the Bank must maintain the confidence of its bondholders and the bankers and brokers who mold the climate of opinion in international financial markets. This is particularly important in the present state of uncertainty caused by the recent currency readjustments, high and widely fluctuating interest rates, illiquidity of giant corporations, rapid movements of short-term capital, severe financial crises in Pakistan and Chile, and the increasing concern over debt repudiation exacerbated two years ago by events in Ghana. All of these circumstances may be temporary, but they could reoccur with increased intensity over the next decade. While economists might agree that the objective risks of large-scale repudiation and default are small, such risks are not always the prime factor in determining the price of capital. Much more important are what bond purchasers imagine the risks to be and what they imagine other bondholders imagine the risks to be; imagination piled upon imagination can result in strangely erratic, and seemingly irrational, behavior in international bond markets.[10]

The World Bank, subject to the constraints imposed by international capital markets, the primary source of its funds, must proceed very cautiously in its approach to debt rescheduling. The Bank is subject to particularly close scrutiny at this time because it has more than doubled its lending capacity over a very short period. It already has about $16 billion in loans outstanding to less developed countries, and this will grow rapidly over the next few years. A large portion of the Bank debt is outstanding in a few less developed countries. The Bank cannot afford to risk its own ability to raise funds by participating vigorously and fully in debt renegotiations. Its interests lie in careful monitoring of the debt position and advising on the debt management of its major borrowers so that debt rollovers can be avoided.

Has the rapid increase in Bank lending to LDCs, combined with the growth of high-cost commercial borrowing by these countries and a reduction in concessionary flows, seriously jeopardized the liquidity positions of many key less developed countries and increased the likelihood of increasingly frequent and large-scale default or debt reschedulings? The Bank is optimistic on this score and bases its optimism on a careful study of the debt situation of a large number of its borrowing countries. I do not dispute this basically optimistic outlook, subject, of course, to the realization that it is exceedingly difficult to make balance of payments predictions in a world filled with uncertainty.

More importantly, however, there is considerable evidence that the Bank has moved quickly and vigorously in building its institutional capabilities to help avoid future debt crises and advise countries in their management of external debt. First, considerable research effort has been channeled into analyzing and projecting the debt position of the most important less developed countries on a continuing basis. This has involved large numbers of highly competent staff in a number of the bank's departments. The Bank has been a leader in developing reliable data and information on external debt and debt servicing. Second, the Bank has become increasingly sophisticated in its blending of IDA credits and Bank loans to take cognizance of the debt-servicing capabilities of its borrowers. Third, the Bank has taken an active role in consortia and consultative groups to help ensure that the total lending package is consistent with development needs and liquidity requirements. All of these developments are encouraging.

On the other side, the Bank has to be aware of some built-in biases. Given the Bank's prominent role and its need to maintain its own financial health, it is highly unlikely that it would ever become a purveyor of "gloom and doom" through its financial projections. Any dire predictions by the Bank are likely to be self-fulfilling. There is always the danger, however, that the Bank's buoyancy in describing financial prospects could contain an element of self-deception. The Bank must walk a thin line between caution and optimism, and avoid tipping the balance too far either way. Another concern is that the Bank needs to take a more active role in advising on exchange rates, trade and monetary policies, and the management of inflation. Bilateral aid agencies no longer seem to have much of a stake in attempting to influence these policies, and the role of the IMF is already very prominent and promises to become increasingly so. A debt-servicing crisis must be regarded as one symptom of a more general balance of payments problem. The policy tools appropriate to the solution of the latter are also crucial for the former. Although the Bank makes loans for specific projects, the repayment of Bank loans is a function, not so much of the viability of the projects it finances, but of an appropriate set of balance of payments policies. The Bank's concerns and interests are vital, and it must begin taking more of a lead in advising on balance of payments policies.

The limited role of the World Bank in debt adjustment is only one aspect of a general problem faced by the Bank: its dependence on international capital markets and the constraints that this places on Bank policy. Because of this dependence, the Bank cannot be the vehicle for transferring large amounts of resources from the developed to the less developed world on a continuing basis. Those who argue for bolder Bank policies toward the developing countries, program lending rather than project lending, renegotiation of debt on liberal terms, and greater transfer of resources, often forget this fundamental fact. When it is brought to their attention, advocates of bolder policies point out the soundness of the Bank's cash flow and profit prospects, and the fact that interest rates are unusually high from an historical perspective and unlikely to remain so, and that, realistically, the risks associated with the Bank's structure of loans are not very great. I would agree that, on balance, project lending is less efficient than program lending in meeting development needs and in transferring re-sources. However, the important arguments for project lending are not based on the development objective, but on the need to convey the image to its bondholders that the Bank is a sober, responsible organization, checking carefully on the use of its loans and the viability of the projects it finances. The Bank is a prisoner of its past policies in this regard. A drastic switch from project to program lending can easily be interpreted as a lessening of the Bank's resolve to protect its cash flow position regardless of the objective merits of doing so.

This is not to say that the Bank has reached its limits in terms of pursuing more imaginative policies. The Bank should be able to increase its role in consortia and consultative groups, pursue more development and country-oriented research rather than project-oriented research, become more involved in monitoring general economic policies, experiment with sector and program loans, and establish more permanent overseas representation. These are serious arguments, however, for proceeding in these directions with a great deal of caution. Furthermore, it must be recognized that the extent to which the Bank can pursue these objectives is related to the amount of soft loans it can provide through the International Development Association (IDA).

If given more autonomy, the IDA, currently an integral part of the World Bank Group, might be better able to pursue some of the bold, development-oriented policies that are needed. For one thing, the IDA could wholeheartedly engage in program lending, argue the case for debt renegotiation as a serious means for effecting resource transfers, and press the case of the less developed countries with their creditors. Second, it can lend on very soft terms, which means that it can be an instrument for large-scale net resource transfers. It is a matter of simple arithmetic combined with simple economic analysis to show that large net resource transfers cannot be made over a considerable period of time with Bank loans at Bank interest rates. Third, the IDA is not expected to make a profit on its loans nor must it pay back principal to its bondholders. It does not operate under the same constraints as the Bank. Finally, an independent IDA might create vested interests in its continuation as a viable organization that might help ensure adequate funding and replenishments in the future.

### Notes

1. For detailed figures regarding the external debt and service payments of selected developing countries, see International Bank for Reconstruction and Development: *Annual Report, 1972*, Statistical Annex, tables 5, 6, 7, and 8; *External Medium- and Long-Term Public Debt Outstanding, Transactions and Payments 1956-1976*. Washington, D.C., 1969. See also *Development Assistance Review*, Paris: OECD, December 1972.

2. P.N. Rosenstein-Rodan, "Notes on the Theory of the Big Push," in Ellis and Wallich (eds.), *Economic Development for Latin America*, London: International Economic Association and Macmillan, 1961.

3. I.M.D. Little and James A. Mirrlees, *Manual of Industrial Project Analysis in Developing Countries*, Paris: OECD Development Center, 1968.

4. Hollis Chenery and Alan Strout, "Foreign Assistance and Economic Development," *American Economic Review*, vol. 56, no. 4, part I, September 1966, pp. 679-733.

5. See Dragoslav Avramovic and Associates, *Economic Growth and External Debt*, Baltimore: Johns Hopkins Press, 1964.

6. For an extensive discussion of debt renegotiations, see, International Bank for Reconstruction and Development, *Multilateral Debt Renegotiations: 1956-1968*, Economics Department Report No. 170, prepared by Patrick B. de Fontenay, April 11, 1969.

7. Robert S. McNamara, *Address to the Board of Governors*, September 21, 1970, Copenhagen, Denmark. Washington, D.C.: International Bank for Reconstruction and Development, pp. 5-6.

8. The reference to the extraordinarily high debt-service ratios of Mexico and Israel and the continued creditworthiness of the two countries in spite of it, indicates the difficulty of assessing creditworthiness (or the lack of creditworthiness) by a single parameter or standard of reference. It points once more to the need of taking into account in the assessment of creditworthiness all factors bearing on the prospects and the performance of the economy.

9. For an excellent analysis of the aid implications of the external debt problem, see, Charles R. Frank, Jr., *Debt and Terms of Aid*, Overseas Development Council, Monograph No. 1, Washington, D.C., 1970; also Charles R. Frank, Jr. and William R. Cline, *Debt Servicing and Foreign Assistance: An Analysis of Problems and Prospects in Less Developed Countries*, U.S. Agency for International Development Discussion Paper No. 19, Washington, D.C., June 1969.

10. For further details on the Bank's borrowing, see International Bank for Reconstruction and Development, *Annual Report, 1972*, pp. 69-73.

# 7

## Relations with Other
## Multilateral Agencies

**Richard H. Demuth***

The Bank's relationship to other parts of the United Nations system, and to the regional development banks, has become a significant aspect of the Bank's activities relatively recently. But there has been some link with the United Nations ever since the Bank began operations.

The nature of the Bank's responsibilities, as set forth in its Articles of Agreement, satisfies the criteria for a "specialized agency" that, under the provisions of the United Nations Charter, is to be "brought into relationship" with the United Nations. Accordingly, soon after the Bank opened its doors, the United Nations proposed that a formal agreement be negotiated. The Bank did not react with enthusiasm. It was, at the time, concerned to establish its credit in the capital markets. For all practical purposes, this then meant the United States, where the financial community, in the light of its post-World War I experiences, tended to distrust investments associated with international lending. The Bank felt that too close an association with the United Nations, regarded as a highly political body, might increase the difficulty of making itself known and trusted and thus adversely affect its ability to raise funds. Ultimately, however, a relationship agreement was entered into, towards the end of 1947. It is noteworthy in the extent to which it reflects the differences between the Bank and most of the other specialized agencies: principally, that the Bank does not rely for its funds on annual contributions from its members and that it employs a weighted voting system rather than one-country, one-vote. (The International Monetary Fund likewise does not depend on annual contributions from governments and employs a weighted voting system.)

Through most of the 1950s, however, the Bank's relationships with the UN system were not very close. In large part, this was because the Bank in its early years functioned almost exclusively as a project-financing agency; there were few areas in which its operations impinged on those of other members of the UN system. Moreover, the aggregate of all the programs of the UN agencies was small, so that there was little need for coordination and little occasion for a concerted attack on development problems. But over the years, the Bank, with its two affiliates, has evolved into a broad-scale development assistance agency, providing not only finance but a wide range of technical assistance. The scope of

---

*At the time of writing, Director, Development Services Department, International Bank for Reconstruction and Development, Washington, D.C.

its lending has extended from the early concentration on infrastructure, particularly transport and power, to agriculture and education, the concerns of other agencies within the UN system; that scope is still expanding. On the UN side, the establishment (with the Bank's assistance) of the UN Special Fund, now the UN Development Programme (UNDP), not only gave occasion for a special Bank relationship, as noted below, but provided the basis for a major expansion, into large-scale operations, on the part of other UN agencies that had until then concentrated on research and other nonoperational activities.

Probably the Bank's most important, certainly its closest, relationship with another international agency is with the International Monetary Fund.[1] Initially, however, there was very little interaction, and the two institutions, notwithstanding their common ancestry and the physical proximity of their headquarters, had little to do with one another. The two institutions do have different areas of responsibility and different emphases, the Fund's major concern being short-term stability, while the Bank's concern is with long-range growth. But they operate in much the same countries, in each of which the government is or should be desirous of formulating and following a set of policies in which both short- and long-term objectives are taken into account.

Although it took time, the Bank and Fund have come to realize that they owe it to their members to reconcile any differences between them and to assure that advice from one is consistent with advice from the other. The institutions have formally expressed their intention that their work should be complementary, and that each should make the fullest possible use of the expertise and information available in the other. There is broad agreement on the desirability of having staff of one institution participate in missions sent by the other, of coordinating the timing of country missions, and of joint briefing and debriefing of such missions. The coordination of country missions is particularly important from the standpoint of governments which must receive the missions and respond to their requests for data, since the Bank and Fund between them probably send out more missions than all the other agencies put together. A complete integration of approach has not yet been achieved and may never be, but cooperation between Bank and Fund is close and constructive.

The next closest relationships are those with the UNDP.[2] The UNDP's principal function is the financing of preinvestment studies; the Bank's is the financing of investment. Both institutions recognize the need to cooperate, because these two functions are essentially successive stages of a single economic process. Preinvestment studies are useful only if the projects studied (assuming the results are favorable) can eventually be financed, while a satisfactory feasibility study is generally a prerequisite to project appraisal and financing. Since the UNDP is the member of the UN family chiefly concerned with financing of preinvestment studies, the Bank finances such studies only when the UNDP, having been given the "right of first refusal," finds itself unable to do so. On the other hand, at the request of the UNDP the Bank reviews all preinvestment projects the UNDP is considering for financing and often serves as executing agency for UNDP-financed projects. When there is a reasonable prospect that such a project will lead to an investment project suitable for Bank financing, but another specialized agency is likely to be designated executing agency, the Bank expresses "special interest" in the project. The executing agency is then instructed by UNDP to consult with the Bank throughout the course of execution of the preinvestment project to assure that the information the Bank would require for appraisal of an investment project will be available.

Cooperation between the Bank and the UNDP is more important than ever, now that the UNDP has adopted "country programming" on a large scale. These programs, formulated by governments in cooperation with the UNDP resident representative, describe the needs in various sectors and propose specific projects to which may be allocated the aggregate of resources that the country concerned may expect to receive from the UNDP over a three- to five-year period. In principle, therefore, the UNDP, and through it the UN system, has thus adapted to its own activity the essence of the Bank's approach to development assistance—to regard the country as the client and to determine priorities before resources are committed. The UNDP Resident Representatives are normally associated with Bank missions concerned with requirements for preinvestment studies, and Bank economic mission reports are made available to the UNDP for its country programming work.

As far as concerns the agencies with responsibility for particular sectors, the Bank entered into formal arrangements for jointly financed programs with the Food and Agriculture Organization of the United Nations (FAO) and with the United Nations Educational, Scientific and Cultural Organization (UNESCO) in 1964, after it decided to expand its work in agriculture and to extend its financing to the education sector. Under the agreements, the agencies act in effect as technical partners of the Bank in their respective fields, providing assistance to governments in identification and preparation of projects for financing by the Bank Group, as well as staff support for Bank missions concerned with the sectors in question. Through this technique, the Bank draws on the expertise and experience available elsewhere in the UN system, rather than attempting to duplicate it on its own staff, while the other two agencies have acquired a financial partner.

Operations under the agreements have not been without difficulty. As noted above, in several important respects the Bank differs from other parts of the UN system. Of particular relevance to the cooperative arrangements are the facts that the Bank is financially independent, takes its decisions on the basis of weighted voting, and has no formal or informal nationality quota system for its staff but recruits on the basis of qualifications alone (although it has been trying in recent years to achieve a more representative balance of nationalities); as a result of all these factors, the Bank is somewhat more insulated from political pressures in its development work than are the other agencies of the UN system.

Moreover, unlike the FAO and UNESCO at the time the agreements with them were negotiated, the Bank is an operating and investment-oriented agency. An effort, largely successful, was made to facilitate the forging of operational links by providing that a separate unit be constituted within each agency to be responsible for the conduct of the cooperative program; that the work program for an indicated future period be agreed periodically; and that there be continuing consultation respecting personnel assignments to specific areas of responsibility. Both the Bank and the other two agencies, as well as their clients, have benefited from the agreements.

A third, and roughly similar, cooperative agreement was recently negotiated with the World Health Organization in connection with the preparation of water supply and sewerage projects. The Bank has thus far not entered into formal agreements with any other UN agencies, although the International Labor Organization and the Bank have cooperated on country missions in the field of employment, and experts from the UN Industrial Development Organization have participated in some Bank missions. Working relationships have been established with the UN Secretariat on a wide range of matters including economic planning, housing, urbanization, and population.

The Bank also has almost continuous contact with the three principal regional development banks, the Inter-American Development Bank (IDB), the Asian Development Bank (AsDB), and the African Development Bank (AfDB). In principle, these three banks, within their respective geographic jurisdictions, are charged with financing the same kinds of projects as the Bank Group finances, and there is no logical basis for allocating areas of responsibility between the World Bank and the regional institutions. The regional banks are at different stages of their own development, and the IBRD has followed a pragmatic approach in working out operational relationships with them. IBRD country reports, project appraisals, and commodity studies are sent routinely to the regional banks. There are frequent exchanges of information and consultations intended to help avoid overlapping or undesirable competition. IBRD operational and economic missions to countries within the region call in at the regional development bank to discuss their findings. The IBRD Permanent Mission in Western Africa, located in Abidjan where the AfDB has its headquarters, maintains an active liaison with that bank, particularly in project identification and preparation. Together with the UNDP and the UN Economic Commission for Africa, the IBRD and the AfDB have set up a coordinating committee for preinvestment studies. There have been a number of instances of joint financing of projects. Joined by representatives of the Inter-American Committee on the Alliance for Progress, the IBRD and the IDB have worked out arrangements for coordinating the schedules of country missions and country program reviews. Finally, the IBRD provided technical assistance in the establishment of the Caribbean Development Bank and cooperates in various ways, which include joint financing operations, with other regional organizations such as the European Investment Bank and the European Development Fund.

To turn from operational relationships to policy, it may be noted that the relationship agreement between the Bank and the UN explicitly provides that neither organization, nor any of their subsidiary bodies, will present any formal recommendations to the other without reasonable prior consultation, and that the UN recognizes that it would be sound policy to refrain from making recommendations to the Bank with respect to particular loans or to terms or conditions of Bank financing, as distinct from the technical aspects of projects or of development plans or programs. Resolutions of the General Assembly, the Economic and Social Council, and the UN Conference on Trade and Development (UNCTAD) do often make recommendations addressed to the Bank, for example that its interest rate should be lower, that it should increase its support of a particular sector of the economy of developing countries, and so on. In addition, the Bank is frequently asked to undertake studies of the feasibility of proposals that might ultimately be implemented by it. It has, for instance, been asked to consider establishment of a multilateral investment insurance agency, a proposed technique for increasing the resources of IDA through establishment of an interest equalization fund, possible improvements in techniques of lending, and a scheme for supplementary financing to compensate developing countries in the event of an unexpected shortfall in their export earnings.

It may be noted that the attitude of the UN General Assembly and UNCTAD on development issues is often very different from that of the Bank's Board of Directors. In part this is attributable to the balance of voting power which, in the UN and its bodies, lies with the developing countries by reason of the one-country, one-vote system, while in the Bank weighted voting power throws the balance in favor of the developed countries. In part the difference is due to the fact that delegations to the UN and its bodies are drawn from foreign affairs ministries, while the Executive Directors of the Bank take their instructions from finance ministries. It is not unusual to find a country's UN delegation expressing one view on an issue and the Executive Director representing that country in the Bank expressing another. The line between developed and developing country positions on the supplementary finance scheme was much less sharply drawn in the Bank than at UNCTAD, for example. And in the exceptional case in which the General Assembly asked the Bank to withhold economic assistance to Portugal and South Africa, and to withdraw loans and credits already granted, because of those countries' "policies of racial discrimination and colonial domination," the Executive Directors, although with some dissents, endorsed the position of the Bank's General Counsel that under the terms of the relationship agreement the Bank is not obligated to comply with the request and, indeed, under the terms of its own Articles is not free to do so.

Nevertheless, I should also emphasize that debates in the UN and its bodies can have constructive outcomes from the Bank's point of view, as witness the discussions that preceded the creation of the two Bank affiliates, the International Finance Corporation and the International Development Association.

Developing countries are prone to use the forum of the UN to press for creation of special funds for special purposes: supplementary finance, disaster relief, the UN Capital Development Fund. In doing so, they sometimes fail to take sufficient account of the fact that, while creation of additional taps may sometimes result in an overall increase in the total of resources available—as happened when the UNDP and the regional development banks were created—this will not always be the case. It is, in fact, becoming increasingly unlikely. Herein lies a risk of policy conflict with the UN bodies, although thus far it has been largely avoided.

# Comment:  The World Bank and the United Nations

Stig Andersen*

Virtually every agency in the United Nations system of organizations has a tendency to, and a remarkable capacity for, showing itself as the centerpiece in the system, with the other agencies having auxiliary functions in relation to its central function. Even highly specialized agencies like the World Health Organization or UNESCO tend to consider themselves the hub of the international development community, with institutions such as the UNDP and the World Bank as mainly sources of finance to supplement their own regular budgets.

The World Bank is no exception from the rule. It tends to see itself not only as the original development agency in the system, but also today, because of the monetary value of its operation, as the principal international partner of the developing countries, with UNDP as a small supplementary source of preinvestment finance, and some of the specialized agencies as sources of technical manpower in certain fields. It reports annually to the Economic and Social Council, but it reviews recommendations and requests from this and other governing bodies in the UN system with, at best, aloofness.

Is there not a more logical way of viewing the UN system of organizations? And would it not be advantageous, especially for the developing countries, to seek in the course of the 1970s to evolve a more coherent system of international development cooperation within which each agency, and the World Bank, would play their assigned coordinated roles?

It would be naïve to expect that in an early future the whole UN development system and the World Bank could be united in one large organization; it is even doubtful that such a monolithic organization would be the most efficient instrument to serve the development of the developing countries. The relative efficiency of such smaller UN organizations as the Universal Postal Union and the International Telecommunications Union depends undoubtedly in part on their modest staff and their relative independence within the system.

However, the seventies could and should see an integration and coordination effort at the international and national level, which would require some limitation in the freedom of action for the individual international agencies concerned, a higher degree of subordination to coordinating bodies, and an obligation to consult effectively between organizations.

*Director, Office of Technical Cooperation, Department of Economic and Social Affairs, United Nations Secretariat, New York.

Two major institutions, at the international and national level respectively, which seem to be most susceptible to development towards increasingly assuming these integration and coordination tasks are the UN Economic and Social Council and the UNDP Resident Representative in each developing country.

First, at the central international level, hardly any other organ in the system can claim the formal authority the Charter endowed to the Economic and Social Council (ECOSOC). Most people would agree that ECOSOC has not lived up to the expectations of the founding fathers, let alone to the even greater needs for interagency cooperation and policy formulation, not foreseen by the founding fathers, which arose with the independence of nearly all nations in Asia and Africa and their accession to membership at the United Nations. However, there is a growing feeling among governments that ECOSOC and the ECOSOC secretariat must be strengthened, and important steps are being taken just this year to bring about long overdue reforms in the working of ECOSOC. These and further reforms that no doubt will have to be introduced during the next decade should lead to ECOSOC becoming the major UN organ in which policies, including operational policies, for international development should be determined. The World Bank could and should participate actively in this process. Even if the Bank does not in an early future change its membership and voting procedures—and a change that would give developing countries a bigger say than is the case at present would seem both desirable and inevitable in the longer term—it may even now decide to seek partly to exercise more influence on, partly to let itself be more susceptible to influence from, ECOSOC's policy-making and coordinating activities. Deliberate efforts in this direction by the Bank's Board of Directors and by its President and staff would without doubt be appreciated and applauded by the governments of developing countries, and governments of the principal donor countries would certainly see virtue in any attempt to seek a higher degree of coordination in international development work.

At the level of each developing country, gratifying progress has been made in the past decade towards coordination of UN development cooperation, notably through the strengthening of the position and authority of the UNDP Resident Representatives. The adoption of the so-called country program approach, which to a large extent only represented a codification of a gradually developed practice, is the latest in a series of reforms that have given the Resident Representative not only a strong coordinating role in each country, but even a considerable decision-making authority. (As from 1972 the Resident Representative can approve UNDP-financed projects costing up to $100,000.)

While there are examples of the World Bank associating the Resident Representative with their country missions, the Bank is alone among the participating agencies under UNDP in not according the Resident Representative its recognition of his primary coordination responsibilities. There are, no doubt, several good reasons why this is so. One of them, though not the only one, is that the post of Resident Representative is not always filled with the highest caliber of development operations officials. The Jackson Report[3] strongly advocated an immediate and radical improvement in this regard; there should be little difficulty in finding ninety-four outstanding international officials to occupy these key posts, and the Bank could very well be of great assistance in achieving that goal. If this improvement took place soon, it would seem possible as well as highly desirable for the Bank to lean more and more on the Resident Representative in each developing country and ultimately, under arrangements to be worked out with the Administrator of UNDP, to accept him as the team leader and coordinator of all development activities carried out by all UN affiliated agencies.

The concept of partnership between international organizations and developing countries in formulating and executing development policies and development projects is universally accepted. However, if one probes a little into what each international organization and each government means by partnership one finds a wide range of ideas. For example, a minister for planning in a developing country has stated: "The UNDP contribution is the only external input which we can treat as an internal resource."

The World Bank would hardly subscribe to such a statement as far as its inputs are concerned, while many UNDP officials might agree to the concept, but have some mental reservations. Under the UN Expanded Program of Technical Assistance, it was largely the developing country concerned that determined the content of the program, with much influence of the specialized agency, but without much central policy control by the then Technical Assistance Board. The UN Special Fund represented a more hard-nosed approach and was much influenced in this direction by the World Bank. The merger of TAB and Special Fund, UNDP, especially after the most recent reforms, is probably swinging the pendulum back towards a preponderance of the recipient country's government in the decision-making, notwithstanding the Administrator's "full accountability" for the funds put at his disposal. Meanwhile, the Bank has no doubt gradually also softened its originally rather tough "banker's" attitude. Its progressively deeper involvement in each country's life and economy has necessitated this development. In this process the deliberations and decisions of many UN bodies have also played a role.

Thus, modifications and adaptations of policies and attitudes in the international organizations are constantly taking place, reflecting not least the overall trend of growing maturity and intellectual power, if not yet a corresponding economic power, of the leaders of developing countries. The seventies should bring these developments and changes in attitudes to the partnership concept a long stride farther.

# Comment: International Economic Diplomacy

**Leon Gordenker\***

It should be apparent from what has been said so far that the United Nations system is enormously complex. This complexity contains important lessons from the past that are going to apply to any development efforts that go into the future.

Deliberate decisions have created and maintained autonomous organizations. Autonomy itself, as Mr. Andersen suggested, has value. Among the values, autonomy at the international level ensures that if there is a large-scale failure in the international system, even one as fundamental as the Second World War, something might survive. The ILO survived the Second World War; the League of Nations did not. Furthermore, the autonomous organizations efficiently represent special interests, which do exist in the world, and thus provide a broad basis for world organization. But autonomy contributes greatly to what the Jackson Report has called "the most complicated structure in the world." That may overstate the situation, but only slightly.

Yet this statement about complexity fails to raise the question as to whether coordinated effort, which is what we are talking about, is really worthwhile in terms of cost. Would the duplication that would result if there were somewhat less time spent on coordination really cost so very much? The local allocations involved in the UN effort, that is, the nonBank effort, are fairly small. The executed projects tend to be in fields where help really is needed. One wonders, therefore, whether all of this extraordinary effort at coordination necessarily has a productive effect. I do not know if there is any way to tell, but I admit that governments firmly believe that coordination is a great thing. This view is supported by their bureaucracies, who thrive on coordination.

The resulting complexity, grounded in efforts to coordinate, has given birth to some splendid bureaucratic artifices. The Administrative Committee on Coordination[4] is perhaps the pinnacle of these artifices; this is an organization of ambassadors of international bureaucracy. Each member of the Administrative Committee of Coordination heads a specialized agency or some agency associated with the UN. Since these agencies tend to multiply every year, the ACC becomes bigger. It is now so big that it possess its own bureaucracy.

At the individual government level, the UN establishes a resident representative. There are some ninety of these so far. The Bank has not so far duplicated

---

*Professor of Politics, Princeton University.

143

this system. If it were to do so, as the Pearson report seems to suggest, then a new coordination problem would arise. Mr. Demuth's comment about competent people in the field at the resident representative level indicates that there are ways in which to reserve positions on coordination at the field level. If the opposite number turns out not to be competent in the judgment of one of the parties involved, the coordination becomes impossible and needless. I will quote a passage from the agreement between the Bank and the UN, which illustrates how far coordination has progressed, how much cooperation there really is—but also how important judgment may be.

Nothing in this agreement shall be construed to require either of them—the UN or the Bank—to furnish any information, the furnishing of which would, in its judgment, constitute a violation of confidence of any of its members or anyone from whom it shall have received such information which would otherwise interfere with the orderly conduct of its operations.

In any case, the Bank and the UNDP clearly have made a good deal of progress in coordinating effort, although as recently as 1968 I was on hand in a UNDP office in Africa where the resident representative said, "What the hell Bank mission is this? I have not heard of them, and they arrived today." It still happens. Perhaps this has less importance as coordination does grow within the international bureaucracy and information is exchanged. Perhaps more important is coordination within governments.

Getting governments to speak with one voice is a difficult problem. Country programming may be of some assistance here. Country programming needs high-grade people on the recipient government side. How to develop such people poses another real problem. In my view, it cannot be solved very quickly. The UN has put a good deal of effort into it. I wonder whether the World Bank has done as much as it could in this regard and whether it should not help more. One of its projects is the Economic Development Institute (EDI), which trains people who take high government positions. One wonders whether this is going as far as it could.

All this intrudes on very delicate ground. What we are really talking about is a kind of political development sponsored, encouraged, and needled from the outside. Governments are as sensitive to this as anything else; they may inevitably come to use the term "neocolonialism." Already there have been at least one or two careful studies of the operations of the international organizations which conclude that they have taken on what the recipient countries usually call neocolonialist aspects.[5]

The Jackson Report explicitly states that the UNDP should move into the technical assistance issues that the IBRD does not upgrade. Mr. Demuth has mentioned the growing use of Bank efforts at coordinating aid. This made some governments so skeptical that in the 1970 report of the UN Economic and Social Council, the Soviet and Bulgarian representatives insisted on inserting a very unusual dissenting statement.[6] If the Bank takes on the coordinating job with more vigor, the question arises as to whether UNDP relationships, which already relate closely to the recipient government, will be damaged at the local level and whether UNDP relationships with the Eastern Europeans will be destroyed. These relationships could conceivably be well worth preserving.[7] In some instances, that I have seen directly, the relationship does work in a coordinative way so that Eastern European aid can be blocked out for one part of the country's program, UN aid for another, and so forth.

There are also some questions as to whether the Bank's adaptation to policy demands emanating from the UN have not come so very late as to suggest that the Bank is not so adaptable as some people would like to believe. It is true that the Bank under Mr. McNamara has moved very rapidly. Yet, looking back over the last twenty-five years, the Bank comes off badly when its record is set against the background of discontent.

It could be argued that the Bank has neglected opportunities by shunning what it considers to be overtly political. The Bank is in politics too. It affects the kind of issues in a developing country that are most important locally; it has a good deal of difficulties with certain kinds of governmental relationships, as for example with the third replenishment of IDA. It might be that the Bank could find ways of moving closer to the UN system with all of its political implications without engulfing the system. This would benefit everybody.

I would like to make a comment about the general policy that related to this. The pronouncements of the Economic and Social Council and the General Assembly, such as the Second Development Decade resolution, are intended to advise governments. There is some doubt in my mind as to whether the governments that most need guidance ever look at these resolutions and ever do anything about them. The question arises as to whether the Bank should attempt to make this kind of policy pronouncement or guidance more important by accepting more of it itself and by feeding in more of its own ideas into the process. This is difficult, and it goes against the grain of accumulated experience; but perhaps it could be done with some more effort and provide valuable theory on which to base actions by governments and international bodies.

What about the social ramifications of the Bank's operations? At the general policy level, the Economic and Social Council and the General Assembly have insisted on more attention to the social ramifications of development work. Does the Bank take these fully into account? Should it be a prime mover in this direction? Should it try to influence governments to pay more attention to social matters that are frequently neglected? For example, if one built a factory or a road on a Bank loan, these have social implications for the surrounding areas. How much attention should be paid to such implications, and how much of this should be built into the Bank's agreement?

Finally, I want to raise the question of the creation of a free-floating bureaucracy. Here I attack both Mr. Andersen and Mr. Demuth, I hope without too much fear. What does coordination mean at the international level? Does it really mean loss of governmental control? Does it mean the construction of bureaucratic fortresses immune from governmental criticism? To what extent can the international bureaucracies themselves, which have their own interests and should have their own standards, inform and teach governments how to be critical? Will they avoid doing this? There is some indication that some of this has happened; whether it is gone far enough is exceedingly doubtful. It is interesting that UN fears, American fears, and Soviet fears on this question tend to merge. Congress, at the moment, is engaged in a serious effort to establish a greater degree of accountability—whatever that means—for all the UN operations. They want to examine the books and learn about cause and effect in their operations. The General Accounting Office has reported in a rather damaging way on some of the organizations.[8] For its part, the Soviet Union regards the creation of large bureaucracies free from much closer control than the United States seeks as an evil in itself and opposes it persistently. On the basis of my own observations I would predict that they would be joined before long by some other governments, governments receiving aid who will become sensitive to what is really a very high degree of influence from the rather small numbers of international officials who have turned to work consistently on the problems that governments frequently cannot work on. All of which would imply greater scrutiny of the workings of the international organizations.

### Notes

1. For further details of the IBRD-IMF relationship, see J. Keith Horsefield, *The International Monetary Fund 1945-1965*, vol. I, Washington, D.C.: 1969.

2. See International Bank for Reconstruction and Development, *Annual Report 1972*, Washington, D.C., esp. pp. 65-67.

3. Sir Robert Jackson, *A Study of the Capacity of the United Nations Development System*, vol. I, New York: United Nations Secretariat, 1969, UN Document DP/S.

4. See Martin Hill, "The Administrative Committee on Co-ordination," in Evan Luard, *The Evolution of International Organisations*, London: Thames and Hudson, 1966.

5. See Leon Gordenker, "The United Nations and Economic and Social Change," in Gordenker, *The United Nations and the International System*, Princeton: Princeton University Press, 1971, pp. 181-283; and Ronald Nairn, *International Aid to Thailand*, New Haven: Yale University Press, 1966, especially Chapter 11. A more extreme approach to these questions is Teresa Hayter, *Aid as Imperialism*, Penguin, 1971.

6. United Nations, Official Record, General Assembly: Session, Supplement No. 3, *Report of the Economic and Social Council*, p. 118.

7. For comments on these relationships, see Gordenker, "Multilateral Aid and Influence on Governmental Policies," in Robert W. Cox, *International Organisation: World Politics*, London: Macmillan, 1969.

8. See especially, Comptroller-General of the United States, *Management Improvements Needed in U.S. Financial Participation in the United Nations Development Program*, U.S. Government Printing Office, B-168767, Washington, D.C.: 1970.

# Selected Bibliography

# Selected Bibliography

Adler, John H. *Absorptive Capacity: The Concept and Its Determinants*, Washington, D.C.: The Brookings Institution, 1965.

Adler, John H. and P. Kuznets (eds.), *Capital Movements and Economic Development*, New York: Macmillan, 1967.

Adler, Robert W. and Raymond F. Mikesell, *Public External Financing of Development Banks in Developing Countries*. Eugene: Bureau of Business and Economic Research, University of Oregon, 1966.

Asher, Robert E. and Edward S. Mason, *The World Bank Since Bretton Woods*, Washington, D.C.: The Brookings Institution, 1973.

Asher, Robert E. "Development Assistance in Development Decade II: The Recommendations of Perkins, Pearson, Peterson, Prebisch, and Others," *International Organisation*, vol. 25, no. 1, 1971, pp. 97-119.

Asher, Robert E. *Development Assistance in the Seventies: Alternatives for the United States*, Washington, D.C.: The Brookings Institution, 1970.

Asher, Robert E. *Multilateral vs. Bilateral Aid: An Old Controversy Revisited*, Washington, D.C.: The Brookings Institution, 1963.

Asian Development Bank. *Agreement Establishing the Asian Development Bank*, Manila: Asian Development Bank, 1968.

Asian Development Bank. *Annual Report for 1968*, Manila: Asian Development Bank, 1969.

Avramovic, Dragoslav. *Debt-servicing and Post-War Growth in International Indebtedness*, Baltimore: Johns Hopkins Press, 1958.

Avramovic, Dragoslav, et al. *Economic Growth and External Debt*, Washington, D.C.: IBRD and IDA, 1964.

Balogh, Lord Thomas. "Multilateral Versus Bilateral Aid," *Oxford Economic Papers*, November 1967.

Balogh, Lord Thomas. "Notes on the Conference (UNCTAD)," *Bulletin of the Oxford University Institute of Economics and Statistics*, vol. 26, 1964.

Bandera, V.N. "Tied Loans and International Payments Problems," *Oxford Economic Papers*, 17, July 1965, pp. 299-308.

Baum, Warren, "The Project Cycle," *Finance and Development*, June 1970.

Baumol, W.J. "On the Social Rate of Discount." *The American Economic Review*, vol. LVIII, no. 4, September 1968, pp. 788-802.

Berrill, Kenneth. "Foreign Capital and the Take-Off," in W.W. Rostow (ed.), *The Economics of Take-Off Into Sustained Growth*, New York: St. Martin's Press, 1963.

Bhagwati, Jagdish N. "Alternative Estimates of the Real Cost of Aid," in Paul Streeten (ed.), *Unfashionable Economics: Essays in Honor of Lord Balogh*, London: Weidenfeld and Nicholson, 1970.

Bhagwati, Jagdish N. *Amount and Sharing of Aid*, Washington, D.C.: Overseas Development Council, Monograph #2, 1970.

Bhagwati, Jagdish N. and Richard S. Eckaus (eds.), *Foreign Aid*, Penguin Books, 1971.

Bhagwati, Jagdish N. and Padma Desai, *India: Planning for Industrialization: Industrialization and Trade Policies since 1951*, Paris and London: Development Centre of the Organization for Economic Co-operation and Development and Oxford University Press, 1970.

Bhagwati, Jagdish N., "The Tying of Aid," New York: UNCTAD Secretariat, TD/7/Supp. 4; Item 125 (ii) of the agenda of the New Delhi Second UNCTAD Conference, February 1968; reprinted in J. Bhagwati and R.S. Eckaus (eds.), *Foreign Aid*, Penguin Books, 1970.

Black, Eugene R. *The Diplomacy of Economic Development*, Cambridge, Mass.: Harvard University Press, 1963.

Carlin, A. "Project versus Program Aid: From the Donor's Viewpoint," *Economic Journal*, vol. 77, 1967.

Center for International Studies, Massachusetts Institute of Technology. "The Objectives of United States Economic Assistance Programs," *Foreign Aid Program (Compilation of Studies and Surveys)*, Special Committee to Study the Foreign Aid Program. US Senate, 85th Congress, 1st Session, 1957.

Chenery, H.B. and A.M. Strout, "Foreign Assistance and Economic Development," *American Economic Review*, vol. 56, no. 4, part 1, September 1966, pp. 679-733.

Cohen, Benjamin I. "Foreign Exchange Constraints in Economic Development and Efficient Aid Allocation: Comment," *Economic Journal*, vol. 76, March 1966, pp. 168-170.

Columbia University School of Law and Institute of International Studies and Overseas Administration, University of Oregon. *Public International Development Financing in Chile*, New York: Columbia University, 1964.

Columbia University School of Law and Institute of International and Overseas Administration, University of Oregon, *Public International Development Financing in Colombia*, New York: Columbia University, 1963.

Cooper, Richard N. *A Note on Foreign Assistance and Capital Requirements for Development*, Santa Monica, California: Rand Corporation, 1965.

Cooper, Richard N. "External Assistance and the Balance of Payments of Donor Countries," Geneva: UNCTAD (E/CONF./46/P/13, March 10), 1964.

Engelmann, Peter. "Sector Surveys and Feasibility Studies: Preparatory Steps in World Bank Practice," Washington, D.C.: IBRD, July 1969.

Fei, John C.H., and D.W. Paauw. "Foreign Assistance and Self-Help: A Reappraisal of Development Finance," *Review of Economics and Statistics*, vol. 47, August 1965, pp. 251-67.

Feis, Herbert. *Foreign Aid and Foreign Policy*. New York: St. Martin's Press, 1964.

Frank, Charles R., Jr. *Debt and Terms of Aid*, Washington, D.C.: The Overseas Development Council, 1970.

Frank, Charles R., Jr. "Debt Servicing and Foreign Assistance: Analysis of Problems and Prospects in Less Developed Countries," AID Discussion Paper No. 19. Washington, D.C.: US Department of State, June 1969.

Fried, Edward R., "International Liquidity and Foreign Aid," *Foreign Affairs*, vol. 48, no. 1, October 1969, pp. 139-49.

Friedman, Milton. "Foreign Economic Aid: Means and Objectives," *Yale Review*, vol. 47, December 1958, pp. 500-516.

Griffin, Keith, "Foreign Capital, Domestic Savings and Economic Development," *Bulletin of the Oxford University Institute of Economics and Statistics*, vol. 32, no. 2, 1970.

Griffin, Keith. *Underdevelopment in Spanish America*, London: George Allen and Unwin, 1969.

Group of Ten, *Report of the Study Group on the Creation of Reserve Assets: Report to the Deputies of the Group of Ten*, Washington, D.C.: US Government Printing Office, 1965.

Gruble, Herbert G. "The Benefits and Costs of Being a World Banker," *The National Banking Review*, vol. 2, December 1964, pp. 189-212.

Gulick, Clarence S. and Joan M. Nelson, "Promoting Effective Development Policies: AID Experience in the Developing Countries," AID Discussion Paper No. 9, Washington, D.C.: US Department of State, 1965.

Hamilton, Edward K. "Toward Public Confidence in Foreign Aid," *World Affairs*, March 1970, p. 296.

Hanson, A.H. *The Process of Planning*, London: Oxford University Press, 1966.

Hirschman, Albert O. *Development Projects Observed*, Washington, D.C.: The Brookings Institution, 1967.

Hirschman, Albert O. and R.M. Bird, *Foreign Aid: A Critique and a Proposal*, Princeton International Finance Section, Princeton University, 1968.

Hirschman, Albert O., *A Bias For Hope*, New Haven and London: Yale University Press, 1971.

International Bank for Reconstruction and Development including International Development Association and International Finance Corporation.

International Bank for Reconstruction and Development. *Annual Report*, Washington, D.C.: 1970, 1971 and 1972.

International Bank for Reconstruction and Development. *Articles of Agreement,* as amended effective December 17, 1965, Washington, D.C.: IBRD, March 1966.

International Bank for Reconstruction and Development. *By-Laws*, as amended through August 21, 1969. Washington, D.C.: IBRD, August 1969.

International Bank for Reconstruction and Development, "Economic Growth, Foreign Capital and Debt-Servicing Problems of the Developing Countries," Washington, D.C.: IBRD, 1963.

International Bank for Reconstruction and Development. *On Estimating the Economic Cost of Capital*, Washington, D.C.: IBRD EC-138, October 21, 1965.

154

International Bank for Reconstruction and Development. *External Medium and Long-Term Public Debt Past and Projected Amounts Outstanding, Transactions and Payments 1956-1976*, Washington, D.C.: IBRD EC-156, December 4, 1967.

International Bank for Reconstruction and Development. *General Conditions Applicable to Loan and Guarantee Agreements*, Washington, D.C.: IBRD, January 31, 1969.

International Bank for Reconstruction and Development. *Multilateral Debt Renegotiation 1956-1968*, Washington, D.C.: IBRD EC-170, April 11, 1969.

International Bank for Reconstruction and Development. *Multilateral Regional Financing Institutions*, Washington, D.C.: IBRD, March 1968.

International Bank for Reconstruction and Development. *Possible Improvements In Techniques of Lending*, a study by the staff of the World Bank for the United Nations Conference on Trade and Development, Washington, D.C.: IBRD, April 1970.

International Bank for Reconstruction and Development. *Preliminary Review of External Public Debt of India*, Washington, D.C.: IBRD EC-51, April 1956.

International Bank for Reconstruction and Development. *Recent Changes in the External Public Indebtedness of Latin American Countries*. Washington, D.C.: IBRD EC-120, October, 1963.

International Bank for Reconstruction and Development. *Supplementary Financial Measures*, Washington, D.C.: IBRD, 1965.

International Bank for Reconstruction and Development. *The World Bank, IDA and IFC: Policies and Operations*, Washington, D.C.: IBRD, June 1969.

International Development Association. *Articles of Agreement*, effective September 24, 1960, Washington, D.C.: IDA, November 1962.

International Development Association. *By-Laws.* Washington, D.C.: IDA, November 30, 1962.

International Development Association. *General Conditions Applicable to Development Credit Agreements*, Washington, D.C.: IDA, January 31, 1969.

Islam, Nurul. *Foreign Capital and Economic Development*, Rutland, Vt.: C.E. Tuttle Co., 1960.

Jackson, Sir Robert. *A Study of the Capacity of the United Nations Development System*, vol. 1, UN Document DP/S, New York: United Nations, 1969.

Johnson, H.G. *Economic Policies Toward Less Developed Countries*, Washington, D.C.: The Brookings Institution, 1967.

Kindleberger, Charles P. *Balance of Payments Deficits and the International Market for Liquidity*, Essays on International Finance, International Finance Section, Princeton: Princeton University Press, 1965.

King, B.F. *Notes on the Mechanics of Growth and Debt*, Washington, D.C.: IBRD, 1968.

King, John. *Economic Development Projects and Their Appraisal: Cases and Principles from the Experience of the World Bank*, Baltimore: Johns Hopkins Press and Economic Development Institute, IBRD, 1967.

Lal, D. "The Cost of Aid Tying: A Study of India's Chemical Industry," New York: UNCTAD Secretariat, 1968 (mimeo).

Lewis, John P. *Quiet Crisis in India*, Washington, D.C.: The Brookings Institution, 1962.

Lieftinck, Peter. *External Debt and Debt-Bearing Capacity of Developing Countries*, Essays in International Finance, International Finance Section, Princeton: Princeton University Press, March 1966.

Little, I.M.D. and J.M. Clifford, *International Aid*, London: George Allen and Unwin, 1965.

Little, I.M.D. and James A. Mirrlees, *Manual of Industrial Project Analysis in Developing Countries*, vols. 1 and 2, Paris: OECD Development Center, 1968.

McNamara, Robert S., *One Hundred Countries, Two Billion People: The Dimensions of Development*, London: Pall Mall Press, 1973.

Mason, Edward S. *Foreign Aid and Foreign Policy*, New York: Harper & Row, 1964.

McKinnon, R.I. "Foreign Exchange Constraints in Economic Development and Efficient Aid Allocation," *Economic Journal*, vol. 74, June 1964, pp. 388-409.

Mikesell, Raymond F. *The Economics of Foreign Aid*, Chicago: Aldine Press, 1968.

Mikesell, Raymond F. *Public Foreign Capital for Private Enterprise*, Essays on International Finance, International Finance Section, Princeton: Princeton University Press, 1966.

Mikesell, Raymond F. *Public International Lending for Development*, New York: Random House, 1966.

Millikan, Max. "India in Transition: Economic Development: Performance and Prospects," *Foreign Affairs*, April 1968.

Montgomery, John D. *The Politics of Foreign Aid: American Experience in Southeast Asia*, New York: Praeger, 1962.

Morgenthau, Hans. "A Political Theory of Foreign Aid," *American Political Science Review*, no. 60, June 1962.

Myrdal, Gunnar. *Asian Drama*, 3 vols., New York: The Twentieth Century Fund, 1968.

Myrdal, Gunnar. *An International Economy*, New York: Harper and Brothers, 1956.

Narain, D. and V.K.R.V. Rao, *Foreign Aid and India's Economic Development*, Bombay: Asia Publishing House, 1963.

Neal, A.D. *The Flow of Resources from Rich to Poor*, Occasional Papers on International Affairs, no. 27, Cambridge, Mass.: Center for International Affairs, Harvard University, 1961.

Nelson, Joan. *Aid, Influence and Foreign Policy*, New York: Macmillan, 1968.

Ohlin, Goran. *Foreign Aid Policies Reconsidered*, Paris: Organization for Economic Cooperation and Development, 1966.

Ohlin, Goran. *Relationship between Aid Requirements, Terms of Assistance and*

156

*Indebtedness of Developing Countries*, Paris: OECD Development Center, 1966.

Organization for Economic Cooperation and Development. *Development Assistance Annual Review*, Paris: 1969, 1970, 1971.

Organization for Economic Cooperation and Development. *The Flow of Financial Resources to Less Developed Countries, 1956-1963.* Paris: OECD, 1965.

Pearson, et al. *Partners in Development*, Report of the Commission on International Development, New York: Praeger, 1969.

Pincus, John A. "The Cost of Foreign Aid," *Review of Economics and Statistics*, November 1963.

Pincus, John A. *Economic Aid and International Cost Sharing*, Baltimore: Johns Hopkins Press, 1965.

Prebisch, Raul. *Change and Development: Latin America's Great Task*, Report submitted to the Inter-American Development Bank, Washington, D.C.: July 1970.

Prebisch, Raul. *Towards a Dynamic Development Policy for Latin America*, Santiago, Chile: UN Economic Commission for Latin America, E/CN 12/680, April 14, 1963.

Prest, A.R., and R. Turvey. "Cost-Benefit Analysis: A Survey," *Economic Journal*, vol. 75, December 1965, pp. 683-735.

Raj, K.N. *Indian Economic Growth: Performance and Prospects*, New Delhi: Allied Publishers, 1965.

Ranis, Gustav. "Trade, aid and what?," *Kyklos*, vol. 17, 1964.

Reddaway, W.B. *The Development of the Indian Economy*, London: George Allen and Unwin, 1962.

Reid, Escott. *The Future of the World Bank*, Washington, D.C.: International Bank for Reconstruction and Development, September 1965.

Rosenstein-Rodan, Paul N. "International Aid for Underdeveloped Countries," *Review of Economics and Statistics*, 43 (2): 1961, pp. 107-138.

Rosenstein-Rodan, Paul N. "The Consortia Technique," *International Organization*, vol. 22, no. 1, 1968, pp. 223-30. Reprinted in Bhagwati and Eckaus (eds.), *Foreign Aid*.

Schmidt, Wilson E. "The Economics of Charity: Loans vs. Grants," *Journal of Political Economy*, vol. 72, August 1964, pp. 387-95.

Schmidt, Wilson E. "Default on International Public Debts," *National Banking Review*, vol. 2, 1965.

Singer, Hans. "International Aid for Economic Development," *International Development Review*, vol. 6, 1964.

Singer, Hans. "Project versus Program Aid: A Rejoinder," *Economic Journal*, vol. 77, 1967.

Streeten, Paul and M. Lipton, (eds.). *The Crisis of Indian Planning*, London: Royal Institute of International Affairs, Oxford University Press, 1968.

Streeten, Paul. "International Capital Movements," Queen Elizabeth House, University of Oxford, 1970 (mimeo).

Streeten, Paul. *The Frontiers of Development Studies*, London and New York: Macmillan and Wiley, 1972.

Ul-Haq, M. "Tied Credits—A Quantitative Analysis," in John Adler and Paul Kuznets (ed.), *Capital Movements and Economic Development*, New York: St. Martin's Press, 1967.

United Nations, including UN Secretariat; UN Conference on Trade and Development; and other UN Agencies.

United Nations, Committee for Development Planning. *Report on the Sixth Session (5-15 January 1970)*, Tingergen Report, UN Document ST/ECA/128, New York: United Nations, 1970.

United Nations, "Accelerated Flow of Capital and Technical Assistance to the Developing Countries: Measurement of the Flow of Long-term Capital and Official Donations to the Developing Countries, Concepts and Methodology," *Report to the Secretary-General*, UN Document No. A/5732, New York: United Nations, 1965.

United Nations, Conference on Trade and Development. "Memorandum Concerning Certain Items on the Agenda of the U.N. Conference on Trade and Development," E/CONF/46/74, Geneva, February 26, 1964.

United Nations, Conference on Trade and Development. *Final Act, United Nations Conference on Trade and Development.* E/CONF/46/L28. Recommendation A IV 2. Geneva: United Nations, 1964.

United States Government, including Agency for International Development; Department of Commerce; Presidential Commission Reports; and US Congress.

Agency for International Development. *Development Assistance in the New Administration* (Perkins Committee), October 25, 1968.

Agency for International Development. "Principles of Foreign Economic Assistance," Washington, D.C.: US Government Printing Office, 1963.

Agency for International Development. *Study on Loan Terms, Debt Burden and Development*, Washington, D.C.: US Government Printing Office, 1965.

Department of Commerce. "Foreign Aid by the United States Government, 1940-51," Washington, D.C.: US Government Printing Office, 1952.

International Development Advisory Board. "Partners in Progress," A Report to the President of the United States (Rockefeller Report), Washington, D.C.: US Government Printing Office, 1951.

United States Congress, Senate Committee on Banking and Currency. *Study of Export-Import Bank and World Bank Hearings.* Washington, D.C.: US Government Printing Office, 1954 (83:2).

Joint Economic Committee of the Congress of the United States. *Twenty Years After: An Appeal for the Renewal of International Economic Cooperation on a Grand Scale.* Report of Subcommittee on International Exchange and Payments. Washington, D.C.: US Government Printing Office, 1966.

Foreign Relations Committee. *Foreign Assistance Act of 1963, Hearings*, Washington, D.C.: US Senate, 89th Congress, 1st Session, 1963.

Committee on Government Operations, Subcommittee on Foreign Aid Expenditures, *United States Foreign Aid in Action: A Case Study*, Washington, D.C.: US Senate, 89th Congress, 2nd session, 1966.

Committee on Foreign Affairs. *Staff Memorandum on International Lending and Guarantee Programs*, Washington, D.C.: House of Representatives, 88th Congress, 2nd Session, 1964.

Legislative Reference Service, Library of Congress. *Some Important Issues in Foreign Aid*. Prepared for Committee on Foreign Relations, U.S. Senate, Washington, D.C.: US Government Printing Office, 1966.

Report to the President from the Task Force on International Development. *U.S. Foreign Assistance in the 1970's: A New Approach* (Peterson Task Force), Washington, D.C.: US Government Printing Office, March 4, 1970.

Wilson, G.M. "World Bank Operations," An address before the Economic Commission of the Council of Europe, Paris, December 16, 1963, Washington, D.C.: IBRD, 1963.

Wolf, C., Jr. *Foreign Aid, Theory and Practice in Southeast Asia*, Princeton: Princeton University Press, 1960.

Wolf, C., Jr. *United States Policy in the Third World*, Boston: Little, Brown, 1970.

Woods, George D. *Statement of George D. Woods to the Ministerial Meeting, Development Assistance Committee*, Organization for Economic Cooperation and Development, Paris: World Bank, 1965.

Wriggins, Howard. "Foreign Assistance and Political Development," in *Development of the Emerging Countries: An Agenda for Research*, Washington, D.C.: The Brookings Institution, 1962, pp. 181-214.

# Index

Abidjan, 136
Administrative Committee on Coordination, 143
Africa, 25, 39, 116, 118
African Development Bank, 55
Afghanistan, 120
Agency for International Development (AID), 54–55, 58–59, 61
Agricultural assistance, 1, 21, 26, 32, 50, 54, 73–74, 134; in India, 90, 91, 92–93, 99, 105, 107–08
Aid-India Consortium, 89–91, 92, 93–95, 97–98, 103, 106; and US, 103–04
Amortization of loans, 18, 19, 45, 66
Andean Pact, 53
Area Departments, 28–29
Argentina, 13, 115, 117, 119
Asia, 39
Asian Development Bank, 55, 136
Australia, 63
Austria, 39, 63

Balance of payments problem, 2, 35, 83, 90; and debt-servicing 114–15, 116–17, 129
Bangladesh, 120
Belgium, 63
Bell, Bernard, 91–92
Bell, David, 103
Bell, John O., 103
Bilateral aid, 6, 21, 59, 98, 129; and grants, 79; terms of, 68, 81, 86, 123; and US, 60–61, 81
Black, Eugene R., 14, 16, 24, 90
Blending, 45, 69–70, 71, 129
Bonds, 14, 16, 30, 37–38, 128, 130
Botswana, 33
Bowles, Chester, 103
Brazil, 39, 115, 117
Bretton Woods, 13, 14, 15
Bulgaria, 144–45

CIAP (Comite Interamericano de la Alianza para el Progreso), 55, 122
Canada, 38, 56, 63, 68
Caribbean Development Bank, 136
Ceylon, 120

Chenery, Hollis, 18, 114
Chile, 53, 115, 117, 119, 128
Colombia, 39
Commercial banks, 120; *see also* Private lending institutions
Committee of 20, 8
Congress (Reform) Party (India), 107
Consortia, 55, 59, 122, 129, 130: *see also* Aid-India Consortium
Cooperatives, 32
Cope, S. Raymond, 65
Copenhagen Annual Meeting, 4, 116
Country development programs, 24, 28, 130, 134, 140, 145–46
Crawford, Sir John, 92, 98
Creditworthiness, 14, 24, 45, 47, 70–71, 120

Debt-servicing, 8, 9, 111–13, 123, 129; and balance of payments, 114–15, 116–17
Denmark, 38, 63
Development Assistance Committee (OECD), 65, 68, 95, 116
Donor governments, 1, 5, 10, 47, 50, 73; and leverage, 80

East Pakistan, 76
Ecological criticism, 5–6
Economic Development Institute, 144
Educational assistance, 1, 21, 26, 33, 54, 134; loans, 66, 73
Egypt, 120
Equity objectives, 5, 27, 30–31
European Development Fund, 136
European Investment Bank, 136
Exchange rates, 129
Export-Import Bank, 111
Exports, 33, 111, 116, 117

Family planning, 26, 54; *see also* Population control
Finland, 38, 63, 69
Food and Agriculture Organization (FAO), 2, 135, 136
Foreign-exchange earnings, 6, 8, 22, 38, 86, 114; and debt-serving, 115–18
France, 16, 50, 63, 118

Friedman, Milton, 99

Gandhi, Indira, 53, 107
General Accounting Office, 2, 56, 60, 146
Germany, 15, 16, 37–38, 63; and India, 95
Ghana, 69–70, 115, 118, 120, 128
Grants, 7, 8, 24, 25, 30, 57, 65, 116; and loans, 65–68, 71–72; and World Bank, 77–81
Greece, 39
"Green Revolution," 59, 92–93, 105
Gross national product, 4, 16; and development, 2, 21, 25–26; Indian, 106, 108

Health, 21, 74
"Horowitz Proposal," 9

IBRD: see World Bank
Ireland, 63
Imports, 80
Income distribution, 31
India, 89–109
Indonesia, 39, 115, 118, 120
Inflation, 117, 129
InterAmerican Committee of the Alliance for Progress, 55, 136
InterAmerican Development Bank, 55, 56, 136
Interest rates, 18, 19, 35, 113–14, 128; World Bank, 65–69, 130
Intermediate loans, 71–72
International Development Association (IDA), 2, 7, 18–19, 28, 34, 84, 137; fund sources, 30, 84; and governments, 55, 63; loan terms, 35, 38, 45–47, 67–73, 85; and project lending, 74–75; and program lending, 75–77
International Finance Corporation (IFC), 16, 18, 24, 53, 137
International Labor Organization (ILO), 14, 32, 136, 143
International Monetary Fund, 7, 8, 16, 24, 28, 51, 63, 117
International Rhine Commission, 14
International Telecommunications Union (ITU), 14, 139
International Trade Centre (Geneva), 32
Iran, 39
Ireland, 69
Israel, 62, 69, 118, 119
Italy, 18, 63
Ivory Coast, 69

Jackson Reports, 141, 143
Japan, 15, 16, 37–38, 39, 58, 63; and India, 95

Keynes, John Maynard, 51
King, Benjamin B., 65
Korea, 69
Kuwait, 63

Land distribution, 32
Latin America, 13, 25, 38–39, 50, 53, 118
League of Nations, 143
"Leverage," 51, 80
Lewis, John, 107
Lewis, W. Arthur, 19
Lilongwe project, 74
"Links" scheme, 8
Liquidity, 7, 8, 114–15, 128
Little, L.M.D., 114
Local-cost financing, 74–75, 80–88
Luxembourg, 63

Malawi, 74
Malaysia, 118
Mason, Edward S., 25, 35
McKinsey and Company, 35
McNamara, Robert S., xiii, 2, 16, 34, 116, 145
Marketing developments, 32
Marshall Plan, 13, 22, 25
Mexico, 39, 118
Middle East, 25
Mirrlees, James A., 114
Multidimensional projects, 73–74
Multilateral lendings, 1, 21, 34; and debt-servicing, 116, 117–18; and grants, 77; growth and advantages, 56–60, 61; and World Bank, 133–38
Multilateral renegotiation of debts, 115, 117–18
Multinational corporations, 10

Nation-states, 10, 113
National personnel quotas, 1, 17, 135
Nationalization, 29
"Neocolonialism," 144
Netherlands, 63
"New Left" critics, 2–4
New Zealand, 38, 69
Nigeria, 47, 69
Nixon, Richard, 62
Norway, 38, 63

Ocean resources, 9, 79
Oil-producing countries, 116
One-flag, one-vote system, 1, 10, 16, 133, 137

PL 480, 90, 104, 105, 108
Pakistan, 39, 45, 60, 83, 120, 128

Part 1 countries, 38, 63, 86
Pearson Commission, 47–50, 74, 144
Per capita assistance, 47, 50
Per capita income, 47, 71, 121
"Performance bargaining," 47, 104–107
Permanent Mission in Western Africa, 136
Peru, 53, 115, 117
Petersen Task Force, 62
Philippines, 119
Population control, 1, 33, 50, 90, 136
Portugal, 137
"Poverty test," 45–47
Power development, 50–51, 73, 107, 134
Private lending institutions, 6, 23, 35, 53, 62, 112–13, 128
Program loans, 21, 75–77, 81, 85–86, 130
Project Departments, 28
Project loans, 14, 73–74, 81, 85, 130

Regional banks, 55, 60, 122
Road development, 66, 100, 101
Rumania, 10
Rural work program lending, 74

Second Development Decade, 4, 6, 27, 76, 116, 145
Second Five Year Plan (India), 90
Sectoral lending, 38–39, 50, 76
Singapore, 118
Smithsonian dollars, 37
Socialist bloc, 10, 28
Soft lending, 18–19, 21, 24–25, 47, 67–73, 77, 130
South Africa, 63, 137
Soviet Union, 15, 145, 146
Spain, 39
Special Drawing Rights, (SDRs), 7, 8, 9, 62–63, 79
Stockholm Conference on Environmental Issues, 6
Subramaniam, 93
Swaminathan, 93
Swaraman, 93
Sweden, 38
Switzerland, 38

Taiwan, 18
Tax structures, 31
Technological assistance, 2, 21, 31, 107, 141, 144
Telecommunications development, 73
Third Five Year Plan (India), 90, 91
Trade surpluses, 7
Transportation development, 33, 50–51, 73, 134

Tunisia, 69–70, 119
Turkey, 39, 69–70, 117, 119

Underemployment, 2, 5, 26, 30–31
United Kingdom, 15, 63, 95, 107
United Nations, 133–144; Charter, 123; General Assembly, 4, 137; Resident Representatives, 135, 143–144
UN Capital Development Fund, 138
UN Conference on Trade and Development, 62
UN Development Programme (UNDP), 29, 32, 134–35, 138, 140–41, 144, 145
UN Economic and Social Council, 139, 140, 144–45
UN Economic Commission for Africa, 136
UN Educational, Scientific and Cultural Organization (UNESCO), 2, 135–36
UN Expanded Program of Technical Assistance, 141
UN Industrial Development Organization, 136
UN Special Fund, 134, 141
UN Technical Assistance Board, 141
United States, 4, 5, 16, 17, 38, 50, 63, 107; aid program, 21; and bilateral aid, 55–56, 61; and AID, 58; in India, 90, 103–105
United States Congress, 2, 5, 56, 58, 60, 146
Universal Postal Union (UPU), 14, 139
Uruguay, 13

Vietnam War, 5

Weighted voting, 16, 27–28, 45, 133, 137
"Whole country" approach, 17
Woodrow Wilson School of Public and International Affairs, xiii
Woods, George, 16, 91, 104
World Bank: Articles of Agreement, 14, 15–17, 22, 74, 75, 133; Board of Directors, 15, 16, 19, 45, 60, 137, 140; Executive Directors, 16, 17, 66, 74, 75, 137; founding, 13–18, 61; loan terms, 65–66, 68–73; President, 16–17, 19, 140; staff, 54, 128, 134, 135
World Health Organization, 136, 139

Yugoslavia, 10, 39

Zambia, 69

# About the Contributors

**John H. Adler** was awarded a law degree by the University of Prague, and a Ph.D. in Economics by Yale University. During the Second World War, he was first an instructor in economics at Oberlin College and then worked with the Federal Reserve System. From 1945 to 1947 he was Deputy Chief of the Finance Division, US War Department, in Vienna. From 1947 to 1950, Mr. Adler was an economist with the Federal Reserve Bank in New York. He has been with the World Bank since 1950 in various capacities, including Director of the Economic Development Institute, Senior Advisor in the Economics Department, and, since 1968, Director of the Programming and Budgeting Department. From 1958 to 1968, Mr. Adler was also a visiting lecturer on Latin-American affairs at the School for Advanced International Studies, Johns Hopkins University. He is the coauthor of several books and author of many articles on economic development, international trade, and public finance.

**Stig Andersen** was educated at the University of Copenhagen from 1944 to 1952. For two years after that he worked for the Danish Government at the Secretariat of the Labor Market Commission. Between 1954 and 1963, Mr. Andersen was with the World Health Organization, first with the Tuberculosis Research Office as a statistician and then as advisor in Sociology and Public Administration to the Government of India. From 1963 to 1970 he was with the UN Development Program in the Philippines, Congo (Kinshasa), and Algeria. Since 1970, Mr. Andersen has been with the Office of Technical Cooperation, United Nations, New York and is currently Director of that office.

**Robert E. Asher** was a Senior Fellow in the Foreign Policy Studies Program at the Brookings Institutions from 1954 to mid-1972. Before that he was employed for a total of nearly twenty years by the United States Government, serving from 1951 to 1954 as Special Assistant to the Assistant Secretary of State for Economic Affairs. He is author of various books and articles, including *Development Assistance in the Seventies: Alternatives for the United States* and *Grants, Loans, and Local Currencies: Their Role in Foreign Aid*. With Edward S. Mason, he is currently completing a comprehensive analytical history of the World Bank Group. He has been a member of the President's Task Force on Foreign Economic Policy, 1960-61, and consultant to the United Nations, the US Department of State, the Council of Economic Advisers, and the US Agency for International Development. Mr. Asher was educated at Dartmouth College, the University of Berlin in Germany, and the University of Chicago. He is now an international economic consultant.

**I.P.M. Cargill** was Director of the South Asia Department at the World Bank from 1968 to 1972 and is now Vice-President for the Asia Region. Prior to that, between 1952 and 1968, he served with the Bank in many positions including Director of Far East Operations from 1961 onwards. During the War, from 1938 to 1947, Mr. Cargill was with the Indian Civil Service and after that with the British Treasury in London and Washington from 1948 to 1952. He was educated at Oxford University.

**Richard H. Demuth** graduated from Princeton University in 1931 and received his law degree from Harvard University in 1934. After having been a lawyer in the 1930s and 1940s, Mr. Demuth joined the World Bank in 1946, first as Assistant to the President and later as Director of the Technical Assistance and Liaison Staff. From 1961 to 1972 he was Director of the Development Services Department, a member of the President's Council, and in overall charge of the Economic Development Institute. Currently, he is a partner in the law firm of Surrey, Karasik and Morse. Mr. Demuth is also a member of the Governing Board of the International Institute for Educational Planning and Chairman of the recently established Consultative Group for International Agricultural Research.

**Charles R. Frank, Jr.** has been Professor of Economics and International Affairs at the Woodrow Wilson School, Princeton University, since 1970. He is currently at the Brookings Institution. He has taught at Yale University, Makerere University College (East Africa), and has lived and studied extensively in Africa. He has been a consultant for many development organizations, including the US Agency for International Development, the World Bank, and the United Nations Economic Commission for Asia and the Far East. He is the author of many books and articles in the fields of economic development and of mathematical economics, including *Statistics and Econometrics, Debt and Terms of Aid*, and *Economic Accounting and Development Planning*. He received the Bachelor of Science in Mathematics in 1959 at Rensselaer Polytechnic Institute, and his Ph.D. in Economics in 1963 at Princeton University.

**William S. Gaud** has been Executive Vice-President of the International Finance Corporation since 1969. From 1961 to 1969 he was with the US Agency for International Development, first as Assistant Administrator for Near East and South Asia, then Deputy Administrator, and finally Administrator of USAID from 1966 to 1969. Mr. Gaud graduated from Yale University in 1929 and then received his law degree from Yale Law School in 1931. He spent over twenty years in private law practice in New York, from 1933 to 1961, interrupted during the Second World War by service in the US Army.

**Leon Gordenker** received his B.A. from the University of Michigan and the Ph.D. degree from Columbia University. He worked as a journalist and from 1945 to 1953 was a member of the United Nations Secretariat, with whom he has since been a consultant. He is the author of *The United Nations and the Peaceful Unification of Korea, The UN Secretary-General and the Maintenance of Peace*, editor of *The United Nations in the International System*, and has published numerous articles. He has been at the Department of Politics, Princeton University, since 1958.

**P.D. Henderson** was Director of the Economics Department of the World Bank when this book was prepared. An Oxford graduate, he is a former Fellow of Economics at Lincoln College, Oxford and a University Lecturer there. While holding these appointments he spent a year as a Commonwealth Fund Fellow at Harvard, and a year as Economic Advisor in the British Treasury. He also served as Dean of Lincoln College, as Chairman of the Oxford Sub-Faculty of Economics, as a consultant in the UK National Economic Development Office, and as a member of the editorial board of *Oxford Economic Papers*. After leaving Oxford he spent two years as Chief Economist of the UK Ministry of Aviation, followed by a period as an advisor in the Harvard Development Advisory Service in Greece and Malaysia. He first came to the World Bank in 1968 as a Visiting Lecturer in the Economic Development Institute. Among other publications, he is joint author of *Nyasaland: The Economics of Federation* (1960), editor of and contributor to *Economic Growth in Britain* (1966), and a contributor to *The British Economy in 1950's* (1962), *Public Enterprise* (1968), *Public Economics* (1969), and *Unfashionable Economics* (1970).

**Michael L. Hoffman** was educated at Oberlin College and the University of Chicago. He taught at Oberlin for two years before joining the US Treasury in 1942, first in the Foreign Funds Control Department and later as their representative to Allied Headquarters in Europe. From 1945 to 1956, Mr. Hoffman was the European Economic Correspondent for *The New York Times*. He then became Director of the Economic Development Institute at the World Bank for five years, followed by a brief period with the Development Advisory Service. Before assuming a position as Associate Director of the Development Services Department until 1972 in the International Bank for Reconstruction and Development, Mr. Hoffman was with the Lambert International Corporation as Executive Vice-President. He is now Director of the Department for International Relations at the Bank.

**L.K. Jha** was educated at Banaras Hindu University, India, and Trinity College, Cambridge, England. He joined the Indian Civil Service in 1936 and has since then held several key governmental positions, including Secretary of Finance, Secretary to the Ministry of Heavy Industry, Secretary to the Prime Minister's Secretariat (under Prime Minister Shastri as well as Mrs. Indira Ghandhi), and Governor of the Reserve Bank of India. From 1969 to 1973, Mr. Jha was the Indian Ambassador to the United States. He is currently Governor of Jammu and Kashmir State in India. Ambassador Jha's association with international affairs began in the late 1950s, when he was elected Chairman of GATT. Since then he has represented India at several international conferences, including those of the World Bank and International Monetary Fund, and has been India's chief spokesman at a number of Aid-India Consortium meetings.

**Ishan Kapur** was educated at the University of Oxford, Columbia University, and the University of Delhi, India. He has been an economist on the UNCTAD Private Overseas Investment Project run jointly by Queen Elizabeth House, Oxford University, and the Institute of Development Studies, Sussex. During 1971-722, Mr. Kapur was on the Research Program in Economic Development at the Woodrow Wilson School of Public and International Affairs, Princeton University. He is now with the European Department of the International Monetary Fund in Washington, D.C.

**J. Burke Knapp** was educated at Stanford University and Oxford University, England, and was a Rhodes Scholar at the latter. He was on the Federal Reserve Board for many years, during and just after the Second World War. In 1950, Mr. Knapp joined the World Bank as Assistant Director of the Economics Department. On a leave of absence after that, he was Economic Advisor to the United States Delegation to the North Atlantic Treaty Organization (NATO), and then US Commissioner, Joint Brazil—United States Economic Development and Technical Cooperation Program in Brazil. From 1952 to 1956, Mr. Knapp was Director of Operations for the Western Hemisphere Department at the World Bank, and since 1956 he has been the Bank's Senior Vice-President.

**John P. Lewis**, Professor of Economics and International Affairs, and Dean of the Woodrow Wilson School, Princeton University, received his Ph.D. from Harvard in 1950. He taught at Union College from 1946 to 1950, and at Indiana University from 1953 to 1964, where he also served as Chairman of the Department of Business Economics and Public Policy from 1961 to 1963. He has been a staff member of the Council of Economic Advisors, the UN Korean Reconstruction Agency, and the Brookings Institution. In 1963-64 he was a member of the President's Council of Economic Advisers, and from 1964 to 1969 he was Minister-Director of the US Agency for International Development Mission to India. His publications include *Reconstruction and Development in South Korea, Business Conditions Analysis,* and *Quiet Crisis in India: Economic Development and American Policy*, as well as several articles.

**Carl I. Ohman** studied law and languages at the University of Lund and economics at the Stockholm School of Economics. From 1962 to 1970 he served with the Ministry of Foreign Affairs, first in Stockholm then at the Swedish Embassies in Madrid (1963-65) and in Cairo (1965-66), dealing mostly with economic matters. From 1967-70, Mr. Ohman again served in Stockholm in the Economics and Trade Department, Division for UNCTAD, GATT, OECD, IBRD, FAO and commodity matters, becoming Head of Section in 1969. He has served for extensive periods on Nordic and Swedish delegations to the Kennedy Round tariff negotiations, the International Grains Conference, the International Sugar Conference, and to meetings within GATT, OECD, UNCTAD, various commodity organizations, etc. Mr. Ohman was Alternate Executive Director for Denmark, Finland, Iceland, Norway, and Sweden at the World Bank from 1970 to 1973, and since then he has been at the Office for International Development Co-operation, Ministry of Foreign Affairs in Sweden.

**Richard W. Richardson** was educated at Cornell University and Johns Hopkins University, and awarded a Ph.D. by the latter in 1957. From 1957 to 1960, Mr. Richardson taught economics at Princeton University, after which he served two years with the International Monetary Fund. Between 1962 and 1968, he was first with the US Bureau of the Budget and then the Associate US Coordinator at the Alliance For Progress. Before assuming his current position as Associate Director of the Twentieth-Century Fund, Mr. Richardson was Chief Economist, US Senate Banking and Currency Committee. He has been a member of President Johnson's Task Force on Foreign Economic Policy in 1964, and on the US Delegation to the First UNCTAD in Geneva. His publications include *Studies in Economic Development* (with B. Okun) and several articles.

**Mahbub Ul Haq** was educated at the Universities of Cambridge (England), Yale, and Harvard, receiving a Ph.D. from Yale in 1957. He has been with the World Bank since 1970, first as Senior Advisor in the Economics Department and now as Director, Policy Planning and Program Review Department. From 1957 to 1970, Mr. Haq was with the Planning Commission of the Government of Pakistan, and from 1967 onwards he was Chief Economist of the Planning Commission and Chief Economic Adviser to the Government. He has also been a consultant to various international organizations including ECAFE, UNCTAD, and IBRD. Mr. Haq is the author of *Strategy of Economic Planning* and numerous articles and papers on the subject of development planning.

**Maurice J. Williams** joined the US economic assistance program in 1958, rising from program officer in the Iran mission to his present Presidential appointment: Deputy Administrator of the Agency for International Development. For three years (1967-1970) Mr. Williams was that agency's Assistant Administrator in charge of programs in the Near East and South Asia (an area from Greece to India). During this period he served as US delegate to World Bank Aid consortia for India, Pakistan and Ceylon as well as the OECD consortium for Turkey. He represented the US Government at international meetings concerned with the Indian debt problem in 1968 and the 1969 Stockholm meeting on Indian population and family planning. Mr. Williams was educated at Northwestern University, the University of Manchester, and the University of Chicago, where he received his M.A. degree in 1949. In 1971, he received the Career Service Award of the National Civil Service League. Mr. Williams is currently Chief US Delegate to the Joint-Economic Commission, between the United States and North Vietnam, for the reconstruction of North Vietnam.